Licensing Law Handbook

LICENSING LAW HANDBOOK

A Practical Guide to Liquor and Entertainment Licensing

Russell Hewitson

Consultant Editor: Tom Moss

The Law Society

ISBN 10: 1–85328–954–X
ISBN 13: 978–1–85328–954–5

Crown copyright material is reproduced with the permission of the Controller of Her Majesty's Stationery Office

Published in 2006 by Law Society Publishing
113 Chancery Lane, London WC2A 1PL

Typeset by J&L Composition, Filey, North Yorkshire
Printed by Antony Rowe Ltd, Chippenham, Wilts

Contents

Preface

The Licensing Act 2003 has radically overhauled the various laws and procedures relating to the sale of alcohol and the provision of entertainment to create a unified structure. Today's licensing practitioners must now consign the once familiar procedures and hearings under the Licensing Act 1964 and other licensing statutes to history, and get to grips with the totally new procedures and forms introduced by the 2003 Act.

My aim in writing this book has been to provide a practical guide to both the new laws and procedures. I hope that it will be useful for all those involved in licensing law and will become their first point of reference. I recall my first experiences of licensing law and practice as a newly qualified solicitor. How I wished then that there was a clear concise and practical guide to licensing law and procedure. My wish now is that this book will fill that gap in relation to the new law and procedures.

Copies of the Act, the Regulations which have been made under it and the guidance issued by the Secretary of State under s.182 of the Act have not been included. This is partly because space does not permit it, but also because these are all easily accessible on the Internet. The new Licensing Authorities have made available on their websites copies of application forms, notices, etc. and so it is hoped that licensing practitioners will find that this book and the information available on the Internet complement each other.

I am immensely grateful to Tom Moss for agreeing to be Consultant Editor and for taking the time during what was a very busy period for him to read my drafts. Tom has many years of licensing experience and his comments after reading my drafts were extremely valuable. Any errors which remain in the book are my responsibility alone.

I am also grateful to the staff of the Law Society, in particular Ben Mullane and Sarah Foulkes for their encouragement and patience.

Finally my thanks go to Andrea and Dominique, my wife and daughter, without whose constant help, support and encouragement this book would not have been possible. This book is dedicated to them.

The law is stated as at 24 November 2005.

Russell Hewitson
Cleadon Village, Sunderland
December 2005

Table of cases

Table of statutes

Table of statutory instruments

Table of treaties and conventions

CHAPTER 1

Introduction

1.1 INTRODUCTION

The Licensing Act 2003 is the culmination of a review of licensing law and procedure which was started in the late 1990s. It introduces radical changes to licensing practices and procedures. The Licensing Bill was introduced into Parliament on 14 November 2002 and on 10 July 2003 it received Royal Assent. The Act came fully into force on 24 November 2005.

The Act establishes a single integrated scheme for licensing premises which are used for the supply of alcohol, to provide regulated entertainment or to provide late night refreshment. Permission to carry on one or more of these activities is now contained in a single authorisation, which will either be a 'premises licence', a 'club premises certificate' in the case of a qualifying club or a 'temporary event notice' in the case of temporary licensable activities.

1.2 BACKGROUND

In April 2000 the Government published a White Paper entitled *Time for Reform: Proposals for the Modernisation of our Licensing Laws* (Cm 4696, 2000). This set out the Government's proposals for modernising and integrating the alcohol, public entertainment, theatre, cinema, night café and late night refreshment house licensing schemes in England and Wales. The key aims of the Government's proposals were to reduce crime and disorder, to encourage tourism, to reduce alcohol misuse and to encourage the self-sufficiency of rural communities.

The Home Secretary in his foreword to the White Paper said:

The current alcohol licensing system is an amalgam of 19th century legislation, intended to suppress drunkenness and disorder, and later additions. The law is complex, and involves a great deal of unnecessary red tape for business. We owe the magistrates and the police a large debt of gratitude for doing their best to make the system work; but it has been impossible to prevent inconsistencies and arbitrary decisions from arising. At the same time, there are too few effective sanctions

1

against premises attracting trouble. The rules governing the admission of children to licensed premises are obscure and deeply confusing. The controls on under-age 'off sales' are inadequate. It is also difficult to find in the present arrangements for licensing the sale of alcohol any real accountability to local residents whose lives are fundamentally affected by the decisions taken. The time has come to develop a better system.

There is a parallel and separate system of public entertainment licensing, under which local authorities issue licences for premises that may or may not also have a liquor licence. These laws too are complex and riddled with anomalies. The intersection of the two licensing systems imposes unnecessary costs and burdens on business.

To complete the picture we are proposing to reform the regulation of late night refreshment services (night cafes) which are subject to yet another separate licensing system, also complex and out of date. Licensing here is meant to prevent disorder and unreasonable disturbance to residents in the neighbourhood, and needs to be re-focused on these key issues.

Our overall aim is to bring about reform which assures the safety of the public, better protects children and safeguards all against crime, disorder and disturbance; the decisions we make on these issues will in turn help to shape the future of our villages, towns and cities.

Following the publication of the White Paper, responsibility for alcohol and entertainment licensing policy was transferred from the Home Office to the Department for Culture, Media and Sport (DCMS).

1.3 THE LICENSING ACT 2003

The Act introduces a unified system to regulate licensable activities. These are the sale and supply of alcohol, the provision of regulated entertainment and the provision of late night refreshment.

The Act is divided into the following nine parts:

Part 1 – licensable activities;
Part 2 – licensing authorities;
Part 3 – premises licences;
Part 4 – clubs;
Part 5 – permitted temporary activities;
Part 6 – personal licences;
Part 7 – offences;
Part 8 – closure of premises;
Part 9 – miscellaneous and supplementary.

The policy behind the new system of licensing for licensable activities is to promote four licensing objectives:

- the prevention of crime and disorder;
- public safety;

- the prevention of public nuisance; and
- the protection of children from harm.

The system of licensing is achieved via the provision of authorisations through personal licences, premises licences, club premises certificates and temporary event notices.

1.4 OVERVIEW OF THE ACT

1.4.1 Licensing authorities

Authorisations to carry on licensable activities are granted by licensing authorities. With minor exceptions these will be the local authority for the area in which the premises are situated or, in the case of personal licences, in which the applicant is normally resident.

The Act provides procedures for regulating the discharge by the licensing authority of its functions. Authorities are required to publish a licensing policy every three years. When drawing this up a licensing authority must take into account the views of those representing the holders of licences and certificates, of local residents and of businesses, of the police and of the fire and rescue authority. Licensing authorities must also take into account the Guidance issued by the Secretary of State under s.182 of the Act (see **2.12**).

1.4.2 Personal licences

A personal licence authorises an individual to sell or supply alcohol, or authorise the sale or supply of alcohol, for consumption on or off premises for which a premises licence is in force for the carrying on of that activity. In order to obtain a personal licence a person must be aged 18 or over, possess a recognised licensing qualification and have not been convicted of a relevant offence or a foreign offence.

Where a person has been convicted of a relevant offence or foreign offence, following notification to the chief officer of police and consideration of any objections from the police the licensing authority must grant a personal licence unless it considers that doing so would undermine the crime prevention objective.

A personal licence lasts for 10 years and is renewable.

1.4.3 Premises licences

A premises licence authorises the licence holder to use premises for licensable activities. The premises licence contains various information including the operating conditions which regulate the use of the premises for licensable activities in line with the licensing objectives.

A premises licence has effect until it is revoked or surrendered. It is otherwise not time limited unless the applicant has requested that it be granted only for a limited period.

Representations concerning the promotion of the licensing objectives may be made about an application for the grant of a premises licence, for example by local residents and businesses, the police, the fire and rescue authority and public bodies with responsibility for environmental health. Once a premises licence has been granted these persons and bodies may seek a review of the licence and its attached conditions.

1.4.4 Club premises certificates

A club premises certificate authorises a qualifying club to use club premises for qualifying club activities. Qualifying club activities are the supply of alcohol by or on behalf of a club to a member of the club, the sale by retail of alcohol by or on behalf of a club to a guest of a member for consumption on the premises and the provision of regulated entertainment by or on behalf of a club for its members and guests.

As with premises licences the right to make representations on the application for a club premises certificate is given to a range of persons and bodies.

1.4.5 Temporary event notices

The Act also introduces new arrangements for the carrying on of licensable activities at temporary events with fewer than 500 people attending. These replace the 'occasional permissions' and 'occasional licences' which existed under the Licensing Act 1964. The new arrangements are based on the organiser of the event notifying the licensing authority about the event and an acknowledgement by that authority of the notification.

1.4.6 Enforcement

On a review of a premises licence or a club premises certificate a licensing authority may suspend or revoke the licence or certificate, exclude specific licensable activities from the licence or certificate or modify operating conditions attaching to the licence or certificate. These powers must be exercised with a view to promoting the licensing objectives.

The Act also gives the police powers to close licensed premises where there is disorderly behaviour and excessive noise.

1.4.7 Offences

The Act contains a range of offences, inspection powers and enforcement provisions.

1.5 HUMAN RIGHTS AND LICENSING

1.5.1 Introduction

The Human Rights Act 1998 came into force on 2 October 2000 and incorporated parts of the European Convention on Human Rights into English law. It gives further effect to the 'Convention rights'. This effect is twofold. First, existing and future legislation must be interpreted in a way which is compatible with the Convention rights (s.3(1)). Secondly, it is unlawful for any public authority to act in a way which is incompatible with a Convention right (s.6(1)).

A 'public authority' includes a court or tribunal, and any person certain of whose functions are of a public nature (s.6(3)). This will include local authorities acting as licensing authorities under the Licensing Act 2003 and they must therefore act compatibly with Convention rights when exercising their licensing functions. In addition magistrates' courts hearing appeals under the Act and chief officers of police exercising their functions under the Act must also act compatibly with Convention rights.

It will not be unlawful if a public authority cannot act compatibly either because of primary legislation or provisions made under primary legislation that cannot be read or given effect in a way that is compatible (s.6(2)). A person who claims that a public authority has acted, or proposes to act, unlawfully may bring proceedings against the authority for breach of its statutory duty in s.6, or rely on the Convention right or rights concerned in any legal proceedings, provided he is, or would be, a victim of the unlawful act (s.7(1)). If the court decides that the act or proposed act is, or would be, unlawful it may grant such relief or remedy, or make such order, within its powers as it considers just and appropriate (s.8).

Section 2(1) indicates that a court or tribunal, when deciding a question which has arisen in connection with a Convention right, must take into account any:

- judgment, decision, declaration or advisory opinion of the European Court of Human Rights;
- opinion of the European Commission of Human Rights given in a report adopted under art. 31 of the Convention as to whether there has been a violation of Convention rights;
- decision of the European Commission of Human Rights in connection with arts. 26 or 27(2) of the Convention as to the admissibility of petitions claiming a violation of Convention rights; and
- decision of the Committee of Ministers taken under art. 46 of the Convention, whenever made or given, so far as, in the opinion of the court or tribunal, it is relevant to the proceedings in which that question has arisen.

1.5.2   Convention rights

Section 1(1) provides that Convention rights are the rights and fundamental freedoms set out in:

- arts. 2–12 and 14 of the Convention;
- arts. 1–3 of the First Protocol; and
- arts. 1 and 2 of the Sixth Protocol,

as read with arts. 16–18 of the Convention.

The Convention rights which have relevance to licensing law are:

- art. 6 – the right to a fair trial;
- art. 1 of the First Protocol – protection of property;
- art. 8 – protection of private and family life; and
- art. 14 – freedom from discrimination.

1.5.3   The right to a fair trial

Article 6(1) provides that:

> In the determination of his civil rights and obligations or of any criminal charge against him, everyone is entitled to a fair and public hearing within a reasonable time by an independent and impartial tribunal established by law. Judgment shall be pronounced publicly but the press and public may be excluded from all or part of the trial in the interest of morals, public order or national security in a democratic society, where the interests of juveniles or the protection of the private life of the parties so require, or to the extent strictly necessary in the opinion of the court in special circumstances where publicity would prejudice the interests of justice.

There will be a determination of a civil right where there is a dispute over a civil right (*James* v. *United Kingdom* (1986) 8 EHRR 123).

The rights of a person involved in licensable activities under the Act will be 'civil rights' under art. 6(1) (*Tre Traktorer AB* v. *Sweden* (A/159) (1991) 13 EHRR 309). This was confirmed by the Joint Committee on Human Rights in its Fourth Report on the Licensing Bill at para. 7:

> As the rights of those in possession of property, and perhaps those entertainers whose freedom of expression would be limited, are civil rights within the meaning of ECHR Article 6.1, the licensing procedures would have to be compatible with the right to a fair hearing by an independent and impartial tribunal under that Article.

Applicants

Applicants for an authorisation under the Act have the right to have their applications determined in manner compatible with art. 6(1). This was confirmed in relation to an application for an on-licence under the Licensing Act 1964 in *R. (on the application of Chief Constable of*

Lancashire) v. *Preston Crown Court* [2001] EWHC Admin 928; [2002] 1 WLR 1332. In this case the right to apply for an on-licence was within 'civil rights and obligations' as it related to the applicant's right to make a living and pursue commercial activity. As authorisations under the Act also relate to commercial activity, they must be determined in a way which is compatible with art. 6(1).

An applicant must have an opportunity to put his case, and there must be 'equality of arms'. In *Dombo Beheer BV* v. *Netherlands* (A/274-A) (1994) 18 EHRR 213 the European Court of Human Rights stated at para. 33 that:

> 'equality of arms' implies that each party must be afforded a reasonable opportunity to present his case – including his evidence – under conditions that do not place him at a substantial disadvantage *vis-à-vis* his opponent.

The Licensing Act 2003 (Hearings) Regulations 2005, SI 2005/44 ('Hearings Regulations'), reg. 8(2) provides that a party to a hearing must request permission for any other person, other than someone representing him, to appear and he must give an indication of how that person will assist the licensing authority. Regulation 23 requires that a hearing take the form of a discussion led by the licensing authority and permits cross-examination only if the licensing authority considers it necessary. A refusal of permission may well infringe art. 6(1).

Objectors

If a person objecting to a licence has a sufficient interest, art. 6(1) will be engaged. Whether a person will have a sufficient interest is a question of fact. An objection may be made by an interested person making a relevant representation. An interested person is defined in s.13(3) as a business or resident in the vicinity of the premises. It is suggested that such persons will have sufficient interest for their rights to be protected by art. 6(1).

Independent and impartial tribunal

Under art. 6(1) the tribunal must be 'independent and impartial'. A body carrying out administrative functions may be a tribunal for the purposes of art. 6(1). A local authority exercising licensing functions will be exercising administrative functions together with a quasi-judicial function and will therefore be a tribunal for the purposes of art. 6(1).

In order to be independent the tribunal must be independent of the parties to the dispute and also independent of the executive. A local authority is part of the executive and therefore not independent. However, where the tribunal is not independent, art. 6(1) will be satisfied if there is a right of appeal to a body which is an independent tribunal (*R. (on the application of Holding &*

Barnes plc) v. *Secretary of State for the Environment, Transport and the Regions* [2001] UKHL 23; [2003] 2 AC 295). The Act provides that there is a right of appeal to the magistrates' court and a further right of appeal to the High Court. This will be sufficient to comply with art. 6(1).

The tribunal must also be 'impartial'. This means that there must not be any bias on the part of any member of the tribunal and that there must be no doubt as to the tribunal's impartiality. The first of these requirements is subjective while the other is objective. The approach which will be taken was laid down by the House of Lords in *Porter* v. *Magill* [2001] UKHL 67; [2002] 2 AC 357, para. 102 as follows:

> The court must first ascertain all the circumstances which have a bearing on the suggestion that the judge was biased. It must then ask whether those circumstances would lead a fair-minded and informed observer to conclude that there was a real possibility, or a real danger, the two being the same, that the tribunal was biased.

In relation to the Act bias may arise where a member of the licensing committee is a councillor for the ward in which the particular premises are situated and he or she makes representations on behalf of an interested party living in the ward. The Guidance at para. 5.32 provides:

> it would be expected that any councillor who is also a member of the licensing committee and who is making such representations on behalf of the interested party would disqualify him or herself from any involvement in the decision-making process affecting the premises licence in question.

1.5.4   Protection of property

Article 1 of the First Protocol to the European Convention of Human Rights provides:

> Every natural or legal person is entitled to the peaceful enjoyment of his possessions. No one shall be deprived of his possessions except in the public interest and subject to the conditions provided for by law and by the general principles of international law.
>
> The preceding provisions shall not, however, in any way impair the right of a State to enforce such laws as it deems necessary to control the use of property in accordance with the general interest or to secure the payment of taxes or other contributions or penalties.

This is a qualified right and so the State may interfere with it in restricted circumstances. Before a State can interfere, the interference must be:

- prescribed by law;
- in pursuit of one or more specified legitimate aims; and
- no more than is necessary in a democratic society (the test for this is whether it is proportionate).

The right may be engaged where the State interferes with a person's possessions. In *Tre Traktorer AB* v. *Sweden* (A/159) (1991) 13 EHRR 309 the argument that a licence was not a possession was rejected. The European Court of Human Rights stated at para. 53:

> The Government argued that a licence to serve alcoholic beverages could not be considered to be a 'possession' within the meaning of Article 1 of the Protocol. This provision was therefore, in their opinion, not applicable to the case. Like the Commission, however, the Court takes the view that the economic interests connected with the running of *Le Cardinal* were 'possessions' for the purposes of Article 1 of the Protocol. Indeed, the Court has already found that the maintenance of the licence was one of the principal conditions for the carrying on of the applicant company's business, and that its withdrawal had adverse effects on the goodwill and value of the restaurant. Such withdrawal thus constitutes, in the circumstances of the case, an interference with TTA's right to the 'peaceful enjoyment of [its] possessions'.

While, the court did not conclude that a licence was a possession it did decide that economic interests in the property in respect of which a licence is held can amount to 'possessions'. Thus economic interests connected with the running of premises under a premises licence or under a club premises certificate should be regarded as 'possessions'. The State will therefore interfere with a property right if the licence or certificate is revoked or varied. In the case of an application for a new licence or certificate a refusal will not be an interference with a property right as there is no economic interest in existence connected with the licence.

Article 1 distinguishes between a 'deprivation' of possessions and 'control' of them. In *Sporrong and Lonnroth* v. *Sweden* (A/52) (1983) 5 EHRR 35 the European Court of Human Rights stated at para. 61 that art. 1:

> comprises three distinct rules. The first rule, which is of a general nature, enounces the principle of peaceful enjoyment of property; it is set out in the first sentence of the first paragraph. The second rule covers deprivation of possessions and subjects it to certain conditions; it appears in the second sentence of the same paragraph. The third rule recognises that the States are entitled, amongst other things, to control the use of property in accordance with the general interest, by enforcing such laws as they deem necessary for the purpose; it is contained in the second paragraph. The Court must determine, before considering whether the first rule was complied with, whether the last two are applicable.

When applying the first rule the court went on to say at para. 69:

> the Court must determine whether a fair balance was struck between the demands of the general interest of the community and the requirements of the protection of the individual's fundamental rights. The search for this balance is inherent in the whole of the Convention and is also reflected in the structure of Article 1.

Once some form of interference has been established the court will apply the following three-part test in order to decide whether the interference is justified:

- it will first consider whether the interference is compatible with the rule of law and is sufficiently accessible and foreseeable;
- it will then consider whether the interference is in the public interest; and
- finally it will consider whether the interference strikes a fair balance between the general interests of the community and the protection of the individual's rights.

Controlling the use of property under the Act by granting premises licences and club premises certificates will advance the general interests of the community, and can be justified by the four licensing objectives contained in the Act (see 1.3).

1.5.5 Right to respect for private and family life

Article 8 provides that:

1. Everyone has the right to respect for his private and family life, his home and his correspondence.
2. There shall be no interference by a public authority with the exercise of this right except such as is in accordance with the law and is necessary in a democratic society in the interests of national security, public safety or the economic well-being of the country, for the prevention of disorder or crime, for the protection of health or morals or for the protection of the rights and freedoms of others.

Article 8 protects private and family life from interference by the State. In relation to licensing interference could arise in the exercise of the powers to inspect and search premises where the premises in question are also someone's home. In such a situation art. 8 will be engaged.

Article 8 also protects people's enjoyment of the amenities of their home, for example against intrusion from noise. In *Moreno Gomez* v. *Spain* (2005) 41 EHRR 40 the European Court of Human Rights held that there had been a violation of art. 8 where the local authority had failed to take action to deal with night-time disturbances and noise pollution caused by night clubs near the applicant's home.

1.5.6 Prohibition of discrimination

Article 14 provides:

The enjoyment of the rights and freedoms set forth in this Convention shall be secured without discrimination on any ground such as sex, race, colour, language, religion, political or other opinion, national or social origin, association with a national minority, property, birth or other status.

Article 14 does not create an independent right and it operates only to prevent discrimination in respect of other Convention rights.

Concern was raised by the Joint Committee on Human Rights when it was considering the Licensing Bill about the exemption in Sched. 1, para. 9 for the provision of entertainment or entertainment facilities for the purposes of, or for purposes incidental to, a religious meeting or service, or at a place of public worship. The Committee in its Fifteenth Report of Session 2002/3 at para. 5.1 said that:

> In our Twelfth Report, we drew the attention of each House to our view that the proposals for exempting places used for public worship from the requirements of the licensing regime, and allowing certain other places associated with places of public worship to obtain licenses without paying the usual fee, might be regarded as discriminating against the occupiers and users of purely secular premises. We were concerned that these exemptions might give rise to a significant risk of violating the right to be free of discrimination under ECHR Article 14, taken together with ECHR Articles 9 (right to freedom of religion, conscience and belief) and 10 (freedom of expression). We were also concerned that there was a risk that the exemptions might – '. . . leave a patchwork of different licensing requirements without a coherent rationale, calling in question the existence of a pressing social need for the restriction on freedom of expression through a licensing regime for public entertainment, and so undermining the Government's claim that such a licensing regime is a justifiable interference with the right to freedom of expression under ECHR Article 10.2'.

The Government's response was summarised in paras. 5.3 and 5.4 as follows:

> So far as is relevant to this issue, the Department pointed out that the exemption for places of public religious worship from the requirements of entertainment licensing law would benefit people who were using the premises for the enjoyment of secular entertainment there. Those people might be of any religious affiliation or of none. In addition, the exemption for religious venues is a recognition of the – '. . . distinct pastoral role in the community played by many of the faiths and the wider responsibility that, for example, the church has in bringing the community together'.
>
> 5.4 The Minister also drew attention to the central role of the churches to the development of music in this country, particularly because churches provide venues large enough for the performance of many pieces of music requiring large forces. For these reasons, the Government argued that Articles 9, 10 and 14 are not engaged, but that, if they were engaged, there is a rational and objective justification for the exemption which does not call into question the pressing social need to regulate public entertainment in general.

CHAPTER 2

Licensing authorities

2.1 INTRODUCTION

The Act transfers responsibility for alcohol licensing from the magistrates' courts to local authorities. This brings the licensing regimes for alcohol, public entertainment, cinemas, theatres, late night refreshment and night cafés under the responsibility of a single authority. The Government in its White Paper entitled *Time for Reform: Proposals for the Modernisation of our Licensing Laws* (Cm 4696, 2000) set out in para. 123 the following reasons for giving local authorities these responsibilities:

- accountability: we strongly believe that the licensing authority should be accountable to local residents whose lives are fundamentally affected by the decisions taken
- accessibility: many local residents may be inhibited by court processes, and would be more willing to seek to influence decisions if in the hands of local councillors
- crime and disorder: local authorities now have a leading statutory role in preventing local crime and disorder, and the link between alcohol and crime persuasively argues for them to have a similar lead on licensing.

2.2 LICENSING AUTHORITIES

Section 3(1) provides that the following are a 'licensing authority':

- the council of a district in England;
- the council of a county in England in which there are no district councils;
- the council of a county or county borough in Wales;
- the council of a London borough;
- the Common Council of the City of London;
- the Sub-Treasurer of the Inner Temple;
- the Under-Treasurer of the Middle Temple; and
- the Council of the Isles of Scilly.

For the purposes of the Act, a licensing authority's area is the area for which the authority acts (s.3(2)).

2.3 THE GENERAL DUTIES OF LICENSING AUTHORITIES

Section 4(1) provides that when carrying out its functions under the Act a licensing authority must do so with a view to promoting the four licensing objectives, which are:

- the prevention of crime and disorder;
- public safety;
- the prevention of public nuisance; and
- the protection of children from harm.

There is no requirement that a licensing authority must achieve the licensing objectives. It just has to carry out its functions with a view to promoting them.

In carrying out its licensing functions a licensing authority must also have regard to its statement of licensing policy published under s.5 and any guidance issued by the Secretary of State under s.182 (s.4(2)) (see **2.12**).

2.4 STATEMENT OF LICENSING POLICY

Section 5 provides that a licensing authority must determine its policy with respect to the exercise of its licensing functions every three years. Before the start of a three-year period it must publish a statement of licensing policy. This policy is referred to in the Act as a 'licensing statement'. The first three-year period began on 7 January 2005 (see Licensing Act 2003 (Licensing Statement Period) Order 2004, SI 2004/2362) and the next three-year period will start on 7 January 2008.

A local authority will usually publish its licensing policy on its website. Copies may also be published on the website of other organisations such as the British Beer and Pub Association.

Before determining its policy for a three-year period, a licensing authority must under s.5(3) consult the following:

- the chief officer of police for the licensing authority's area;
- the fire and rescue authority for its area;
- such persons as the licensing authority considers to be representative of holders of premises licences issued by that authority, for example the local licensed victuallers' association (for public houses), the Cinema Exhibitors' Association (for film exhibitions), the Theatrical Management Association (for theatres);
- such persons as the licensing authority considers to be representative of holders of club premises certificates issued by that authority, for example the Club and Institute Union;

13

- such persons as the licensing authority considers to be representative of holders of personal licences issued by that authority, for example a trade association or a professional body; and
- such other persons as the licensing authority considers to be representative of businesses and residents in its area, for example a local chamber of commerce or a residents' association.

The Guidance at para. 3.4 provides:

> The views of all these persons/bodies listed should be given appropriate weight when the policy is determined. It is recognised that in some areas, it may be difficult to identify persons or bodies representative for all parts of industry affected by the provisions of the 2003 Act, but licensing authorities must make reasonable efforts to identify the persons or bodies concerned.

A licensing authority is not precluded from consulting with other persons or bodies in addition to those it is required to consult under s.5(3). The Guidance at para. 3.5 provides that:

> For example, certain authorities may consider it essential to consult the Crime and Disorder Reduction Partnerships (CDRPs), British Transport Police, local Accident and Emergency Departments, bodies representing consumers, local police consultative groups or those charged locally with the promotion of tourism. They may also consider it valuable to consult local performers, performers' unions (such as the Musicians' Union and Equity) and entertainers involved in the cultural life of the local community.

While a licensing authority is free to decide the full extent of its consultation beyond those it is required to consult, the Guidance at para. 3.6 issues the following warning:

> When undertaking consultation exercises, licensing authorities should have regard to cost and time. Licensing authorities should note that the Secretary of State will establish fee levels to provide full cost recovery of all licensing functions including the preparation and publication of a statement of licensing policy, but this will be based on the statutory requirements. Where licensing authorities exceed these requirements, they should note that they would have to absorb those costs themselves.

During each three-year period a licensing authority must keep its licensing policy under review and make any revisions it considers appropriate. Before making a revision, the licensing authority must carry out a consultation exercise. If a revision is made, the licensing authority must publish a statement of the revision or the revised licensing statement.

2.5   THE CONTENTS OF A STATEMENT OF LICENSING POLICY

The Guidance recommends that a licensing policy should begin by stating the four licensing objectives (para. 3.8). It should then make it clear that:

1. Licensing is about regulating the carrying on of licensable activities on licensed premises, by qualifying clubs and at temporary events within the terms of the Act, and that the conditions attached to various authorisations will be focused on matters which are within the control of individual licensees and others in possession of relevant authorisations, so that these matters will centre on the premises being used for licensable activities and the vicinity of those premises (para. 3.11).

2. In addressing the matter of vicinity, the licensing authority will primarily focus on the direct impact of the activities taking place at the licensed premises on members of the public living, working or engaged in normal activity in the area concerned. Whether or not incidents can be regarded as being 'in the vicinity' of licensed premises is a question of fact and will depend on the particular circumstances of the case. In cases of dispute, the question will ultimately be decided by the courts (para. 3.11).

3. Licensing law is not the primary mechanism for the general control of nuisance and antisocial behaviour by individuals once they are away from the licensed premises and, therefore, beyond the direct control of the individual, club or business holding the licence, certificate or authorisation concerned (para. 3.11).

In addition the Guidance specifically considers that a licensing policy should consider:

- the cumulative impact of licensed premises;
- licensing hours;
- children;
- integration with other strategies;
- duplication of regulatory control;
- standardised conditions;
- enforcement; and
- administration, exercise and delegation of functions.

2.5.1   The cumulative impact of licensed premises

While 'cumulative impact' is not mentioned specifically in the Act, the potential impact on the promotion of the licensing objectives of a significant number of licensed premises concentrated in one area is a proper matter for a licensing authority to consider in developing its licensing policy statement. An example is the potential impact on crime and disorder or public nuisance on a town or city centre of a large concentration of licensed premises in that part of the local licensing authority area (Guidance, para. 3.13).

The Guidance, para. 3.14 provides:

> It is however important that applicants, responsible authorities and interested parties should know through the statement of licensing policy, whether the licensing authority already considers that a particular concentration of licensed premises in a particular part of its area is considered to be already causing a cumulative impact on one or more of the licensing objectives. Whether an area is nearing this point should be one of the issues on which local residents are consulted.

If a licensing authority decides that an approach to cumulative impact in its licensing policy statement is appropriate and necessary 'it should indicate in the statement that it is adopting a special policy of refusing new licences whenever it receives relevant representations about the cumulative impact on the licensing objectives from responsible authorities and interested parties which it concludes after hearing those representations should lead to refusal' (Guidance, para. 3.16). There should be an evidential basis for this and the Guidance at para. 3.17 provides that:

> For example, Crime and Disorder Reduction Partnerships will often have collated information which demonstrates cumulative impact as part of their general role on anti-social behaviour; and crime prevention strategies may have already identified cumulative impact as a local problem. Similarly, environmental health officers may be able to demonstrate concentrations of valid complaints relating to noise disturbance.

The Guidance at para. 3.18 sets out the following steps to be followed by a licensing authority when deciding whether to adopt a cumulative impact policy within the statement of licensing policy:

- identification of concern about crime and disorder or public nuisance;
- consideration of whether it can be demonstrated that crime and disorder and nuisance are arising and are caused by the customers of licensed premises (and if so identifying the area from which problems are arising and the boundaries of that area) or that the risk factors are such that the area is reaching a point when a cumulative impact is imminent;
- consultation with those persons and bodies specified in s.5(3) as part of the general consultation required in respect of the whole statement of licensing policy;
- subject to that consultation, inclusion of a special policy about future premises licence or club premises certificate applications from that area within the terms of this Guidance in the statement of licensing policy; and
- publication of the special policy as part of the statement of licensing policy required by the Act.

Once a cumulative impact policy has been adopted, the Guidance at para. 3.19 states that there will be:

a rebuttable presumption that applications for new premises licences or club premises certificates or material variations will normally be refused, if relevant representations to that effect are received, unless it can be demonstrated that the operation of the premises involved will not add to the cumulative impact already being experienced. Applicants would need to address the special policy issues in their operating schedules in order to rebut such a presumption. However, a special policy must stress that this presumption does not relieve responsible authorities or interested parties of the need to make a relevant representation before a licensing authority may lawfully consider giving effect to its special policy. If no representation is received, it would remain the case that any application must be granted in terms that are consistent with the operating schedule submitted. However, responsible authorities, such as the police, or interested parties, can make a written representation maintaining that it is necessary to refuse the application for the promotion of the prevention of crime and disorder and referring to information which had been before the licensing authority when it developed its statement of licensing policy.

A cumulative impact policy should only be adopted in relation to on-licensed premises and the Guidance at paras. 3.22 and 3.23 provides:

3.22 It would normally not be justifiable to adopt a special policy on the basis of a concentration of shops, stores or supermarkets selling alcohol for consumption off the premises. Special policies will address the impact of a concentration of licensed premises selling alcohol for consumption on the premises which may give rise to large numbers of people who have been drinking alcohol on the streets in a particular area.

3.23 A special policy should never be absolute. Statements of licensing policy should always allow for the circumstances of each application to be considered properly and for licences and certificates that are unlikely to add to the cumulative impact on the licensing objectives to be granted. Following receipt of representations in respect of a new application for or a variation of a licence or certificate, the licensing authority must consider whether it would be justified in departing from its special policy in the light of the individual circumstances of the case. The impact can be expected to be different for premises with different styles and characteristics. For example, while a large nightclub or high capacity public house might add to problems of cumulative impact, a small restaurant or a theatre may not. If after such consideration, the licensing authority decides that an application should be refused, it will still be for the licensing authority to show that the grant of the application would undermine the promotion of one of the licensing objectives and if it would, that necessary conditions would be ineffective in preventing the problems involved.

In addition, there are other limitations on the use of a cumulative impact policy:

17

1. It should never be used as a ground for revoking an existing licence or certificate when relevant representations are received about problems with those premises (Guidance, para. 3.24).
2. It should never be used to justify rejecting applications to vary an existing licence or certificate except where those modifications are directly relevant to the policy (as would be the case with an application to vary a licence with a view to increasing the capacity limits of the premises) and are strictly necessary for the promotion of the licensing objectives (Guidance, para. 3.25).
3. It cannot justify and should not include provisions for a terminal hour in a particular area. The Guidance at para. 3.26 states that:

> For example, it would be wrong not to apply the special policy to applications that include provision to open no later than, for example, midnight, but to apply the policy to any other premises that propose opening later. The effect would be to impose a fixed closing time akin to that under the 'permitted hours' provisions of the Licensing Act 1964. Terminal hours dictated by the Licensing Act 1964 were abolished to avoid the serious problems that arise when customers exit licensed premises simultaneously. Attempting to fix a terminal hour in any area would therefore directly undermine a key purpose of the 2003 Act.

4. It must not impose quotas – based on either the number of premises or the capacity of those premises – that restrict the consideration of any application on its individual merits or which seek to impose limitations on trading hours in particular areas (Guidance, para. 3.27). Quotas that indirectly have the effect of predetermining the outcome of any application should not be used because they have no regard to the individual characteristics of the premises concerned. There are many different types of premises, for example public houses, night clubs, restaurants, hotels, theatres, concert halls and cinemas which sell alcohol, serve food and provide entertainment, each with contrasting styles and characteristics and the Guidance at para. 3.27 states that proper regard should be given to those differences and the differing impact they will have on the promotion of the licensing objectives.

A cumulative impact policy must be reviewed on a regular basis. The Guidance at para. 3.20 provides:

> Once adopted, special policies should be reviewed regularly to assess whether they are needed any longer or need expanding. While a special policy is in existence, applicants will need to demonstrate why the operation of the premises would not add to the cumulative impact being experienced.

A licensing policy should also indicate the other mechanisms both within and outside the licensing regime that are available for addressing problems caused by any customers behaving badly and unlawfully. The Guidance at para. 3.28 suggests that these include:

- planning controls;
- positive measures to create a safe and clean town centre environment in partnership with local businesses, transport operators and other departments of the local authority;
- the provision of CCTV surveillance in town centres, ample taxi ranks, provision of public conveniences open late at night, street cleaning and litter patrols;
- powers of local authorities to designate parts of the local authority area as places where alcohol may not be consumed publicly;
- police enforcement of the general law concerning disorder and antisocial behaviour, including the issuing of fixed penalty notices;
- the prosecution of any personal licence holder or member of staff at such premises who is selling alcohol to people who are drunk;
- the confiscation of alcohol from adults and children in designated areas;
- police powers to close down instantly for up to 24 hours any licensed premises or temporary event on grounds of disorder, the likelihood of disorder or noise emanating from the premises causing a nuisance; and
- the power of the police, other responsible authorities or a local resident or business to seek a review of the licence or certificate in question.

2.5.2 Licensing hours

In relation to licensing hours, the Guidance at para. 3.29 provides that:

> the statement of policy should generally emphasise the consideration which will be given to the individual merits of an application. The Government strongly recommends that statements of policy should recognise that longer licensing hours with regard to the sale of alcohol are important to ensure that the concentrations of customers leaving premises simultaneously are avoided. This is necessary to reduce the friction at late night fast food outlets, taxi ranks and other sources of transport which lead to disorder and disturbance.

Licensing hours should be set on an individual basis and fixed trading hours within a designated area should not be used. The Guidance at para. 3.30 states:

> The term 'zoning' is used in this Guidance to refer to the setting of fixed trading hours within a designated area. As experience in Scotland suggests that zoning leads to the significant movement of people across boundaries in search of premises opening later and puts greater pressure on town and city centres than is necessary, it should not be adopted as a policy. Zoning can result in greater disturbance in the streets at particular times and concentrations of disturbance and noise, particularly where licensing authorities seek to adopt fixed 'terminal hours' as a matter of policy. It also assumes that the representations of residents in one area should be treated less favourably than others in other areas simply because they live in busy central areas of towns and cities or because residential housing is less dense than in other areas. It is acceptable for

a statement of policy to make clear that stricter conditions with regard to noise control will be expected in areas which have denser residential accommodation, but this should not limit opening hours without regard to the individual merits of any application.

In relation to premises which sell alcohol for consumption off the premises, the Guidance at para. 3.31 provides:

> With regard to shops, stores and supermarkets, the Government strongly recommends that statements of licensing policy should indicate that the norm will be for such premises to be free to provide sales of alcohol for consumption off the premises at any times when the retail outlet is open for shopping unless there are very good reasons for restricting those hours. For example, a limitation may be appropriate following police representations in the case of some shops known to be a focus of disorder and disturbance because youths gather there. Statements of licensing policy should therefore reflect this general approach.

2.5.3 Children

The Guidance, para. 3.36 provides that a licensing policy must not:

> seek to limit the access of children to any premises unless it is necessary for the prevention of physical, moral or psychological harm to them. Licensing policy statements should not attempt to anticipate every issue of concern that could arise in respect of children with regard to individual premises and as such, general rules should be avoided. Consideration of the individual merits of each application remains the best mechanism for judging such matters.

A licensing policy should highlight areas that will give rise to particular concern in respect of children. The Guidance, para. 3.37 suggests that these should include premises:

- where entertainment or services of an adult or sexual nature are commonly provided;
- where there have been convictions of members of the current staff at the premises for serving alcohol to minors or with a reputation for underage drinking;
- with a known association with drug taking or dealing;
- where there is a strong element of gambling on the premises (but not, for example, the simple presence of a small number of cash prize gaming machines); and
- where the supply of alcohol for consumption on the premises is the exclusive or primary purpose of the services provided at the premises.

The Guidance, para. 3.38 provides that:

> In the context of paragraph 3.37 above, it is not possible to give an exhaustive list of what amounts to entertainment or services of an adult or sexual nature.

Applicants, responsible authorities and licensing authorities will need to apply common sense to this matter. However, such entertainment or services, for example, would generally include topless bar staff, striptease, lap-, table- or pole-dancing, performances involving feigned violence or horrific incidents, feigned or actual sexual acts or fetishism, or entertainment involving strong and offensive language.

A licensing policy should make clear the range of alternatives which may be considered for limiting the access of children where that is necessary for the prevention of harm to them. The Guidance, para. 3.39 provides that these, which can be adopted in combination, include:

- limitations on the hours when children may be present;
- limitations or the exclusion of the presence of children under certain ages when particular specified activities are taking place;
- limitations on the parts of premises to which children might be given access;
- age limitations (below 18);
- requirements for accompanying adults (including for example, a combination of requirements which provide that children under a particular age must be accompanied by an adult); and
- full exclusion of those people under 18 from the premises when any licensable activities are taking place.

Representations may be made by a responsible authority in relation to the protection of children, and the Guidance at para. 3.41 provides:

A statement of licensing policy should therefore indicate which body the licensing authority judges to be competent in this area and therefore to which applications will need to be copied. In most cases, this may be the Area Child Protection Committee. However, in some areas, the Committee's involvement may not be practical and the licensing authority should consider alternatives. For example, the local authority social services department. It would be practical and useful for statements of licensing policy to include the correct descriptions of the responsible authorities in any area and appropriate contact details.

In relation to premises which give film exhibitions, the Guidance, para. 3.41 provides that a licensing policy:

should make clear that in the case of premises giving film exhibitions, the licensing authority will expect licensees or clubs to include in their operating schedules arrangements for restricting children from viewing age-restricted films classified according to the recommendations of the British Board of Film Classification or the licensing authority itself. Where a licensing authority intends to adopt its own system of classification, its statement of policy should indicate where the information regarding such classifications will be published and made available to licensees, clubs and the general public.

21

2.5.4 Integration with other strategies

A licensing policy should provide clear indications of how the licensing authority will secure the proper integration of its licensing policy with local crime prevention, planning, transport, tourism, race equality schemes and cultural strategies and any other plans introduced for the management of town centres and the night-time economy (Guidance, para. 3.45). As many of these strategies will not be directly related to promoting the licensing objectives but will indirectly affect them, it is important that they are coordinated and integrated.

Crime prevention

The Guidance at para. 3.46 provides:

> Licensing policy statements should indicate that conditions attached to premises licences and club premises certificates will, so far as possible, reflect local crime prevention strategies. For example, the provision of closed circuit television cameras in certain premises. Where appropriate it should reflect the input of the local Crime and Disorder Reduction Partnership.

Cultural strategies

In connection with cultural strategies, the Guidance, para. 3.47 provides that:

> licensing policy statements should include clearly worded statements indicating that they will monitor the impact of licensing on the provision of regulated entertainment, and particularly live music and dancing. Care will be needed to ensure that only necessary, proportionate and reasonable licensing conditions impose any restrictions on such events. Where there is any indication that such events are being deterred by licensing requirements, statements of licensing policy should be revisited with a view to investigating how the situation might be reversed. Broader cultural activities and entertainment may also be affected. In developing their statements of licensing policy, licensing authorities should also consider any views of the local authority's arts committee where one exists.

Transport

The Guidance, para. 3.50 provides:

> A statement should describe any protocols agreed between the local police and other licensing enforcement officers and indicate that arrangements will be made for them to report to local authority transport committees so that those committees may have regard to the need to disperse people from town and city centres swiftly and safely to avoid concentrations which produce disorder and disturbance when developing their policies. When developing the statement licensing authorities should have regard to the existing policies and strategies of the relevant local transport authority, as set out in their local Transport Plan.

Tourism, employment, planning and building control

The Guidance at para. 3.51 provides that:

A statement should also indicate:

- that arrangements have been made for licensing committees to receive, when appropriate, reports on the needs of the local tourist economy for the area to ensure that these are reflected in their considerations;
- the licensing authority's intention to keep their licensing committee apprised of the employment situation in the area and the need for new investment and employment where appropriate;
- that planning, building control and licensing regimes will be properly separated to avoid duplication and inefficiency. Applications for premises licences for permanent commercial premises should normally be from businesses with planning consent for the property concerned. Licensing applications should not be a re-run of the planning application and should not cut across decisions taken by the local authority planning committee or following appeals against decisions taken by that committee. Similarly, the granting by the licensing committee of any variation of a licence which involves a material alteration to a building would not relieve the applicant of the need to apply for planning permission or building control where appropriate. Proper integration should be assured by licensing committees, where appropriate, providing regular reports to the planning committee on the situation regarding licensed premises in the area, including the general impact of alcohol related crime and disorder. This would enable the planning committee to have regard to such matters when taking its decisions and avoid any unnecessary overlap.

Promotion of racial equality

The Guidance at para. 3.52 provides:

A statement of licensing policy should also recognise that:

- the Race Relations Act 1976, as amended by the Race Relations (Amendment) Act 2000, places a legal obligation on public authorities to have due regard to the need to eliminate unlawful discrimination; and to promote equality of opportunity and good relations between persons of different racial groups;
- local authorities are also required under the 1976 Act, as amended, to produce a race equality scheme, assess and consult on the likely impact of proposed policies on race equality, monitor policies for any adverse impact on the promotion of race equality, and publish the results of such consultations, assessments and monitoring;
- Home Office guidance on how to prepare race impact assessments is available at www.raceimpact.homeoffice.gov.uk;
- the statement of licensing policy should therefore refer to this legislation and in turn, the statement of policy should be referenced in the race equality scheme.

23

2.5.5 Duplication of regulatory control

A licensing policy should according to the Guidance para 3.53:

> include a firm commitment to avoid duplication with other regulatory regimes so far as possible. For example, legislation governing health and safety at work and fire safety will place a range of general duties on the self-employed, employers and operators of venues both in respect of employees and of the general public when on the premises in question. Similarly, many aspects of fire safety will be covered by existing and future legislation. Conditions in respect of public safety should only be attached to premises licences and club premises certificates that are 'necessary' for the promotion of that licensing objective and if already provided for in other legislation, they cannot be considered necessary in the context of licensing law. Such regulations will not however always cover the unique circumstances that arise in connection with licensable activities, particularly regulated entertainment, at specific premises and tailored conditions may be necessary.

2.5.6 Standardised conditions

Standardised conditions should not be imposed on all licences and certificates. The Guidance, para. 3.55 provides:

> Statements of policy should make clear that a key concept underscoring the 2003 Act is for conditions to be attached to licences and certificates which are tailored to the individual style and characteristics of the premises and events concerned. This is essential to avoid the imposition of disproportionate and overly burdensome conditions on premises where there is no need for such conditions. Standardised conditions should therefore be avoided and indeed, may be unlawful where they cannot be shown to be necessary for the promotion of the licensing objectives in any individual case.

A licensing authority can have a pool of common conditions which applicants can use. Paragraph 3.55 goes on to provide:

> However, it is acceptable for licensing authorities to draw attention in their statements of policy to pools of conditions from which necessary and proportionate conditions may be drawn in particular circumstances.

2.5.7 Enforcement

A licensing policy should deal with the enforcement issues, and the Guidance, paras. 3.56 and 3.57 provides:

> 3.56 As part of their statement of policy, the Government strongly recommends that licensing authorities should express the intention to establish protocols with the local police on enforcement issues. This would provide for a more efficient deployment of licensing authority staff and police officers who are commonly engaged in enforcing licensing law and the inspection of licensed premises.

3.57 In particular, these protocols should also provide for the targeting of agreed problem and high risk premises which require greater attention, while providing a lighter touch in respect of low risk premises which are well run. In some local authority areas, the limited validity of public entertainment, theatre, cinema, night café and late night refreshment house licences has in the past led to a culture of annual inspections regardless of whether the assessed risks make such inspections necessary. The 2003 Act does not require inspections to take place save at the discretion of those charged with this role. The principle of risk assessment and targeting should prevail and inspections should not be undertaken routinely but when and if they are judged necessary. This should ensure that resources are more effectively concentrated on problem premises.

2.5.8   Administration, exercise and delegation of functions

The Guidance at paras 3.61 and 3.62 provides:

3.61 The 2003 Act provides that the functions of the licensing authority (including its determinations) are to be taken or carried out by its licensing committee (except those relating to the making of a statement of licensing policy or where another of its committees has the matter referred to it). The licensing committee may delegate these functions to subcommittees or in appropriate cases, to officials supporting the licensing authority. Where licensing functions are not automatically transferred to licensing committees, the functions must be carried out by the licensing authority as a whole and not by its executive. Statements of licensing policy should indicate how the licensing authority intends to approach its various functions. Many of the decisions and functions will be purely administrative in nature and statements of licensing policy should underline the principle of delegation in the interests of speed, efficiency and cost-effectiveness.

3.62 Where under the provisions of the 2003 Act, there are no relevant representations on an application for the grant of a premises licence or club premises certificate or police objection to an application for a personal licence or to an activity taking place under the authority of a temporary event notice, these matters should be dealt with by officers in order to speed matters through the system. Licensing committees should receive regular reports on decisions made by officers so that they maintain an overview of the general situation.

2.6   CHALLENGING A STATEMENT OF LICENSING POLICY

A licensing policy may be challenged by judicial review on the ground that it is unlawful. Circumstances where this could be appropriate might be where the licensing authority has not consulted properly under s.5(3) before determining its statement of licensing policy or where the policy contains material which does not relate to the licensing objectives. A successful challenge to a licensing policy was brought in *British Beer and Pub Association* v. *Canterbury City Council* [2005] EWHC 1318; *The Times*, 11 July 2005, where the licensing policy was found to be unlawful as it purported to dictate the contents of an application for a premises licence and impose conditions beyond those which were consistent with the Act. Relief was not however granted as the licensing authority proposed an addendum to the policy to mitigate the problems.

It may be possible to challenge a licensing policy under the Human Rights Act 1998, for example if the policy infringes the protection of property under art. 1 of the First Protocol. It is unlikely that a challenge could be brought under art. 6(1) (the right to a fair trial) as the preparation of a licensing policy is not the 'determination of civil rights and obligations' (see *R. (on the application of Aggregate Industries UK Ltd)* v. *English Nature* [2002] EWHC 908; [2003] Env LR 3 where this was decided in relation to a development plan and its statements of policy and it is submitted that a licensing policy could be treated in the same way).

2.7 LICENSING COMMITTEES

Section 6 provides that each licensing authority, except the Sub-Treasurer of the Inner Temple or the Under-Treasurer of the Middle Temple, must establish a licensing committee consisting of at least 10, but not more than 15, members of the authority. The Inner Temple and the Middle Temple will discharge all the licensing functions themselves.

Each licensing committee discharges all the licensing authority's licensing functions, except for the determination and publication of the licensing policy (s. 7(1)). The licensing authority may decide that its licensing committee must also discharge additional functions of the authority that are related to its licensing functions, and if it decides to do so it must consider any relevant report prepared by the licensing committee before acting in any such matter, unless it is urgent. This ensures that the licensing committee will have an input into any matter relating to the authority's licensing functions.

Where a matter concerns other functions in addition to licensing functions, a licensing authority may choose to refer the matter either to its licensing committee, having first consulted it, or to another of its committees. If it decides to refer the matter to another committee, then when that committee considers the matter it must, unless the matter is urgent, consider any report prepared by the licensing committee. Alternatively, if it decides to refer the matter to the licensing committee, this committee must, in its considerations, consider any report about the matter prepared by any of the authority's other committees, unless the matter is urgent.

If a licensing committee is unable to discharge any of its functions because some of its members are prevented from considering or voting on a matter, for example where they are disqualified under the licensing authority's standing orders because they have a financial interest in the matter, then the matter must be referred back to the licensing authority for it to discharge its functions in relation to the matter (s. 7(9)).

2.8 THE LICENSING REGISTER

Section 8 requires every licensing authority to keep a register containing:

- a record of each premises licence, club premises certificate and personal licence which it has issued;
- a record of each temporary event notice it has received;
- a record of the following matters:
  - an application for the grant of a premises licence;
  - an application relating to the theft, loss or destruction of or damage to a premises licence or summary;
  - a notice of surrender of a premises licence;
  - an application by way of a provisional notice in respect of premises;
  - a notice of a change of name or address of a holder of a premises licence;
  - an application for a variation of a premises licence;
  - an application for a variation of the designated premises supervisor;
  - a request from a designated premises supervisor for removal from a premises licence;
  - an application for the transfer of a premises licence;
  - an interim authority notice;
  - an application for the review of a premises licence;
  - an application for a club premises certificate;
  - an application relating to the theft, loss or destruction of or damage to a club premises certificate or summary;
  - a notice of surrender of a club premises certificate;
  - a notice of a change of name of a club or alteration of its rules;
  - an application to vary a club premises certificate;
  - an application for the review of a club premises certificate;
  - a notice of the withdrawal of a temporary event notice;
  - a counter notice following a police objection to a temporary event notice;
  - a copy of a temporary event notice given following the making of modifications to a temporary event notice with police consent;
  - an application relating to the theft, loss or destruction of or damage to a temporary event notice;
  - a notice of the surrender of a personal licence;
  - an application for the grant or renewal of a personal licence;
  - an application relating to the theft, loss or destruction of or damage to a personal licence;
  - a notice of the change of name or address of a personal licence holder;
  - a notice given to it by a magistrates' court to notify its determination made after closure order;

- an application for the conversion of an old licence into a premises licence; and
- an application for the conversion of a club certificate into a club premises certificate; and

- such other information as may be prescribed. The Licensing Act 2003 (Licensing Authority's Register) (Other Information) Regulations 2005, SI 2005/43 has prescribed that each licensing authority must record in its register:

  - the operating schedule which accompanies an application for a premises licence, provided that the name and address of the premises supervisor, if any, shall be removed from the schedule before it is recorded, and the plan of the premises to which the application relates;
  - the schedule of works and plans of the work being or about to be done at the premises which accompany an application for a provisional statement;
  - the revised operating schedule which accompanies an application to vary a premises licence, provided that the name and address of the premises supervisor, if any, shall be removed from the schedule before it is recorded;
  - the club operating schedule and plan of the premises to which the application relates which accompany an application for a club premises certificate;
  - the revised club operating schedule which accompanies an application to vary a club premises certificate;
  - the ground or grounds for reviews set out in applications for a review of a premises licence or club premises certificate and the determination of the magistrates' court on its consideration of a closure order; and
  - the existing licensable activities and existing qualifying club activities and plans of the premises which accompany applications for the conversion of existing licences and existing club certificates.

Regulations may require a register to be in a prescribed form and kept in a prescribed manner. No such regulations have been made.

A licensing authority must provide facilities for making the information contained in the entries in its register available for inspection in a legible form by any person during office hours and without payment (s.8(3)). It must on request supply a person with a copy of the information contained in any entry in its register in legible form, and may charge such reasonable fee as it may determine (s.8(4) and (5)).

The Secretary of State may arrange for the duties conferred on licensing authorities to keep a register to be discharged by means of one or more central registers, and may require licensing authorities to participate in and contribute towards the cost of any such central registers (s.8(6) and (7)). The Guidance at para. 4.16 states that:

> The licensing authorities, supported by the Government, are considering the development of a central database which will, among other things, include details of all personal licence holders. Future developments relating to the creation of a central database will be reported on the DCMS website.

The Government has set up a central licensing register project to work with licensing authorities and other key stakeholders to examine ways in which a central register might best be developed. The Government has indicated that the first stage of its development would involve only personal licences and possibly temporary event notices, with other licences likely to be part of later phases (Consultation on Fee Levels to be Established by Regulation under the Licensing Act 2003, para. 4.19).

2.9 NOTIFICATION TO PERSONS WITH AN INTEREST IN THE PREMISES

Section 178 provides for a person with a 'property interest' in premises affected by licensing matters to be notified of any changes in the register kept under s.8.

A person has a property interest in premises if:

- he has a legal interest in the premises as freeholder or leaseholder;
- he is a legal mortgagee (within the meaning of the Law of Property Act 1925) in respect of the premises;
- he is in occupation of the premises; or
- he has a prescribed interest in the premises (at the time of writing, no interests have been prescribed).

In order to receive notification, a person with a property interest must give notice of his interest to the licensing authority. This notice must be in the prescribed form which is set out in the Licensing Act 2003 (Premises Licences and Club Premises Certificates) Regulations 2005, SI 2005/42, Sched. 1 and be accompanied by the prescribed fee of £21 (Licensing Act 2003 (Fees) Regulations 2005, SI 2005/79 ('Fees Regulations'), reg. 8 and Sched. 6). The notice has effect for a period of 12 months beginning with the date it is received by the licensing authority. It must be renewed annually.

Once a notice has been given, and while it remains in effect, any changes relating to the premises to which the notice relates made in the register must be notified forthwith by the licensing authority to the person who gave the notice. The notification must also set out the right under s.8 to request a copy of the information contained in any entry in the register.

It is submitted that the requirement to 'forthwith' notify a change means that it may be notified as soon as is reasonably practicable rather than on the same day the change is made to the register. This would accord with the view taken by the Privy Council in *Sameen* v. *0* [1963] AC 597 in relation to the meaning of 'forthwith' in the Civil Procedure Code of Ceylon.

2.10 PROCEEDINGS OF THE LICENSING COMMITTEE

Each licensing committee may establish one or more subcommittees consisting of three members of the licensing committee. The procedure to be adopted by the licensing committee and its subcommittees is set out in the Hearings Regulations, as amended by the Licensing Act 2003 (Hearings) (Amendment) Regulations 2005, SI 2005/78 (see further **Chapter 24**). Subject to these regulations, each licensing committee may regulate its own procedure and that of its subcommittees.

2.11 DELEGATION OF FUNCTIONS BY A LICENSING COMMITTEE

A licensing committee may arrange for its functions to be discharged by a subcommittee or by an officer of the licensing authority. Where a function has been delegated to a subcommittee, the subcommittee may in turn arrange for an officer of the licensing authority to discharge that function; however, this power is subject to any direction given by the licensing committee to the subcommittee. More than one subcommittee or officer may discharge the same function concurrently.

The following functions may not however be delegated to an officer:

- the determination of an application for a premises licence where representations have been made;
- the determination of an application for a provisional statement where representations have been made;
- the determination of an application for a variation of a premises licence where representations have been made;
- the determination of an application to vary the designated premises supervisor following a police objection;
- the determination of an application for a transfer of a premises licence following a police objection;
- the consideration of a police objection made to an interim authority notice;
- the determination of an application for a club premises certificate where representations have been made;

- the determination of an application to vary a club premises certificate where representations have been made;
- the decision to give a counter notice following a police objection to a temporary event notice;
- the determination of an application for the grant of a personal licence following a police objection;
- the determination of an application for the renewal of a personal licence following a police objection;
- the revocation of a licence where convictions come to light after its grant;
- the determination of an application for the review of a premises licence where relevant representations have been made;
- the determination of an application for the review of a club premises certificate where relevant representations have been made; and
- a review following a closure order where relevant representations have been made.

When the Gambling Act 2005 comes into force the functions of a licensing authority in respect of a premises licence under part 8 of that Act and in respect of temporary use notices under part 9 of that Act will be delegated to the licensing committee of the authority established under the Licensing Act 2003, and may be further delegated to officers of the authority. The only matter that may not be subdelegated under part 9 is the decision whether or not to issue a counter notice; this decision must be made by the licensing committee.

In addition, the Violent Crime Reduction Bill proposes that neither the determination of interim steps pending a summary review nor the review itself where relevant representations have been made can be delegated to an officer.

2.12 MINISTERIAL GUIDANCE

The Secretary of State is required under s.182 to issue guidance ('the Guidance') to licensing authorities on how they are to discharge their functions under the Act. He may, from time to time, revise the Guidance. The present Guidance was issued on 7 July 2004 and para. 1.4 provides:

> The Guidance is provided for licensing authorities carrying out their functions. Furthermore it provides information for magistrates hearing appeals against licensing decisions. It is also being made widely available for the benefit of operators of licensed premises, their legal advisers and the general public. It is a key mechanism for promoting best practice, ensuring consistent application of licensing powers across the country and for promoting fairness, equal treatment and proportionality. The police remain key enforcers of licensing law. The Guidance has no binding effect on police officers who, within the terms of their force orders and the law, remain operationally independent. However, the Guidance is provided to support and assist police officers in interpreting and

implementing the 2003 Act in the promotion of the prevention of crime and disorder, public safety, prevention of public nuisance and the protection of children from harm.

The Guidance must be published in such manner as the Secretary of State considers appropriate, and it is published on the DCMS website and on UK Online. In addition, a local authority or any other organisation is free to publish the Guidance on its own website or provide an appropriate link to either of these websites.

Nothing in the Guidance should be taken as indicating that any requirement of licensing law or any other law may be overridden (including the obligations placed on the authorities under human rights legislation). The Guidance does not in any way replace the statutory provisions of the Act or add to its scope.

Extracts of the Guidance are included where appropriate throughout the text of this book.

2.13   INFORMATION

Information which is held by or on behalf of a licensing authority or a responsible authority is subject to strict controls. It may be supplied to a licensing authority, or to a responsible authority, in order to facilitate the exercise of the authority's functions under the Act, but cannot be otherwise disclosed (s.185).

2.14   PROCEDURES FOR GIVING NOTICES

Section 184 sets out the rules in relation to any document which is required by the Act to be given to any person.

Where a document has to be given to a licensing authority, it must be given by addressing it to the licensing authority and leaving it at or sending it by post to its principal office or any other office at which it will accept such documents.

In any other case the document may be given to the person in question by delivering it to him, or by leaving it at his proper address, or by sending it by post to him at that address. In the case of a body corporate other than a licensing authority a document may be given to the secretary or clerk of that body; in the case of a partnership it may be given to a partner or a person having the control or management of the partnership business; and in the case of an unincorporated association other than a partnership it may be given to an officer of the association.

A person's proper address will be his last known address except that:

- for a body corporate or its secretary or clerk, it will be the address of the registered office of that body or its principal office in the United Kingdom;
- for a partnership, a partner or a person having control or management of the partnership business, it will be the address of the principal office of the partnership in the United Kingdom; and
- for an unincorporated association other than a partnership or any officer of the association, it will be the address of its principal office in the United Kingdom.

Where a document is to be given to a person in his capacity as the holder of a premises licence, club premises certificate or personal licence or as the designated premises supervisor under a premises licence, his proper address will be the address recorded for him in the licensing register.

CHAPTER 3

Licensable activities

3.1 INTRODUCTION

The Act sets out in s.1 the types of licensable activity which require authorisation under the Act by means of a premises licence, a club premises certificate or a temporary event notice.

Section 1(1) provides that 'licensable activities' are:

- the sale by retail of alcohol;
- the supply of alcohol by or on behalf of a club to, or to the order of, a member of the club;
- the provision of regulated entertainment; and
- the provision of late night refreshment.

In addition, certain licensable activities are 'qualifying club activities' if they occur on club premises. In effect they are the activities which qualify a club for the grant of a club premises certificate (see **Chapter 17**). Section 1(2) provides that 'qualifying club activities' are:

- the supply of alcohol by or on behalf of a club to, or to the order of, a member of the club;
- the sale by retail of alcohol by or on behalf of a club to a guest of a member of the club for consumption on the premises where the sale takes place; and
- the provision of regulated entertainment where that provision is by or on behalf of a club for members of the club or members of the club and their guests.

The provision of late night refreshment in a qualifying club is an exempt supply and does not require authorisation (Sched. 3, para. 3).

3.2 THE SALE BY RETAIL OF ALCOHOL

Section 1(1) provides that there are two types of licensable activity so far as alcohol is concerned: the sale by retail of alcohol and the supply of alcohol by or on behalf of a club to or to the order of a member of the club otherwise than by way of sale.

3.2.1 Sale by retail

The Act defines 'sale by retail' in s.192, in relation to any alcohol, as a sale of alcohol to any person, other than a sale of alcohol that:

- is:
  - to a trader for the purposes of his trade;
  - to a club, which holds a club premises certificate, for the purposes of that club;
  - to the holder of a personal licence for the purpose of making sales authorised by a premises licence;
  - to the holder of a premises licence for the purpose of making sales authorised by that licence; or
  - to the premises user in relation to a temporary event notice for the purpose of making sales authorised by that notice;
- is made from premises owned by the person making the sale, or occupied by him under a lease to which the provisions of the Landlord and Tenant Act 1954 Part 2 apply; and
- is made for consumption off the premises.

There is no longer an exemption for large quantities and a wholesaler will therefore require a premises licence to sell alcohol in wholesale quantities to members of the public. Sales made to other traders for the purposes of their trade will not be a licensable activity. Similarly, sales made to holders of premises licences, club premises certificates or personal licences will not be a licensable activity if the sale is for the purposes authorised by the premises licence or for the purposes of the qualifying club. The wholesale sale of alcohol to premises users operating under a temporary event notice will also not be a licensable activity. In cases of doubt it will be advisable to check with the local licensing authority to see whether the sale is a licensable activity.

Another effect of the definition is that a person may require a premises licence if he sells alcohol to his friends from his house. All sales of alcohol to members of the public, even in wholesale quantities, from any premises will require an authorisation and there will need to be a designated premises supervisor for the premises if the authorisation is in the form of a premises licence.

3.2.2 Alcohol

Not everything which contains alcohol will be treated as alcohol under the Act. Section 191 defines 'alcohol' as spirits, wine, beer, cider or any other fermented, distilled or spirituous liquor, but not including:

- alcohol which does not exceed a strength of 0.5 per cent at the time of the sale or supply;
- perfume;
- flavouring essences recognised by the Commissioners for HM Revenue and Customs as not being intended for consumption as or with dutiable alcoholic liquor;
- Angostura bitters;
- alcohol which is, or is included in, a medicinal product;
- denatured alcohol, that is alcohol which has been made unfit for drinking by the addition of another substance but is still useful for other purposes (formerly called methylated spirits);
- methyl alcohol, that is methanol;
- naphtha, that is inflammable oil obtained by the distillation of organic substances; or
- alcohol contained in liqueur confectionery.

For these purposes:

- 'beer', 'cider', 'dutiable alcoholic liquor', 'spirits', 'wine' and 'strength' are defined in the Alcoholic Liquor Duties Act 1979;
- 'denatured alcohol' has the same meaning as in the Finance Act 1995, s.5, that is, any dutiable alcoholic liquor which has been subject to a process of being mixed in the manner prescribed by statutory instrument (currently the Denatured Alcohol Regulations 2005, SI 2005/1524) with a prescribed substance;
- 'liqueur confectionery' means confectionery which:

  - contains alcohol in a proportion not greater than 0.2 litres of alcohol of a strength not exceeding 57 per cent per kilogram of the confectionery, and
  - either consists of separate pieces weighing not more than 42 g or is designed to be broken into such pieces for the purpose of consumption; and

- 'medicinal product' has the same meaning as in the Medicines Act 1968, s.130.

3.3 THE SUPPLY OF ALCOHOL BY OR ON BEHALF OF A CLUB TO, OR TO THE ORDER OF, A MEMBER OF THE CLUB

There are two types of club. A proprietary club is run as a business and the club assets are owned by the proprietor of the business. In the case of a proprietary club there is a retail sale when a member of the club purchases alcohol and a premises licence will be required. A members' club is a club where all the assets are owned by the members jointly, for example a working men's club. The alcohol in a members' club is treated as being owned equally by all the members and so when a member purchases alcohol in the club there is a release to that member of the proprietary rights of the other members. The Act makes the supply of alcohol by a club to its members a licensable activity.

3.4   THE PROVISION OF REGULATED ENTERTAINMENT

'Regulated entertainment' is defined in Sched. 1 as:

- a performance of a play;
- an exhibition of a film;
- an indoor sporting event;
- a boxing or wrestling entertainment;
- a performance of live music;
- any playing of recorded music;
- a performance of dance; or
- entertainment of a similar description to a performance of live music, any playing of recorded music or a performance of dance;

where the entertainment takes place in the presence of an audience and is provided for the purpose, or for purposes which include the purpose, of entertaining that audience.

3.5   THE PROVISION OF LATE NIGHT REFRESHMENT

Under the Act authorisation is required for the provision of late night refreshment. Section 1(5) provides that:

> Schedule 2 makes provision about what constitutes the provision of late night refreshment for those purposes (including provision that certain activities carried on in relation to certain clubs or hotels etc, or certain employees, do not constitute provision of late night refreshment and are, accordingly, not licensable activities).

Late night refreshment is the supply of hot food or hot drink to the public, for consumption on or off the premises, between 11 pm and 5 am or the supply of hot food or hot drink to any persons between those hours on or from premises to which the public has access.

Food or drink is 'hot' for the purposes of the Act if it is heated on the premises or elsewhere before it is supplied for the purpose of enabling it to be consumed at above ambient air temperature, or if it may be heated on the premises for this purpose after it is supplied.

The Act provides that the provision of hot drinks by vending machines in certain circumstances, the supply free of charge of hot food or hot drink and the supply by a registered charity are exempt supplies which will not constitute the provision of late night refreshment.

3.6 AUTHORISATION FOR LICENSABLE ACTIVITIES AND QUALIFYING CLUB ACTIVITIES

Section 2 provides that a licensable activity may only be carried on in accordance with the following appropriate authorisations:

- a premises licence (see **Chapter 7**);
- a club premises certificate (see **Chapter 17**);
- a temporary event notice (see **Chapter 20**).

Section 2(3) provides that there is nothing in the Act to prevent two or more authorisations having effect concurrently in respect of the whole or a part of the same premises or in respect of the same person. This would enable, for example, a qualifying club that wished to provide entertainment to members of the public on certain days to hold both a club premises certificate to cover its normal operation and a premises licence to authorise the provision of entertainment in respect of the same premises. Another example would be where premises have both a premises licence authorising the sale of alcohol in the bar area and another premises licence authorising a different licensable activity in the bar or in another part of the premises.

A club which is not a qualifying club will be able to carry out licensable activities under either a premises licence or a temporary event notice. A club which has a club premises certificate is not prevented from having a premises licence or a temporary event notice as well.

CHAPTER 4

Regulated entertainment

4.1 INTRODUCTION

The Act provides that the provision of regulated entertainment is a licensable activity. Section 1(4) provides that Sched. 1 sets out what constitutes the provision of regulated entertainment. The provision of regulated entertainment includes both the provision of entertainment and the provision of entertainment facilities.

4.1.1 The provision of entertainment

Entertainment is identified in the Act as the following:

- the performance of a play;
- an exhibition of a film;
- an indoor sporting event;
- boxing or wrestling entertainment;
- a performance of live music;
- any playing of recorded music;
- a performance of dance; or
- entertainment of a similar description to live music, recorded music or dance.

The entertainment must take place in the presence of an audience and be provided for the purpose of, or for purposes which include, entertaining that audience. There is no requirement that the audience must be made up of or include any members of the public. Activities which do not involve entertaining an audience are not licensable and the Guidance, para. 5.12 provides:

the following activities do not amount to regulated entertainment under the regime:

- education – teaching students to perform music or to dance;
- activities which involve participation as acts of worship in a religious context;
- the demonstration of a product – for example, a guitar – in a music shop; or

- the rehearsal of a play or rehearsal of a performance of music to which the public are not admitted.

4.1.2 Entertainment facilities

Entertainment facilities are facilities for enabling people to take part in entertainment for the purpose of being entertained or for purposes which include the purpose of being entertained. This applies only to making music, dancing and entertainment of a similar description to making music or dancing. Thus 'entertainment facilities' would include, for example, a dance floor provided in a venue for patrons to use, whereas 'entertainment' might involve dance performed for an audience.

4.1.3 Requirements for regulated entertainment

In order for the provision of entertainment or entertainment facilities to be regulated, two conditions must be satisfied:

- the entertainment or entertainment facilities must be provided:

  - to any extent for the public or a section of the public;
  - exclusively for members and their guests of a club which is a qualifying club in relation to the provision of regulated entertainment; or
  - where neither of the above applies, for consideration and with a view to profit; and

- the premises on which the entertainment takes place, or entertainment facilities provided, are made available for the entertainment to take place.

For the purposes of the first condition entertainment is, or entertainment facilities are, to be regarded as provided for consideration only if any charge (which includes any charge for the provision of goods or services):

- is made by or on behalf of:

  - any person concerned in the organisation or management of that entertainment; or
  - any person concerned in the organisation or management of entertainment facilities who is also concerned in the organisation or management of the making of music, dancing or entertainment of a similar description in which the facilities enable persons to take part; and

- is paid by or on behalf of some or all of the persons for whom that entertainment is, or those facilities are, provided.

Where the entertainment consists of the performance of live music or the playing of recorded music, a person performing or playing the music is not concerned in the organisation or management of the entertainment by reason only that he chooses the music to be performed or played, determines the manner in which he performs or plays it or provides any facilities for the purposes of his performance or playing of the music. So a disc jockey or musician who is not responsible for the organisation or management of the performance will not have to obtain a licence if he is paid to play at a private event.

The charge for the entertainment must be made by those involved in some way in the organisation or management of the entertainment. The Guidance at para. 5.16 provides:

> This means that, for example, a wedding reception for invited guests (at which no charge intended to generate a profit is made to those guests) at which a live band plays and dancing takes place is not regulated entertainment where the organiser or manager of those facilities is not also concerned in the organisation or management of the entertainment and therefore not a licensable activity. Similarly, for example, a party organised in a private house by and for friends at which music and dancing is provided and a charge or contribution is made solely to cover the costs of the entertainment is not a licensable event. Furthermore, any charge made by musicians or other performers or their agents to the organiser of a private event does not make that entertainment licensable unless the guests attending are themselves charged for the entertainment with a view to achieving a profit as explained above.

Where entertainment takes place spontaneously, the premises have not really been made available to those who took part in the spontaneous entertainment, and so the Guidance, para. 5.19 provides:

> The spontaneous performance of music, singing or dancing does not amount to the provision of regulated entertainment and is not a licensable activity. The relevant part of the 2003 Act to consider in this context is paragraph 1(3) of Schedule 1 to the Act. This states that the second condition which must apply before an activity constitutes the provision of regulated entertainment is that the premises (meaning 'any place') at which the entertainment is, or entertainment facilities are, provided are made available for the purpose, or purposes which include the purpose, of enabling the entertainment concerned to take place. In the case of genuinely spontaneous music (including singing) and dancing, the place where the entertainment takes place will not have been made available to those taking part for that purpose.

Unless temporary entertainment is being provided (see **Chapter 20**) or the entertainment or location is exempt, a premises licence or club premises certificate will need to be obtained from the relevant licensing authority in order to provide regulated entertainment.

4.2 TYPES OF ENTERTAINMENT

The various types of entertainment are defined in Sched. 1, part 3.

4.2.1 The performance of a play

The performance of a play is defined as a performance of any dramatic piece, whether involving improvisation or not, which is given wholly or in part by one or more persons actually present and performing, and in which the whole or a major proportion of what is done by the person or persons performing, whether by way of speech, singing or action, involves the playing of a role.

The performance of a play will include rehearsals if they take place in the presence of an audience and if one of the purposes for which they are provided is entertaining that audience. The Guidance, para. 5.12 provides that the rehearsal of a play or rehearsal of a performance of music to which the public are not admitted does not amount to regulated entertainment.

4.2.2 An exhibition of a film

An 'exhibition of a film' means any exhibition of moving pictures. An exhibition of moving pictures is the showing of moving pictures to an audience as opposed to the display of moving objects on a screen (*British Amusement Catering Trades Association* v. *Westminster City Council* [1989] AC 147).

The provision of entertainment consisting of the exhibition of a film will not amount to the provision of regulated entertainment if:

- its sole or main purpose is to demonstrate any product, advertise any goods or services, or provide information, education or instruction;
- it consists of or forms part of an exhibit put on show for any purposes of a museum or art gallery.

4.2.3 An indoor sporting event

An 'indoor sporting event' is defined as a sporting event which takes place wholly inside a building and at which the spectators present at the event are accommodated wholly inside the building. A 'sporting event' is defined as any contest, exhibition or display of any sport, and 'sport' includes any game in which physical skill is the predominant factor, and any form of physical recreation which is also engaged in for purposes of competition or display. Thus it would include such events as darts tournaments, gymnastics and indoor athletic meetings. 'Building' is defined as any roofed structure, other than a structure with a roof which may be opened or closed, and includes a vehicle, vessel or moveable structure. This means that structures with a moving roof, such as the Millennium Stadium in Cardiff (and the Centre Court at

42

Wimbledon once it has its moving roof installed), are excluded and are treated as outdoor premises.

Pub games, for example pool or darts, do not necessarily need to be licensed as they are not generally played for the entertainment of spectators. However if for example a darts exhibition match or championship were staged in a pub for spectators, that would amount to regulated entertainment and require a licence. The Guidance, para. 5.15 provides:

> Games commonly played in pubs and social and youth clubs like pool, darts, table tennis and billiards may fall within the definition of indoor sports in Schedule 1, but normally they would not be played for the entertainment of spectators but for the private enjoyment of the participants. As such, they would not normally constitute the provision of regulated entertainment, and the facilities provided (even if a pub provides them with a view to profit) do not fall within the limited list of entertainment facilities in that Schedule . . . It is only when such games take place in the presence of an audience and are provided to, at least in part, entertain that audience, for example, a darts championship competition, that the activity would become licensable.

4.2.4   Boxing or wrestling entertainment

A boxing or wrestling entertainment is any contest, exhibition or display of boxing or wrestling. It does not matter whether the entertainment takes place outside or inside.

4.2.5   A performance of live music

'Music' includes vocal or instrumental music or any combination of the two. There is no requirement as to a maximum number of performers (the 'two in a bar' rule which existed under previous legislation no longer applies) and all kinds of live music are now on an equal footing no matter how many performers are involved.

There is an exemption for live music which is incidental to an activity which is not itself regulated entertainment or the provision of entertainment facilities. Spontaneous singing, for example of 'Happy Birthday', is not licensable and nor are carol singers singing from door to door, just deciding to sing in a particular place or even turning up unannounced in a pub and singing.

4.2.6   Any playing of recorded music

The playing of recorded music is a licensable activity where it is done for the entertainment of an audience – for example karaoke. There is an exemption for recorded music which is incidental to an activity which is not itself regulated entertainment or the provision of entertainment facilities.

4.2.7 A performance of dance

This is not defined in the Act but is self-explanatory.

4.2.8 Entertainment of a similar description to live music, recorded music or dance

This is a sweeping up provision and covers entertainment of a similar kind to music or the performance of dance, for example a skating performance to music.

4.2.9 Modification of the definition

The Secretary of State may add to, vary or remove any of the descriptions of entertainment in the Act.

4.3 ENTERTAINMENT FACILITIES

'Entertainment facilities' are facilities for enabling people to take part in making music, dancing or entertainment of a similar description for the purpose, or for purposes which include the purpose of being entertained. No audience is necessary but the customers must be active participants.

4.3.1 Making music

'Music' is defined to include vocal or instrumental music or any combination of the two; a karaoke bar would be included within the definition of 'entertainment facilities' as the participants take part in the making of music.

4.3.2 Dancing

There is no definition of 'dancing' in the Act but dance venues will include discotheques.

4.3.3 Any combination of making music and dancing

This is a sweeping up provision.

4.3.4 Modification of the definition

The Secretary of State may add to, vary or remove any of the descriptions of entertainment facilities in the Act.

4.4 EXEMPTIONS

There are eight general exemptions in part 2 of Sched. 1 where the provision of regulated entertainment does not amount to a licensable activity.

4.4.1 Film exhibitions for the purposes of advertisement, information or education

Entertainment which consists of the exhibition of a film is outside the definition of the provision of regulated entertainment if its sole or main purpose is to demonstrate any product, advertise any goods or services, or provide information, education or instruction. Thus educational films shown in schools or special advertisements shown at product display stands in shopping centres are exempt.

4.4.2 Film exhibitions in museums and art galleries

The exhibition of a film is not the provision of regulated entertainment if it consists of or forms part of an exhibit put on show for any purposes of a museum or art gallery.

4.4.3 Music incidental to certain other activities

The provision of entertainment which consists of the performance of live music or the playing of recorded music is not the provision of regulated entertainment if it is incidental to some other activity which is neither entertainment nor the provision of entertainment facilities. So a jukebox in a pub will not be required to be authorised unless say a dance floor is also provided or it is not incidental to some other activity.

The Guidance at para. 5.18 provides:

Common sense dictates that live or recorded music played at volumes which predominate over other activities at a venue could rarely be regarded as incidental to those activities. So, for example, a juke box played in a public house at moderate levels would normally be regarded as incidental to the other activities there, but one played at high volume would not benefit from this exemption. Stand-up comedy is not regulated entertainment and musical accompaniment incidental to the main performance would not make it a licensable activity. But there are likely to be some circumstances which occupy a greyer area.

4.4.4 Use of television or radio receivers

The provision of any entertainment or entertainment facilities is not the provision of regulated entertainment if it consists of the simultaneous reception and playing of a programme included in a programme service within the meaning of the Broadcasting Act 1990. Live broadcast entertainment is therefore exempt. However showing pre-recorded entertainment, for example a video or a DVD, would require a licence.

4.4.5 Religious services, places of worship, etc.

The provision of any entertainment or entertainment facilities for the purposes of or for purposes incidental to a religious meeting or service, or at a place of public religious worship, is not the provision of regulated entertainment. This will exempt the singing of hymns during a church service.

4.4.6 Garden fêtes, etc.

The provision of any entertainment or entertainment facilities at a garden fête, or at a similar function or event, will not amount to the provision of regulated entertainment unless the fête, function or event is promoted with a view to applying the whole or part of its proceeds for purposes of private gain.

'Private gain' is construed in accordance with the Lotteries and Amusements Act 1976, s.22. The proceeds of any entertainment, lottery or gaming promoted on behalf of a society which is established and conducted either wholly for purposes other than purposes of any commercial undertaking, or wholly or mainly for the purpose of participation in or support of athletic sports or athletic games which are applied for any purpose calculated to benefit the society as a whole, will not be applied for purposes of private gain by reason only that their application for that purpose results in benefit to any person as an individual.

4.4.7 Morris dancing, etc.

The provision of any entertainment or entertainment facilities is not the provision of regulated entertainment if it is the provision of a performance of morris dancing or any dancing of a similar nature or a performance of unamplified, live music as an integral part of such a performance, or facilities for enabling persons to take part in such entertainment.

4.4.8 Vehicles in motion

The provision of any entertainment or entertainment facilities on premises consisting of or forming part of a vehicle at a time when the vehicle is not permanently or temporarily parked is not to be regarded as the provision of regulated entertainment. This will exempt music or videos provided on coaches or other vehicles.

4.5 PARTICULAR PREMISES AND EVENTS

4.5.1 Church halls

Church halls and similar premises require a premises licence for the provision of regulated entertainment unless they come within one of the exemptions listed above. No fee is payable for such a premises licence unless it also authorises the use of the premises for the supply of alcohol or the provision of late night refreshment. If the supply of alcohol is included as a licensable activity then a designated premises supervisor must be named on the premises licence application. A church hall could also use a temporary event notice (see **Chapter 20**).

4.5.2 Village halls

A premises licence is required for the provision of regulated entertainment in village halls. However, as with church halls, there is an exemption from the payment of fees in relation to the provision of regulated entertainment at village halls, parish or community halls or other premises of a similar nature unless the licence also authorises the use of the premises for the supply of alcohol or the provision of late night refreshment. A village hall could also use a temporary event notice (see **Chapter 20**).

4.5.3 Scout and guide halls

A premises licence is required for a scout hall or similar premises where regulated entertainment is provided for the public or if a charge is made to a private audience with a view to profit, including for a charity. If the public is not invited and a charge is made to a private audience such as family and friends in order to cover costs, then this will not be the provision of regulated entertainment and a licence will not be required. A licence will also not be required if persons invited to a private performance without being charged are asked to make a voluntary donation to a charity at their own choice. However, if the performance is to any extent open to members of the public, whether they are charged or not, a licence will be required. A scout hall could also use a temporary event notice (see **Chapter 20**).

4.5.4 Schools and sixth form colleges

Schools and sixth form colleges will require a premises licence to stage regulated entertainment to which the public is invited or where a fee is charged and with a view to profit. They are exempt from the payment of a fee where the regulated entertainment is provided by and at the school or college and for the purposes of the school or college. A licence is not required if the public is not invited to the event and a charge to cover costs is made to a private audience, such as family and friends. A school could also use a temporary event notice (see **Chapter 20**).

4.5.5 Shops

A premises licence is not required if a customer or sales assistant demonstrates or tries out a musical instrument in a shop. If a shop holds an event at which musicians play instruments for the purpose of entertaining customers then a premises licence or a temporary event notice will be required.

4.5.6 Rehearsal halls

Rehearsals will not require a licence unless the rehearsal is provided for the entertainment of the public or the members and their guests of a qualifying club in relation to the provision of regulated entertainment or for consideration and with a view to profit.

4.5.7 Circuses

If a circus or pleasure fair provides regulated entertainment, or there are to be supplies of alcohol or the provision of late night refreshment, a premises licence or a temporary event notice will be required.

4.5.8 Village greens, market squares, seaside promenades, etc.

Anyone wishing to carry out a licensable activity on a public space such as a village green, market square or seaside promenade should make enquiries with the local authority to find out whether there is a premises licence in existence for the particular public space which covers the licensable activity to be carried out. No additional licence would then need to be obtained in order to carry out that licensable activity, although the consent of the local authority holding the licence would usually be required, as would permission to use the land.

4.5.9 Punch and Judy shows

A Punch and Judy show will require a premises licence or a temporary event notice when performed for the public, for members and their guests of a qualifying club, or to a private audience for consideration and with a view to profit by the organiser. However, a Punch and Judy show at a private children's party will not require a licence.

4.5.10 Private homes and gardens

Any performances of live music that take place in a private home and/or garden for a private party or a wedding will not be licensable unless the host takes the unusual step of charging his guests to attend with a view to making a profit.

CHAPTER 5

Late night refreshment

5.1 INTRODUCTION

The Act provides that the provision of late night refreshment is a licensable activity (s.1(1)). This means that a premises licence will be required by establishments such as take-aways, fish and chip shops, mobile catering vehicles and fast food outlets which wish to provide late night refreshment. It is possible for the supply of alcohol, the provision of regulated entertainment and the provision of late night refreshment to be carried on under one premises licence.

The inclusion of late night take-aways and fast food outlets in the Act has extended the licensing regime which operated in most of London to all of England and Wales. The rationale behind this is to protect local residents because premises which serve late night refreshment can be used by customers who may have been drinking at other premises earlier in the evening, thereby creating the potential for disorder on and near the premises. There is also a potential for nuisance and disturbance for local residents as large numbers of customers may gather at places serving late night refreshments.

The effect is that if a business, such as a supermarket, a garage, a take-away or a fast food outlet is heating food or drink for customers to consume on or off the premises between 11 pm and 5 am, or provides facilities for customers that enable the food or drink to be heated above the ambient temperature, a late night refreshment licence will be required. However if a business is selling only cold food and drink and not providing facilities to enable the food or drink to be heated on the premises, then a licence authorising the provision of late night refreshment will not be required.

In relation to premises where the main licensable activity is not the provision of late night refreshment, the Guidance at para. 5.22 provides that:

> It is not expected that the provision of late night refreshment as a secondary activity in licensed premises open for other purposes such as public houses, cinemas or nightclubs or casinos should give rise to a need for significant additional conditions. The Secretary of State considers that the key licensing objectives in connection with late night refreshment are the prevention of crime and disorder

and public nuisance, and it is expected that both will normally have been adequately covered in the conditions relating to the other licensable activities on such premises.

5.2   WHAT IS LATE NIGHT REFRESHMENT?

Section 1(5) provides for Sched. 2 to make provisions about what constitutes late night refreshment.

A person provides late night refreshment if:

- at any time between the hours of 11.00 pm and 5.00 am, he supplies hot food or hot drink to members of the public, or a section of the public, on or from any premises, whether for consumption on or off the premises; or
- at any time between those hours when members of the public, or a section of the public, are admitted to any premises, he supplies, or holds himself out as willing to supply, hot food or hot drink to any persons, or to persons of a particular description, on or from those premises whether for consumption on or off the premises;

unless the supply is an exempt supply.

5.3   HOT FOOD OR HOT DRINK

Food or drink supplied on or from any premises is 'hot' if the food or drink, or any part of it:

- before it is supplied, is heated on the premises or elsewhere for the purpose of enabling it to be consumed at a temperature above the ambient air temperature and, at the time of supply, is above that temperature, for example fish and chips; or
- after it is supplied, may be heated on the premises for the purpose of enabling it to be consumed at a temperature above the ambient air temperature, for example in a microwave in the premises provided by the business for that purpose.

The second limb of this definition will include shops and supermarkets which open late and provide a microwave in which customers can heat up food which they have bought. Whether this was the intention is not clear as the Guidance at para. 5.20 provides:

shops, stores and supermarkets selling food that is immediately consumable from 11.00pm will not be licensable as providing late night refreshment unless they are selling hot food or hot drink. The legislation will impact on those premises such as night cafés and take away food outlets where people may gather at any time from 11.00pm and until 5.00am giving rise to the possibility of disorder and disturbance. The licensing regime will not catch premises only selling immediately consumable food, such as, bread, milk or cold sandwiches in all night grocers' shops and which do not tend to attract these problems.

5.4 EXEMPT SUPPLIES

Certain supplies are exempt from being late night refreshment and so do not require authorisation.

5.4.1 Clubs, hotels, etc. and employees

The first exemption relates to the supply to members of certain clubs, supply to guests in hotels and similar premises, supply to employees of a particular employer, supply to persons in particular trades, professions or vocations, and guests of any of the above.

The supply of hot food or hot drink on or from any premises at any time is an exempt supply if, at that time, a person will neither be admitted to the premises, nor be supplied with hot food or hot drink on or from the premises, unless:

- he is a member of a recognised club, that is a members' club which meets the general qualifying conditions for a club premises certificate;
- he is a person staying at a hotel, a guest house, lodging house or hostel, a caravan site, camping site or any other premises the main purpose of maintaining which is the provision of facilities for overnight accommodation, for the night in question;
- he is an employee of a particular employer, for example at a staff canteen;
- he is engaged in a particular trade, he is a member of a particular profession or he follows a particular vocation, for example a tradesman carrying out work at particular premises; or
- he is a guest of the above persons.

Where a club is not a recognised club, the supply of hot food or hot drink to a member or his guest will not be exempt and will require authorisation.

5.4.2 Premises licensed under other statutes

There are two exemptions here and both have effect only in London.

The supply of hot food or hot drink on or from any premises is an exempt supply if it takes place during a period for which the premises may be used for a public exhibition of a kind described in the Greater London Council (General Powers) Act 1966, s.21(1) by virtue of a licence under that section. The premises concerned are the Alexandra Palace, Central Hall, Earls Court, Olympia, the Royal Festival Hall, the Royal Horticultural Halls and Seymour Hall.

The second exemption relates to premises which may be used as near beer premises, where certain non-alcoholic beverages are sold, within the meaning of the London Local Authorities Act 1995, s.14 by virtue of a licence under s.16 of that Act. These premises consist to a significant degree of the sale of drinks such as non-alcoholic beers and lagers accompanied by live entertainment and/or companions for their customers. Such premises are common in London's Soho area.

5.4.3 Miscellaneous exempt supplies

The following supplies of hot food or hot drink are exempt supplies:

- the supply of hot drink which consists of or contains alcohol;
- the supply of hot drink by means of a vending machine where the payment for the hot drink is inserted into the machine by a member of the public, and the hot drink is supplied directly by the machine to a member of the public;
- the supply of hot food or hot drink free of charge, and these will not be regarded as supplied free of charge if, in order to obtain them, a charge must be paid for admission to the premises, or for some other item;
- the supply of hot food or hot drink by a charity which is registered under s.3 of the Charities Act 1993, or by a charity which by virtue of subs. (5) of that section is not required to be so registered, or a person authorised by such charities; and
- the supply of hot food or hot drink on a vehicle at a time when the vehicle is not permanently or temporarily parked.

The supply of hot drink which consists of or contains alcohol is exempt under the 2003 Act as late night refreshment because it is caught by the provisions relating to the sale or supply of alcohol (Guidance, para. 5.23). The supply of hot food or hot drink free of charge is not a licensable activity. However where any charge is made either for admission to the premises or for some other item in order to obtain the hot food or hot drink it will not be regarded as 'free of charge'. Supplies by a registered charity or anyone authorised by a registered charity are also exempt. Similarly supplies made on vehicles – other than when they are permanently or temporarily parked – are also exempt (Guidance, para. 5.24).

CHAPTER 6

Personal licences

6.1 INTRODUCTION

Part 6 of the Act has introduced a new system of personal licences for controlling the sale or supply of alcohol. Any person who wants to sell alcohol by retail or to supply it by or on behalf of a club or to the order of a member of the club must possess a personal licence. A personal licence is separate from a premises licence and the rationale behind this is to make it easier for individuals to move between licensed premises without the need to have to apply for a transfer of licence, allowing greater flexibility. No matter which licensing authority issues the personal licence it will be valid for use anywhere in England and Wales. A personal licence is not required for the provision of regulated entertainment or late night refreshment. It is only required for the sale or supply of alcohol under a premises licence.

While the Act provides that all supplies of alcohol under a premises licence must be made by or under the authority of a personal licence holder, there is no requirement that every person employed in the licensed premises must hold a personal licence. It is sufficient that an employee working in licensed premises and who does not hold a personal licence is supplying alcohol on the authority of a personal licence holder (s.19(3)). Nor is it necessary for the personal licence holder to be on the premises at all times to physically authorise every sale of alcohol, and the Guidance at para. 7.67 states:

> the fact that every supply of alcohol must be made under the authority of a personal licence holder does not mean that only personal licence holders can make such sales or that they must be personally present at every transaction. A personal licence holder may authorise members of staff to make sales of alcohol during the course of an evening, but may be absent at times from the premises when a transaction takes place. However, the personal licence holder will not be able to escape responsibility for the actions of those he authorises to make such sales.

A premises licence which specifies that the supply of alcohol is a licensable activity must also specify a person to be the designated premises supervisor (see **Chapter 9**). This is the person who is responsible for the day-to-day running of the premises. The designated premises supervisor must always hold a personal licence. There may be other individuals at the premises who hold a personal licence but only one of them can be the designated premises supervisor.

6.2 DEFINITION OF PERSONAL LICENCE

A personal licence is defined in s.111 as a licence which is granted by a licensing authority to an individual authorising that person either to supply alcohol or to authorise its supply in accordance with a premises licence. The supply of alcohol includes selling alcohol by retail, or supplying it by or on behalf of a club or to the order of a member of the club. Where club premises operate under a club premises certificate a personal licence is not required in order to supply alcohol to members or their guests.

A personal licence does not authorise its holder to supply alcohol anywhere other than from premises which have a premises licence authorising the supply of alcohol, or from other premises under the authority of a temporary event notice.

6.3 WHO CAN APPLY FOR A PERSONAL LICENCE?

Section 117(1) provides that an individual may apply for a personal licence. It is not possible for an application to be made by a corporate body.

The requirements for the grant of a personal licence are laid down in s.120(2) and the effect of these is that an application for a personal licence can be made by any individual who:

- is at least 18 years old;
- possesses an accredited licensing qualification or is a person of a description prescribed by regulation;
- has not had a personal licence forfeited within the five years immediately preceding the date when the application was made; and
- has not been convicted of any relevant offence or foreign offence.

There is no requirement that an applicant for a personal licence be employed in the licensing trade or have business interests associated with the use of the licence.

A person can only hold one personal licence at a time. A person who has applied for a personal licence cannot make an application for another personal licence until the first application has been withdrawn or determined by the licensing authority (s.118(1)). If the holder of a personal licence is subsequently granted another personal licence, then that second licence will be void (s.118(2)).

6.4   APPLICATION FOR A PERSONAL LICENCE

An application for a personal licence must be made either to the licensing authority for the area in which the applicant is ordinarily resident or, if the applicant is not ordinarily resident in the area of any particular licensing authority, to any licensing authority (s.117(2)). This is referred to in the Act as the 'relevant licensing authority' and it takes responsibility for the personal licence once it has been granted. This means that it will deal with the renewal (see **6.13**). The licensing authority which issues a personal licence remains the relevant licensing authority even if the holder moves out of its area.

The application form, the information it must contain and the documentation which must accompany it are prescribed by the Licensing Act 2003 (Personal Licences) Regulations 2005, SI 2005/41 ('Personal Licences Regulations').

In order to apply for a personal licence, an applicant must submit to the relevant licensing authority:

- a completed application form;
- two photographs of himself which are:
    - taken against a light background so that his features are distinguishable and contrast against the background;
    - 45 mm by 35 mm;
    - with full face uncovered and without sunglasses and, unless the applicant wears a head covering because of his religious beliefs, without a head covering;
    - on photographic paper; and
    - one of the photographs is endorsed with a statement verifying the likeness of the photograph to the applicant by a solicitor, notary, a person of standing in the community, such as a bank or building society official, a police officer, a civil servant or a minister of religion or any individual with a professional qualification;
- the applicant's licensing qualification;
- either a criminal conviction certificate issued under the Police Act 1997, s.112, a criminal record certificate issued under the Police Act 1997, s.113A, or the results of a subject access search under the Data Protection Act 1998 of the Police National Computer by the National Identification Service. Whichever of these is produced, it must not have been issued more than one month before the application for the personal licence is submitted to the licensing authority;
- a declaration by the applicant, in the prescribed form, that either he has not been convicted of a relevant offence or a foreign offence or that he has been convicted of a relevant offence or a foreign offence accompanied by

details of the nature and date of the conviction and any sentence imposed on him in respect of it; and

* the fee of £37.00 (prescribed by the Fees Regulations).

It is suggested that some form of seniority will be required for the person endorsing the photograph, for example a bank or building society manager rather than a junior employee. Individuals with professional qualifications would presumably include persons such as doctors, accountants, solicitors, barristers, legal executives and teachers.

6.5   THE APPLICATION FORM

6.5.1   Obtaining an application form

A relevant licensing authority must provide a potential applicant with an application form on request. An electronic version may be provided on a licensing authority's website which a potential applicant can download, print off and complete (Personal Licences Regulations, reg. 10). An application cannot be rejected purely because it has been made on a form which was not provided by the relevant licensing authority but which in all other respects complies with the requirements of the Personal Licences Regulations, reg. 11.

6.5.2   Completing the application form

Guidance in completing the application form may be obtained from the DCMS website or the relevant licensing authority. The form may be completed by being either typed or written legibly in block capitals. All answers must be inside the boxes and written in black ink.

The application form is divided into five parts, as follows.

Part 1 – personal details

This section asks for details of the applicant, such as his full name, any previous names, confirmation that the applicant is 18 years old or over, the address where the applicant is ordinarily resident (the licensing authority will use this address to correspond with the applicant unless he specifies an alternative correspondence address, such as his business address), the applicant's telephone number and fax number and finally the applicant's e-mail address if he would prefer the licensing authority to correspond with him by e-mail.

Part 2 – licensing qualification

This section asks the applicant to indicate his licensing qualification and to give details, such as the name of his qualification, the date it was issued and the name of the issuing body.

Part 3 – previous or outstanding applications for a personal licence

The applicant must indicate whether he currently holds a personal licence, has an outstanding application for a personal licence waiting to be dealt with or has had a personal licence forfeited within the previous five years.

Part 4 – checklist

This part is made up of a checklist of the enclosures which must be sent with the application so that the applicant can make sure that the application is complete before it is submitted.

Part 5 – declaration

By signing this part the applicant is making a declaration that the information in the application form is correct to the best of his knowledge and belief. If he signs and has not complied with the declaration, he may be making a false statement in relation to the application. This is an offence which on conviction may incur a fine not exceeding level 5 on the standard scale.

6.5.3 Making an application

Regulation 9 of the Personal Licences Regulations provides that an application must be made in writing. However notwithstanding this requirement an application can also be made electronically, provided:

- the text of the application is transmitted by electronic means, is capable of being accessed by the recipient, is legible in all material respects, and is capable of being read and reproduced in written form and used for subsequent reference;
- the person to whom the application is to be given has agreed in advance that an application may be given by electronic means; and
- forthwith on sending the text of the application by electronic means, the application is given to the recipient in writing.

As the application must be accompanied by a fee and other documents, where the text of the application is transmitted by electronic means, the application will not be treated as being made until the fee and other documents have been received by the relevant licensing authority.

Table 6.1 Checklist for a personal licence application

	Original to relevant licensing authority
Completed application form	
Two photographs of the applicant, one of which is endorsed as a true likeness	
Completed disclosure of criminal convictions and declaration form	
Criminal record details	
Payment of the fee	
Licensing qualification	
Fee of £37	

6.6 DETERMINATION OF AN APPLICATION

6.6.1 Mandatory grant

If an application has been made in accordance with the procedural requirements, s.120(2) provides that the application must be granted if the applicant:

- is at least 18 years old;
- possesses an accredited licensing qualification or is a person of a prescribed description;
- has not had a personal licence forfeited in the five years immediately preceding the date when the application was made; and
- has not been convicted of any relevant offence or foreign offence.

The licensing authority has no discretion to refuse an application where these criteria are met. There is no longer a 'fit and proper' test as there was under previous legislation. In the Guidance, para. 4.1 'the Government stresses that the "fit and proper" test associated with the old alcohol licensing regime has been abolished and the tests established by the 2003 Act are the only ones which may now be applied'.

There appears to be nothing to stop a person aged under 18 years old from applying for a personal licence provided that he is 18 years old when the licensing authority considers his application.

6.6.2 Mandatory refusal

If the applicant does not satisfy the first three of the conditions in s.120(2), in other words he is not at least 18 years old, does not possess an accredited licensing qualification or is not a person of a prescribed description, or if he has had a personal licence forfeited in previous five years, then the application must be rejected (s.120(3)).

6.6.3 Discretionary grant

If the applicant satisfies the first three conditions in s.120(2) but fails to satisfy the final condition, in other words he has been convicted of a relevant offence or foreign offence, then the licensing authority must give notice of this to the chief officer of police for its area (s.120(4)).

If the chief officer of police is then satisfied that granting the licence would undermine the crime prevention objective, he must, within 14 days beginning on the day he received the notice, give the licensing authority an objection notice stating the reasons why he is satisfied that granting the licence would undermine the crime prevention objective. The personal licence must be granted if the police do not give an objection notice within the 14-day period or if an objection notice is withdrawn.

If the police give an objection notice within the 14-day period, the licensing authority must hold a hearing to consider it, unless the applicant, the chief officer of police and the licensing authority all agree that a hearing is not necessary. The hearing must be held within 20 working days beginning with the day after the end of the 14-day period for the police to give an objection notice (Hearings Regulations, reg. 5 and Sched. 1, para. 12). Notice of the hearing must be given to the applicant and the chief office of police no later than 10 working days before the day or the first day on which the hearing is to be held (Hearings Regulations, reg. 6(4) and Sched. 2, para. 12). The applicant must be given the notice of objection with the notice of hearing (Hearings Regulations, reg. 7(2) and Sched. 3, para. 11).

The licensing authority must reject the application for the personal licence if, having regard to the objection notice, it considers it necessary to do so on crime prevention grounds; otherwise the personal licence must be granted.

It is expected that if an objection notice is given by the police, the application for the personal licence will be rejected. The Guidance, para. 4.8 provides:

> The Secretary of State recommends that, where the police have issued an objection notice, refusal of the application should be the normal course unless there are, in the opinion of the licensing authority, exceptional and compelling circumstances which justify granting the application. For example, certain offences can never become spent. However, where an applicant is able to demonstrate that the offence in question took place so long ago and that he or she no longer has any propensity to re-offend, a licensing authority may consider that the individual circumstances of the case are so exceptional and compelling and any risk to the community so diminished that it is right to grant the application.

6.7 NOTIFICATION OF THE GRANT OR REFUSAL OF A PERSONAL LICENCE

When a personal licence has been granted, the licensing authority must give notice of its decision to the applicant and the chief officer of police, and where the chief officer of police has objected to the grant and has not withdrawn his objection, the notice must set out the reasons why the licensing authority has granted the application (s.122(1)). If the personal licence is not granted, notice must be given to the applicant and the chief officer of police setting out the reasons for the refusal (s.122(2)).

Notice must be given forthwith (see **2.9**) on making the determination, and must be accompanied by information regarding the right of a party to appeal against the determination.

6.8 ISSUING OF A PERSONAL LICENCE

Section 125 provides that a personal licence once granted must be issued forthwith (see **2.9**).

A personal licence must:

- specify the holder's name and address;
- identify the licensing authority which granted it;
- contain a record of each relevant offence and each foreign offence of which the holder has been convicted, the date of each conviction and the sentence imposed in respect of it; and
- be in the prescribed form.

Regulation 5 of the Personal Licences Regulations prescribes the form of a personal licence. A personal licence must take the form of a physical document in two separate parts. The first part must be produced in durable form, be of a size no larger than 70 mm by 100 mm and contain the holder's name and address, the licensing authority which granted it, a photograph of the holder, a number allocated by the licensing authority that is unique to the licence, an identifier for the licensing authority granting the licence and the date of the expiry of the licence. The second part must contain a record of each relevant offence and each foreign offence of which the holder has been convicted, the date of each conviction and the sentence imposed in respect of it together with all the matters in the first part of the licence with the exception of the photograph of the holder.

6.9 ACCREDITED LICENSING QUALIFICATIONS

Section 120 defines a 'licensing qualification' as:

- a qualification which is both accredited by the Secretary of State and awarded by a body accredited by the Secretary of State;
- a qualification awarded before the coming into force of s.120 which the Secretary of State certifies is to be treated as if it were a qualification which is both accredited by the Secretary of State and awarded by a body accredited by the Secretary of State; or
- a qualification obtained in Scotland or Northern Ireland or in an EEA State (other than the United Kingdom) which is equivalent to such a qualification which is both accredited by the Secretary of State and awarded by a body accredited by the Secretary of State. For this purpose 'EEA State' means a state which is a contracting party to the Agreement on the European Economic Area signed at Oporto on 2 May 1992, as adjusted by the protocol signed at Brussels on 17 March 1993.

Details of the licensing qualifications which have been accredited by the Secretary of State can be found at **www.culture.gov.uk**, together with details of the syllabus for courses leading to an accredited qualification.

A person does not have a recognised licensing qualification if he is a person of prescribed description. The only persons who have been prescribed so far are the holders of three ancient privileges which have all been abolished by the Act, so these were only relevant during the transitional period.

6.10 CONVICTIONS FOR A RELEVANT OFFENCE OR FOREIGN OFFENCE

An applicant must disclose whether or not he has a conviction for a relevant offence or a foreign offence, unless it has become spent for the purposes of the Rehabilitation of Offenders Act 1974.

6.10.1 Relevant offence

Section 113(1) provides that an offence is a relevant offence if it is one of those listed in Sched. 4. These include offences under the Act, under previous licensing legislation, under the Theft Act 1968 and under the Misuse of Drugs Act 1971.

6.10.2 Foreign offence

A foreign offence is an offence (other than a relevant offence) under the law of a country outside England and Wales (s.113(3)). This will include offences committed in Scotland and Northern Ireland. Offences under foreign laws which are equivalent to relevant offences will not necessarily exist in exactly the same form as relevant offences.

An applicant must disclose whether or not he has a conviction for a foreign offence unless it has been spent for the purposes of the Rehabilitation of Offenders Act 1974.

The Act does not prescribe how an applicant should disclose a foreign offence. However the Personal Licences Regulations provide that in order to disclose whether or not an applicant has been convicted of a foreign offence, he must submit a declaration, in the prescribed form, that either he has not been convicted of a foreign offence or that he has been convicted of a foreign offence accompanied by details of the nature and date of the conviction and any sentence imposed on him in respect of it. This declaration also relates to relevant offences. The form of declaration is set out in Sched. 3 to the Personal Licences Regulations.

It is not expected that an applicant will disclose all foreign offences, only those equivalent to a relevant offence. The Guidance, para. 4.5 provides that 'All applicants would also be expected to make a clear statement as to whether or not they have been convicted outside England and Wales of a relevant offence or an equivalent foreign offence.' If a foreign offence which is not equivalent to a relevant offence is disclosed, the police will be notified by the relevant licensing authority but may not be able to object on the basis of that foreign offence as they can only object where the chief officer of police considers that the foreign offence is comparable to a relevant offence (s.120(5)).

6.10.3 Spent convictions

A conviction for a relevant offence or a foreign offence must be disregarded if it is spent for the purposes of the Rehabilitation of Offenders Act 1974 (s.114).

Under the Rehabilitation of Offenders Act 1974, s.1 all convictions (other than those involving a prison sentence in excess of 30 months) are 'spent' and no longer need to be disclosed after a specified period of time which depends on the particular sentence. The length of the rehabilitation period is specified in the Rehabilitation of Offenders Act 1974, s.5 and varies from 6 months for an absolute discharge to 10 years for a prison sentence of more than 6 months but not more than 30 months. Where the sentence exceeds 30 months' imprisonment, the conviction cannot be spent.

Section 7(3) of the Rehabilitation of Offenders Act 1974 provides that at any stage in any proceedings before a judicial authority, the authority can admit spent convictions or require evidence as to spent convictions if it is satisfied that justice cannot otherwise be done. A licensing authority will be a judicial authority for these purposes (see *Adamson* v. *Waveney District*

Council (1997) 161 JP 787, 793). Thus where justice cannot be done otherwise than by admitting a spent conviction, it may be admitted. This does not mean that the licensing authority has a discretion to admit a spent conviction (see *R.* v. *Hastings Magistrates' Court ex p. McSpirit* (1994) 162 JP 44; *Adamson* v. *Waveney District Council* (1997) 161 JP 787, 793).

6.10.4 Establishing a conviction

The Act does not set out how an applicant should establish whether or not he has a conviction for a relevant offence or foreign offence; however the Personal Licences Regulations provide that an applicant must submit a declaration in the prescribed form that either he has not been convicted of a relevant offence or foreign offence or that he has been convicted of a relevant offence or foreign offence, accompanied by details of the nature and date of the conviction and any sentence imposed on him in respect of it. The form of declaration is set out in Sched. 3 to the Personal Licences Regulations.

In addition an applicant must also submit with his application:

- a criminal conviction certificate issued under the Police Act 1997, s.112 (commonly referred to as 'basic disclosure');
- a criminal record certificate issued under the Police Act 1997, s.113A; or
- the results of a subject access search under the Data Protection Act 1998 of the Police National Computer by the National Identification Service.

Only one of these needs to be submitted with the application, and whichever is submitted it must not have been issued more than one month before the application for the personal licence is submitted to the relevant licensing authority.

The original intention was that an applicant would rely on a basic disclosure from the Criminal Records Bureau. However it is not possible at the present time to obtain a basic disclosure in England and Wales. An enhanced or standard disclosure could be used but these are not issued to individuals, only to organisations, and they contain information not specifically required by the Act.

It is however possible to obtain a basic disclosure from Disclosure Scotland as this is available to any person resident in the UK. This costs £13.60 plus an additional charge of 50p when using a credit or debit card. Until a basic disclosure is available in England and Wales, this will be the recommended method of complying with the requirements of the Act.

6.10.5 Obtaining a basic disclosure from Disclosure Scotland

Where an applicant's current address is in the UK and he has been living at that current address for more than 12 months, an application for a basic disclosure can be made on-line at **www.disclosurescotland.co.uk/**

disclosureOnline/BDO_Instr.htm. An applicant needs to have the following information when making an on-line application:

- his current name;
- any previous names;
- his date of birth;
- details from at least one form of identification from the following:

    - national insurance number;
    - passport number;
    - driving licence number;

- the details of any previous disclosure issued by Disclosure Scotland;
- details of at least a five-year address history including county and postcode; and
- credit or debit card details (at present Disclosure Scotland only accepts MasterCard, Visa, Switch or Solo).

If an applicant has not lived at his current address for at least 12 months, he must apply using the paper application form. An application form can be obtained by:

- telephone: 0870 609 6006 (calls charged at national rates);
- fax: 0870 609 6996 (calls charged at national rates);
- e-mail: **info@disclosurescotland.co.uk**; or
- writing to Disclosure Scotland, PO Box 250, Glasgow, G51 1YU.

An application for a basic disclosure which is not to be returned to the applicant's home address and is not paid by personal credit/debit card must be supported by copies of two documents, one of which must be a utility bill (or other document which confirms the applicant's home address) and the applicant's passport, driving licence or birth certificate. Where an on-line application is required to be supported by these documents, the applicant must include the 16-digit reference number when forwarding the documents. An application will not be processed until these documents are received and checked.

6.10.6   Criminal conviction certificate

A criminal conviction certificate (basic disclosure) either gives the prescribed details of every conviction, other than those which are spent, of the applicant which are recorded in central records or states that there are no such convictions. An application for a certificate must be made in the prescribed manner and form and any fee must be paid. At the time of writing the Police Act 1997, s.112 is yet not in force in England and Wales and so it is not possible to obtain a criminal conviction certificate.

6.10.7 Criminal record certificate

Disclosure may be made by a means of a criminal record certificate (enhanced or standard disclosure) issued under the Police Act 1997, s.113A. This provision will be inserted into the Police Act 1997 in due course by the Serious Organised Crime and Police Act 2005, s.163. Section 113A consolidates the existing provisions for criminal record certificates.

A criminal record certificate is available to people who have regular contact with the under 18s, the elderly, sick or handicapped people; those involved in the administration of the law (e.g. police officers); and others employed in other sensitive areas and professions.

A criminal record certificate must be issued by the Secretary of State to a person who applies in the prescribed manner and form countersigned by a registered person and who pays the prescribed fee. The application form and fees are currently prescribed by the Police Act 1997 (Criminal Records) Regulations 2002, SI 2002/233 as amended. The application must be accompanied by a statement by the registered person that the certificate is required for the purposes of an exempted question. An 'exempted question' means a question in relation to which the Rehabilitation of Offenders Act 1974, s.4(2)(a) or (b) has been excluded by an order of the Secretary of State under s.4(4) of that Act.

The certificate either gives prescribed details of every relevant matter relating to the applicant which is recorded in central records or states that there is no such matter. The certificate will include details of convictions, including convictions 'spent' under the Rehabilitation of Offenders Act, and cautions held at national level. The Secretary of State must send a copy of the criminal record certificate to the registered person who countersigned the application.

A registered person is a person who is listed in a register maintained by the Secretary of State. The Secretary of State must include in the register any person who applies to him in writing to be registered and who satisfies the following conditions:

- a person applying for registration must be a body corporate or unincorporate, a person appointed to an office by virtue of any enactment, or an individual who employs others in the course of a business;
- a body applying for registration must satisfy the Secretary of State that it is likely to ask exempted questions, or is likely to countersign applications at the request of bodies or individuals asking exempted questions; and
- a person other than a body applying for registration must satisfy the Secretary of State that he is likely to ask exempted questions.

6.10.8   Subject access search

The National Identification Service is operated by the Metropolitan Police on behalf of all UK police forces, and is responsible for the national collection of fingerprints and criminal records. It is also deals with subject access searches which disclose to individuals under the Data Protection Act information held on them on the Police National Computer. This search makes no allowance for the Rehabilitation of Offenders Act and so everything is included in the result even though it is officially no longer relevant.

Section 7 of the Data Protection Act 1998 states that a 'data subject' (the person to whom the personal data refer) is entitled, upon written request, to be informed whether or not personal data are held or processed about them. If personal data are being held or processed, the 'data subject' is allowed to be given a copy of the personal data held, the reasons why the data are being held or processed and information as to what other bodies the information may be passed on to.

However some exemptions exist to prevent disclosure of this information in certain circumstances, for example:

- the prevention and detection of crime;
- the apprehension and prosecution of offenders;
- the interests of national security.

An application for a subject access search should be made to the police force which covers the region or area the applicant resides in. The application form should be obtained from the appropriate police force. A fee of £10 is payable and the application must be accompanied by proof of identity which shows the applicant's full name, current address and date of birth, for example a passport, medical card, driving licence, bank statement or utility bill. All documents must be originals and photocopies will not be accepted unless stamped and signed by a Justice of the Peace or solicitor.

A subject access search application must be processed within a maximum of 40 days.

6.11   APPEALS

If a licensing authority rejects an application for the grant of a personal licence or rejects an application for renewal, the applicant may appeal against the decision (Sched. 5, para. 17(1)). In addition, where a licensing authority grants an application for a personal licence or for renewal, any chief officer of police who gave an objection notice may appeal against the decision (Sched. 5, para. 17(2) and (3)).

The holder of a personal licence which is revoked because of convictions which have come to light after it was granted or renewed may also appeal against the revocation (Sched. 5, para. 17(4)).

A chief officer of police who gave notice to the relevant licensing authority that continuation of the licence would undermine the crime prevention objective may appeal against a decision of the authority not to revoke the licence, as long as the notice has not been withdrawn (Sched. 5, para. 17(5)).

Any appeal must be made to a magistrates' court (Sched. 5, para. 17(6)). The appeal must be commenced by the service of a notice on the designated officer for the magistrates' court within 21 days beginning with the date on which the appellant was notified by the licensing authority of its decision (Sched. 5, para. 17(7)). In the case of an appeal by a chief officer of police, the holder of the personal licence, as well as the licensing authority, is to be treated as a respondent (Sched. 5, para. 17(8)).

Where a licence holder gives notice of appeal against a decision not to renew his licence, the licensing authority or the magistrates' court to which the notice has been given may, on such conditions as it thinks fit, order that the licence is to continue or order that the licence is to be reinstated, if it has already ceased to have effect, until either the time at which the appeal is dismissed or abandoned or, where the appeal is allowed, the time the licence is renewed (Sched. 5, para. 17(10) and (11)).

6.12 DURATION OF A PERSONAL LICENCE

A personal licence is granted for an initial period of 10 years from the date on which it was granted. Once granted the licensing authority that issued the personal licence remains the relevant licensing authority for it and may subsequently renew it for further 10-year periods.

6.13 RENEWAL OF A PERSONAL LICENCE

An application to renew a personal licence may only be made during the two-month period which starts three months before the time the licence will expire (s.117(6)). This is a strict requirement and failure to meet it will mean that a new application for a personal licence will have to be made. This means that an application must be made not more than three months and not less than one month before the existing licence expires.

Provided an application is made within the prescribed two-month time limit, the existing personal licence will continue to have effect until the renewal application is either determined or withdrawn, even if the application is not determined until after the date on which the existing licence would expire, subject to the provisions on revocation, forfeiture and suspension and surrender (s.119).

A renewal application must be made to the licensing authority which granted the personal licence originally, even if the applicant has moved since the licence was originally granted and no longer resides in that licensing authority's area (s.119(3)).

The Guidance, para. 4.17 provides that:

Renewal of the personal licence every ten years provides an opportunity to ensure that the arrangements ensuring that all convictions for relevant and foreign offences have been properly notified to the relevant licensing authority have worked and nothing has been missed, and that all such convictions have been properly endorsed upon the licence. It also provides an opportunity to ensure that the photograph of the holder on the personal licence is updated to aid identification.

6.13.1 Applying for renewal

In order to apply for a renewal, an applicant must submit the following to the relevant licensing authority:

- a completed application form. The application form is prescribed and is set out in Sched. 2 to the Personal Licences Regulations;
- the applicant's current personal licence or a statement of the reasons as to why this cannot be produced;
- two photographs of himself which are:
  - taken against a light background so that his features are distinguishable and contrast against the background;
  - 45 mm by 35 mm;
  - full face uncovered and without sunglasses and, unless the applicant wears a head covering because of his religious beliefs, without a head covering;
  - on photographic paper; and
  - one of the photographs endorsed with a statement verifying the likeness of the photograph to the applicant by a solicitor, notary, a person of standing in the community, such as a bank official, police officer, civil servant or minister of religion, or any individual with a professional qualification;
- either a criminal conviction certificate issued under the Police Act 1997, s.112, a criminal record certificate issued under the Police Act 1997, s.113A or the results of a subject access search under the Data Protection Act 1998 of the Police National Computer by the National Identification Service. Whichever of these is produced, it must not have been issued more than one month before the application for the personal licence is submitted to the licensing authority;

- a declaration by the applicant, in the prescribed form, that either he has not been convicted of a relevant offence or a foreign offence or that he has been convicted of a relevant offence or a foreign offence accompanied by details of the nature and date of the conviction and any sentence imposed on him in respect of it; and
- the fee of £37 (prescribed by the Fees Regulations).

6.13.2 Obtaining the application form and making an application

The procedures for obtaining and completing the form and making an application are the same as those described in **6.5.1–3**.

6.13.3 Dealing with the application

If the application for renewal is in order and the prescribed requirements have been met, the application for renewal must be granted.

Section 121 contains provisions which govern the determination of a renewal application where it appears to the licensing authority that the applicant has, since the personal licence was originally granted or last renewed, been convicted of any relevant offence or foreign offence which is not spent for the purposes of the Rehabilitation of Offenders Act 1974. Where it appears that there are convictions, the licensing authority must give notice to the chief officer of police for its area. If the chief officer of police is then satisfied that renewing the personal licence would undermine the crime prevention objective, he must, within 14 days beginning with the day he received the notice from the licensing authority, give an objection notice to the licensing authority setting out the reasons why he is objecting.

In deciding whether or not to object, the chief officer of police may take into account any unspent conviction, whether occurring before or after the personal licence was originally granted or last renewed, for a relevant offence or a foreign offence which he considers is comparable to a relevant offence.

If an objection notice is not given within the 14-day period, or if one is given and later withdrawn, the personal licence must be renewed. Where an objection notice is given a hearing must be held to consider it, unless the applicant, the chief officer of police and the licensing authority all agree that a hearing is not necessary. The hearing must be held within 20 working days beginning with the day after the end of the 14-day period for the police to give an objection notice (Hearings Regulations, reg. 5 and Sched. 1, para. 13). Notice of the hearing must be given to the applicant and the chief officer of police no later than 10 working days before the day or the first day on which the hearing is to be held (Hearings Regulations, reg. 6(4) and Sched. 2, para. 13). The applicant must be given the notice of objection with the notice of hearing (Hearings Regulations, reg. 7(2) and Sched. 3, para. 12). The licensing authority can only reject the application if it is necessary to do so for the promotion of the crime prevention objective. In all other cases, it must grant the application.

On the renewal of a personal licence the licensing authority must give notice of its decision to the applicant and the chief officer of police, and where the chief officer of police has objected to the renewal and has not withdrawn it, the notice must set out the reasons why the licensing authority has granted the application (s.122(1)). If the personal licence is not renewed, notice must be given to the applicant and the chief officer of police setting out the reasons for the decision (s.122(2)).

6.14 CONVICTIONS DURING THE APPLICATION PROCESS

Where an applicant for the grant or renewal of a personal licence is convicted of a relevant offence or a foreign offence during the period following submission of his application and its determination, he must as soon as reasonably practicable notify the licensing authority of his conviction (s.123(1)). Failure to notify the licensing authority without having a reasonable excuse is an offence punishable on summary conviction by a fine not exceeding level 4 on the standard scale (s.123(2) and (3)).

Where a licensing authority has granted or renewed a personal licence and it subsequently discovers that the applicant was convicted during the application period of a relevant offence or a foreign offence, it must give a notice of the conviction to the chief officer of police for its area (s.124(2)). If the chief officer of police is satisfied that continuation of the licence would undermine the crime prevention objective, having taken into account any unspent conviction for a relevant offence or a foreign offence comparable to a relevant offence which occurred before the end of the application period, he must, within 14 days beginning with the day he received the notice from the licensing authority give the authority an objection notice setting the reasons why he is so satisfied (s.124(3)).

Where an objection notice is given within the 14-day period, and it is not withdrawn, the licensing authority must hold a hearing to consider the objection notice, unless the holder of the licence, the chief officer of police and the authority agree it is unnecessary, and having regard to the notice, must revoke the licence if it considers it necessary for the promotion of the crime prevention objective to do so (s.124(4)). The hearing must be held within 20 working days beginning with the day after the end of the period within which the chief officer of police may give an objection notice (Hearings Regulations, reg. 5 and Sched. 1, para. 14). Notice of the hearing must be given to the personal licence holder and the police no later than 10 working days before the day or the first day on which the hearing is to be held (Hearings Regulations, reg. 6(4) and Sched. 2, para. 14). The personal licence holder must be given the notice of objection with the notice of hearing (Hearings Regulations, reg. 7(2) and Sched. 3, para. 13).

Whether the licensing authority revokes or decides not to revoke the personal licence it must notify the offender and the chief officer of police of the decision and its reasons for making it (s.124(5)). The notice must be given forthwith (see **2.9**) on making the determination and it must be accompanied by information regarding the right of a party to appeal against the determination.

Any decision to revoke a personal licence does not have effect until the end of the period for appealing against the decision, or if the decision is appealed against, until the appeal is disposed of (s.124(6)).

6.15 CONVICTIONS DURING THE CURRENCY OF A PERSONAL LICENCE

6.15.1 Notifying the court of the personal licence

If a personal licence holder is charged with a relevant offence, he must produce his personal licence to the magistrates' court no later than when he first appears before them in connection with the offence (s.128(1)). If he cannot produce his licence, he must explain to the court why it is not available and provide details of the licensing authority which issued the licence to him.

A person charged with a relevant offence who is subsequently granted a personal licence after his first appearance in a magistrates' court in connection with the offence must produce the licence or its details and an explanation for its absence at the next appearance in court in connection with the offence (s.128(3)).

Where a personal licence has been produced to the court or the court has been notified of its existence, a personal licence holder charged with a relevant offence must notify the court of any application to renew the licence which is made or withdrawn, or of any surrender, renewal or revocation of the licence at the next appearance in court in connection with the offence (s.128(4)).

Failure without reasonable excuse to provide a court with the relevant details concerning a personal licence is an offence punishable on summary conviction with a fine not exceeding level 2 on the standard scale (s.128(6) and (7)).

6.15.2 Forfeiture or suspension of a personal licence

If a court in England or Wales convicts a personal licence holder of a relevant offence, it may order that the licence be forfeited or be suspended for a period up to six months (s.129(2)). When deciding whether to make an order for forfeiture or suspension the court may consider any previous conviction of the licence holder for a relevant offence which is not spent for the purposes of the Rehabilitation of Offenders Act 1974 (s.129(3)). The court making an order forfeiting or suspending a personal licence may suspend the order pending an appeal against it (s.129(4)).

An appellate court can suspend an order forfeiting or suspending a personal licence (s.130). The power is exercisable on such terms as the court thinks fit by the court to which a person convicted of a relevant offence has appealed, applied for leave to appeal, stated a case or applied for a quashing order (s.130(7)). The appellate court must give notice of any suspension to the relevant licensing authority (s.130(8)). If the original order forfeited the licence and the appellate court suspends that order it will be reinstated for the period during which the order is suspended (s.130(9)).

6.15.3   The court's duty to notify the relevant licensing authority

Where a court convicts a personal licence holder of a relevant offence it must, as soon as is reasonably practicable, under s.131 send a notice to the relevant licensing authority a notice containing details of:

- the name and address of the convicted licence holder;
- the nature and date of the conviction; and
- the sentence passed including any order for forfeiture or suspension of the licence.

A copy of the notice must also be sent to the licence holder.

The Guidance, para. 4.24 provides that:

> The sentence of the court has immediate effect despite the fact that an appeal may be lodged against conviction or sentence (although the court may suspend the forfeiture or suspension of the licence pending the outcome of any appeal). On receipt of such a notification, the licensing authority should contact the holder and request his licence so that the necessary action can be taken. The holder must then produce his licence to the authority within 14 days. It is expected that the chief officer of police for the area in which the holder resides would be advised if he or she does not respond promptly. On receipt of the licence, the details of the conviction should be recorded in the authority's records and endorsed on the licence, as should any period of suspension if so ordered. The licence should then be returned to the holder. If the licence is declared forfeit, it should be retained by the licensing authority.

If a personal licence holder appeals against the conviction or sentence imposed for a relevant offence the appeal court must, as soon as is reasonably practicable, notify the relevant licensing authority if the conviction is quashed or a new sentence substituted (s.131(3)). A copy of the notice given to the licensing authority must be sent to the licence holder. Where the Court of Appeal is asked to consider the leniency of a sentence imposed on a personal licence holder following conviction for a relevant offence, the court must notify the relevant licensing authority of any action taken, and a copy of the notice must also be sent to the licence holder (s.131(4)).

6.15.4   The licence holder's duty to notify the relevant licensing authority

Whether or not a court dealing with a personal licence holder for a relevant offence is aware of the existence of the licence a duty is imposed on the personal licence holder, as soon as is reasonably practicable after conviction, to notify the relevant licensing authority of the nature and date of the conviction and any sentence imposed as a result (s.132(2)). Similar provisions apply where the existence of a personal licence is not known to a court hearing an appeal or the Court of Appeal to which a reference has been made concerning leniency of a sentence. As soon as reasonably practicable following determination of the appeal or referral the personal licence holder must give notice of the determination to the relevant licensing authority. Any such notice given to the relevant licensing authority must be accompanied by the personal licence or an explanation for its omission (s.132(3)). A personal licence holder who fails, without reasonable excuse, to comply with the obligation to notify the licensing authority of a conviction or other relevant matter commits an offence punishable on summary conviction by a fine not exceeding level 2 on the standard scale (s.132(4) and (5)).

6.16   SURRENDER OF A PERSONAL LICENCE

A holder of a personal licence may decide that he wishes to surrender his licence and can do so by giving notice that he wishes to do so to the relevant licensing authority (s.116(1)). Such a notice must be accompanied by the personal licence or, if that is not practicable, by a statement setting out the reasons why the licence cannot be produced (s.116(2)). Once a notice of surrender is given the personal licence lapses on receipt of the notice by the relevant licensing authority (s.116(3)).

6.17   THEFT OR LOSS OF A PERSONAL LICENCE

A holder of a personal licence who has lost his licence, or had it stolen, damaged or destroyed, can apply to the relevant licensing authority for a copy of his licence (s.126(1)). The fee for issuing a copy of a licence is £10.50 (prescribed by the Fees Regulations). There is no prescribed application form and a letter will suffice.

A licensing authority can only issue a copy of a licence if it is satisfied that the licence has been lost, stolen, damaged or destroyed, and where it has been lost or stolen, the holder of the licence has reported the loss or theft to the police (s.126(3)). The copy which is issued must be certified by the authority to be a true copy, and must be a copy of the licence in the form in which it existed immediately before it was lost, stolen, damaged or destroyed.

A certified copy has the same effect under the Act as the original licence (s.126(5)).

6.18 DUTY TO NOTIFY CHANGES

The holder of a personal licence must, as soon as is reasonably practicable, notify the relevant licensing authority of any change in his name or address as stated in the personal licence (s.127(1)). The notification must be accompanied by the fee, which is £10.50 (prescribed by the Fees Regulations). There is no prescribed form of notification and a letter will suffice.

The notice must be accompanied by the personal licence or, if that is not practicable, by a statement setting out the reasons why the licence cannot be produced (s.127(3)).

A personal licensee who fails to give notice of any change in his name or address commits an offence and, on summary conviction, may be fined a sum not exceeding level 2 on the standard scale (s.127(4) and (5)).

6.19 UPDATING A PERSONAL LICENCE

Where a relevant licensing authority:

- renews a personal licence;
- revokes or decides not to revoke a personal licence where convictions come to light after the licence has been granted or renewed;
- receives a notice of convictions during the application period;
- receives notification of a change in the licence holder's name or address;
- receives notification from a court of convictions; or
- receives notification from a licence holder of convictions;

or an appeal against a decision made in respect of a personal licence is disposed of, then the licensing authority must make any appropriate amendments to the licence (s.134(1)).

Where notice is given of an order to forfeit or suspend a personal licence, the relevant licensing authority must endorse the licence with the terms of the order (s.134(2)). Any such endorsement must be cancelled if a notice is subsequently received that the order has been quashed (s.134(3)).

In order to allow the licence to be updated, a licensing authority which is not in possession of the personal licence may require the licensee to produce it to the authority within a period of 14 days beginning with the day on which he is notified that the authority requires the licence (s.134(4)). A personal licensee who then fails to produce his licence commits an offence and, on summary conviction, may be fined a sum not exceeding level 2 on the standard scale (s.134(5) and (6)).

6.20 DUTY TO PRODUCE A PERSONAL LICENCE

A constable or an officer of a licensing authority who has been authorised by the authority may require the holder of a personal licence who is on the premises in order make or authorise the supply of alcohol under a premises licence or a temporary event notice to produce his licence for inspection (s.135(2)). An authorised officer of a licensing authority must produce evidence of his authority if requested (s.135(3)). A personal licensee who fails to produce his licence, without a reasonable excuse, commits an offence and, on summary conviction, may be fined a sum not exceeding level 2 on the standard scale (s.135(5) and (6)).

CHAPTER 7

Premises licences

7.1 INTRODUCTION

Part 3 of the Act introduces the concept of a licence which relates to premises which are to be used for licensable activities called a 'premises licence'.

7.2 PREMISES LICENCES

A premises licence is defined by s.11 as a licence granted under Part 3 of the Act, in respect of any premises, which authorises the premises to be used for one or more licensable activity.

7.2.1 The definition of premises

The term 'premises' is defined in s.193 to mean any place and includes a vehicle, vessel or moveable structure. While this definition appears to be broad, s.176 prohibits the sale or supply of alcohol at certain places, and there are also places and activities specified in ss.173, 174 and 175 which are exempt from the requirement to have a premises licence.

'Any place'

A premises licence is required for licensable activities which occur at, on or in 'any place'. This means that not only do licensable activities which take place inside buildings, for example public houses, theatres, etc., require a premises licence but licensable activities which take place outside, for example open air concerts and plays, require a premises licence. Where the licensable activity takes place at several places a separate premises licence is required for each place; for example a circus will require a separate licence for each performance site.

Where the place of sale of alcohol is different from the place of supply, s.190 treats the sale as having happened at the place from which the alcohol is appropriated to the contract. This will cover Internet, mail order and telephone sales, and so the sale will be regarded as having taken place at the warehouse from which the alcohol is to be delivered and not the Internet or the call centre handling the sale. The requirement for a premises licence will therefore apply to the warehouse rather than the call centre.

'Vehicle, vessel or moveable structure'

A 'vehicle' is defined in s.193 to mean a vehicle intended or adapted for use on roads. This definition will include vehicles which are towed such as caravans or trailers. A 'vessel' is also defined in s.193 to include a ship, boat, raft or other apparatus constructed or adapted for floating on water. There is no definition of 'moveable structure' but it would presumably include a tent or inflatable building.

The situation where vehicles, vessels and moveable structures are not permanently located in one place is dealt with in s.189. Where a vessel is not permanently moored or berthed in a particular place, a premises licence will be required as the vessel will treated as though it were premises situated at the place where it is normally moored or berthed. A vehicle or moveable structure which is not permanently located in the same place will be treated as premises located at any place where it is parked or set. This means for example that a fast food van which provides late night refreshment in a number of locations will need a separate premises licence in respect of each location, as will a business which provides alcohol from a marquee at events such as fairs and village fêtes. Each application must be made to the relevant authority for that particular location and so applications may have to be made to several relevant authorities.

The provisions in the Act relating to provisional statements do not apply to vessels, vehicles or moveable structures (s.189(5)).

7.2.2 Premises excluded from premises licences

Certain premises are 'excluded premises' which means that no sale by retail or supply of alcohol can take place on or from them. These fall into the following two categories:

- service areas on 'special roads', which has the same meaning as in the Highways Act 1980 except that it also includes a trunk road; these will thus include service areas on motorways and trunk roads; and
- premises used primarily as a garage or which form part of premises which are primarily so used.

The Secretary of State may by order amend this definition of excluded premises so as to include or exclude any other premises of such description as may be specified in the order.

Garage premises

Premises which are used primarily as a garage or which form part of premises which are primarily used as a garage are excluded premises.

Premises are used as a garage if they are used for one or more of the following activitities:

- the retailing of petrol;
- the retailing of derv;
- the sale of motor vehicles; or
- the maintenance of motor vehicles.

This exclusion maintains the position under the Licensing Act 1964. It will be for a licensing authority to decide in the light of the facts whether or not on the balance of probabilities premises are used primarily as a garage. This will be relevant where for example the premises comprise a petrol filling station and a convenience store which sells items such as food, newspapers, etc. The test is not whether the premises are primarily used as a shop. For premises to be excluded there must be significantly more use as a garage than for any other use.

In order to determine the primary use, it will be necessary to look at the intensity of use of the premises by customers. It is accepted that this will usually be proved by evidence such as an analysis of till receipts over a recent period of time.

In *Green* v. *Inner London Justices* (1994) *Licensing Review* 13 the gross turnover from fuel sales was compared to the net turnover from other sales, but this was held not to be an accurate method bearing in mind the taxes and duties on fuel. If figures for turnover are used, they must be net of taxes and duties. In *R.* v. *Liverpool Crown Court ex p. Goodwin* [2002] LLR 698 the court said that the test must be to consider the intensity of use by customers at the premises and that evidence such as customer lists might be highly material. Having regard to the appearance of the premises and how they were known in the locality was 'erroneous'.

The Guidance, para. 5.28 provides:

> The approach to establishing primary use so far approved by the courts has been based on an examination of the intensity of use by customers of the premises. For example, if a garage shop in any rural area is used more intensely by customers purchasing other products than by customers purchasing non-qualifying products or services, it may be eligible to seek authority to sell or supply alcohol.

It would therefore appear that in determining the primary use a consideration of the intensity of use of the premises by customers will be used and a comparison of the net turnovers may be taken into account.

7.2.3 Exempt premises

Certain licensable activities will not require a premises licence if they are carried on at premises which are exempt. Section 173(1) provides that an activity is not a licensable activity if it is carried on:

- aboard an aircraft, hovercraft or railway vehicle engaged on a journey;
- aboard a vessel engaged on an international journey;
- at an approved wharf at a designated port or hoverport;
- at an examination station at a designated airport;
- at a royal palace;
- at premises which, at the time when the activity is carried on, are permanently or temporarily occupied for the purposes of the armed forces of the Crown;
- at premises in respect of which a certificate issued under s.174 (exemption for national security) has effect; or
- at such other place as may be prescribed.

Journeys

The period during which an aircraft, hovercraft, railway vehicle or vessel is engaged on a journey includes any period ending with its departure when preparations are being made for the journey, and any period after its arrival at its destination when it continues to be occupied by the passengers, or any of them, who made the journey or any part of it.

An international journey is either a journey from a place in the United Kingdom to an immediate destination outside the United Kingdom, or a journey from a place outside the United Kingdom to an immediate destination in the United Kingdom.

'Railway vehicle' has the meaning given by the Railways Act 1993, s.83 (see **21.5.2**).

Designated airports, ports and hoverports

Only certain parts of designated airports, ports and hoverports are exempt. In relation to airports, only the part of the airport which is an 'examination station' is exempt. This area has the meaning given by the Customs and Excise Management Act 1979, s.22A and is essentially that part of an airport beyond the security check in, i.e. 'airside'. In respect of ports and hoverports this area is an approved wharf which has the meaning given by the Customs and Excise Management Act 1979, s.20A, i.e. 'wharfside'. These are areas to which the non-travelling public do not have access and are subject to stringent by-laws. This exemption allows refreshment of all kinds to be provided to travellers at all times of the day and night. Other parts of designated ports, hoverports and airports are subject to the normal licensing controls.

All ports, airports and hoverports which have already been designated for the purposes of the Licensing Act 1964 continue to be treated as designated for the purposes of the Act. The Secretary of State may by order designate a port, hoverport or airport in the future if it appears to him to be one at which there is a substantial amount of international passenger traffic. Alternatively an order may be made to remove designation from any port, airport or hoverport.

Royal palaces

Royal palaces are exempt from the need to have a premises licence.

Premises used by the armed forces

Premises used by the armed forces are exempt. These include premises which are permanently or temporarily occupied by the armed forces.

Premises exempt on national security grounds

A Cabinet minister or the Attorney General may issue a certificate under s.174 in respect of any premises if he considers that it is appropriate to do so for the purposes of safeguarding national security. The effect of the certificate will be that any activities carried on at the premises will not be licensable activities. The certificate may identify the premises by means of a general description but there are no other requirements as to its contents. It is expected that this power will be used where the inspection of a particular premises for purposes of the licensing regime would give rise to a security risk.

A document purporting to be a certificate is to be received in evidence and treated as being a certificate unless the contrary is proved. A document which purports to be certified by or on behalf of a minister of the Crown as a true copy of a certificate given by a minister of the Crown is evidence of that certificate.

A minister of the Crown may cancel a certificate issued by him or any other minister of the Crown.

7.2.4 Exempt lotteries

A lottery such as a raffle or tombola where one or more of the prizes consists of or includes alcohol will be exempt under s.175 from requiring a premises licence if:

- the lottery is promoted as incidental to an exempt entertainment. 'Exempt entertainment' has the same meaning as in the Lotteries and Amusements

Act 1976, s.3(1) and so means a bazaar, sale of work, fête, dinner, dance, sporting or athletic event or other entertainment of a similar character;

- after the deduction of all relevant expenses, the whole proceeds of the entertainment (including those of the lottery) are applied for purposes other than private gain. 'Private gain' is construed in accordance with the Lotteries and Amusements Act 1976, s.22 and so the proceeds of any entertainment, lottery or gaming promoted on behalf of a society which are applied for any purpose calculated to benefit the society as a whole shall not be held to be applied for purposes of private gain by reason only that their application for that purpose results in benefit to any person as an individual;
- the alcohol consists of or includes alcohol in a sealed container, for example a bottle of wine;
- no prize in the lottery is a money prize. 'Money' has the meaning given by the Lotteries and Amusements Act 1976, s.23 and includes a cheque, postal order, money order or banknote;
- a ticket or chance in the lottery is not sold or issued, or the result of the lottery is not declared, other than at the premises where the entertainment takes place and during the entertainment. 'Ticket' has the meaning given by the Lotteries and Amusements Act 1976, s.23 and includes any document evidencing the claim of a person to participate in the chances of the lottery; and
- the opportunity to participate in a lottery or in gaming is not the only or main inducement to attend the entertainment. 'Gaming' has the same meaning as in the Gaming Act 1968, s.52 and means the playing of a game of chance for winnings in money or money's worth, whether any person playing the game is at risk of losing any money or money's worth or not.

The following are relevant expenses:

- the expenses of the entertainment, excluding expenses incurred in connection with the lottery;
- the expenses incurred in printing tickets in the lottery; and
- such reasonable and proper expenses as the promoters of the lottery appropriate on account of any expenses they incur in buying prizes in the lottery.

The provisions of the Lotteries and Amusements Act 1976 will in due course be repealed and replaced by the Gambling Act 2005.

7.3 APPLICANTS FOR PREMISES LICENCES

Section 16 sets out a wide list of persons or bodies who can apply for a premises licence. It also provides that a person may not apply for a premises licence unless he is aged 18 or over.

The full list of persons or bodies who can apply for a premises licence is as follows:

- a person who carries on, or proposes to carry on, a business which involves the use of the premises for the licensable activities to which the application relates;
- a person who makes the application pursuant to any statutory function discharged by that person which relates to those licensable activities, for example a local authority, a fire and rescue authority and the Prison Service;
- a person who makes the application pursuant to any function discharged by that person by virtue of Her Majesty's prerogative;
- a recognised club, which is a club which satisfies the first three requirements in s.62 (see **17.3**);
- a charity (for these purposes 'charity' has the same meaning as in the Charities Act 1993, s.96(1) which provides that it means any institution, corporate or not, which is established for charitable purposes and is subject to the control of the High Court in the exercise of the court's jurisdiction with respect to charities);
- the proprietor of an educational institution (for these purposes 'educational institution' means either a school or an institution within the further or higher education sector within the meaning of the Education Act 1996, s.4) or a college (including any institution in the nature of a college), school, hall or other institution of a university, in circumstances where the university receives financial support under the Further and Higher Education Act 1992, s.65 and 'proprietor' in relation to a school within the meaning of the Education Act 1996, s.4 has the same meaning as in s.579(1) of that Act, and in relation to an educational institution other than such a school means the governing body of that institution within the meaning of the Further and Higher Education Act 1992, s.90(1));
- a health service body, (for these purposes 'health service body' means either an NHS trust established by virtue of the National Health Service and Community Care Act 1990, s.5, a primary care trust established by virtue of the National Health Service Act 1977, s.16A, or a local health board established by virtue of the National Health Service Act 1977, s.16BA);
- a person who is registered under part 2 of the Care Standards Act 2000 in respect of an independent hospital, (for these purposes 'independent hospital' has the same meaning as in the Care Standards Act 2000, s.2(2) which provides that a hospital which is not a health service hospital is an independent hospital);
- the chief officer of police of a police force in England and Wales; and
- a person of such other description as may be prescribed.

7.3.1 Persons who propose to carry on a business involving licensable activities on the premises

The principal category of those who are eligible to apply for a premises licence will be those persons who propose to carry on a business involving licensable activities on the premises. If the applicant is an individual then he must be aged 18 or over. Additionally, for these purposes, a 'person' includes a business or partnership, and the Guidance, para. 5.40 provides that:

> Licensing authorities should not require the nomination of an individual to hold the licence. It is not for the licensing authority to decide who is the most appropriate person to hold the licence. For example, in respect of most leased public houses, a tenant may run or propose to run the business at the premises in agreement with a pub owning company. Both would be eligible to apply for the appropriate licence and it is for these businesses or individuals to agree contractually amongst themselves who should do so. It is not for the licensing authority to interfere in that decision. However, in the case of a managed public house, the pub operating company should apply for the licence as the manager (an employee) would not be entitled to do so. Similarly, with cinema chains, the normal holder of the premises licence would be the company owning the cinema and not the cinema manager (an employee of the main company).

There is no requirement that an applicant for a premises licence must have a legal or equitable interest in the premises or a contractual right to use them. So an application for a premises licence could be made by someone who was proposing to buy the premises and use them for licensable activities. While there is nothing to prevent an application being made before premises have been built, extended or altered, a developer could not make an application unless he proposed subsequently to use the premises for a licensable activity. A developer in such a situation should apply instead for a provisional statement (see **Chapter 13**).

7.3.2 Joint applications

It is possible for a joint application to be made for a premises licence, though this is likely to be rare as each applicant must be carrying on a business which involves the use of the premises for licensable activities at the premises. In the case of a tenanted public house for example it would be far easier for the tenant to show this than for a pub owning company which was not itself carrying on licensable activities.

Where a public house is owned, or a tenancy is held, jointly by a husband and wife or other partnerships of a similar nature and both parties actively involve themselves in the business of carrying on licensable activities at the premises, then the husband and wife or the partners could make a joint application for the premises licence even if they were not formally partners in business terms. According to the Guidance this is unlikely to lead to the same issues of clouded accountability that could arise where two separate businesses applied jointly for the licence (para. 5.42). If the application is then granted the premises licence would identify the holder as both people and any subsequent applications, for example for a variation of the licence, would have to be made jointly. Before making a joint application consideration should be given as to whether it will provide sufficient flexibility for the business or whether a single application, given that it would be possible later to apply for transfer and interim authority, would be preferable.

7.3.3 Multiple licences

There is no bar on there being more than one premises licence in force at any given time in respect of the same premises. For example a property could have a premises licence authorising the sale of alcohol which was held by one person and another person could hold a premises licence for those premises or part of those premises which authorised regulated entertainment. So the fact that there is already a premises licence in force should not prevent another premises licence being applied for.

7.4 MAKING AN APPLICATION

An application for a premises licence must be made to the 'relevant licensing authority' (s.17(1)). In the majority of cases this will be the authority in whose area the premises are situated. Where part of the premises is situated in one authority area and another part of the premises is situated in the area of another authority, the relevant licensing authority will be the authority in whose area the greater or greatest part of the premises is situated (s.12(3)(a)). If the premises are split equally between neighbouring authorities, then the applicant must nominate which of the authorities is to be the relevant licensing authority (s.12(3)(b)).

An applicant must submit the following to the relevant licensing authority:

- a completed application form;
- an operating schedule;
- a plan of the premises in the prescribed form;
- if the application requests the authorisation to supply alcohol, the written consent of the proposed designated premises supervisor in the prescribed form; and
- the fee.

A copy of the application must be sent to each of the responsible authorities (see **7.9**). The application must also be advertised (see **7.8**).

7.5 THE APPLICATION FORM

An application for a premises licence must be in the prescribed form which is set out in Sched. 2 to the Licensing Act 2003 (Premises Licences and Club Premises Certificates) Regulations 2005, SI 2005/42 ('Premises Licences Regulations').

7.5.1 Completing the application form

For the procedures for completing the form see **6.5.2**. Care must be taken when completing the application form as any mistakes will be built into the new licence.

In the opening statement, the name of the applicant or applicants applying for the premises licence should be inserted.

The application form is then divided into four parts.

Part 1

The applicant must set out the following details of the premises:

- the postal address;
- the telephone number at the premises, if any; and
- the non-domestic rateable value of the premises.

If the premises have no postal address, the location of the premises should be described or the Ordnance Survey map reference should be given.

The trading name of the premises should also be included.

The non-domestic rateable value of the premises will determine the fee to be paid both for the initial application and annually. The non-domestic rateable value is based on the annual rent that the premises could have been let for on the open market at a particular date. It can be checked on the Valuation Office Agency website (**www.voa.gov.uk**).

Part 2

Part 2 deals with details of the applicant. The applicant must state in which capacity he is applying for a premises licence. If he is applying as an individual, a limited company, a partnership, an unincorporated association or a statutory corporation he must confirm that he is carrying on or proposing to carry on a business which involves the use of the premises for licensable activities, or that he is making the application pursuant to a statutory function or a function discharged by virtue of Her Majesty's prerogative.

The applicant must then give further details such as his name and address, telephone number, e-mail address (this is optional) and confirmation, where relevant, that he is at least 18 years old.

Part 3

Part 3 contains the operating schedule (see **Chapter 8**). It starts by requiring the applicant to state when he wants the premises licence to start and if he wants it only to be valid for a limited period of time, when he wants it to end.

If 5,000 or more people are expected to attend the premises at any one time, the applicant must state the number expected to attend. This question is asked in order to determine whether an additional fee is payable. The figure of 5,000 relates to the maximum number of people on the licensed premises at any one time. It does not relate to areas which do not form part of the licensed premises; for example more than 5,000 people may attend a country show but a beer tent at that show is unlikely to hold 5,000 people all at the same time and so would not trigger the additional fee.

The applicant must then give a general description of the premises, for example the type of premises, their general situation and layout and any other information which could be relevant to the licensing objectives. Where the application includes off-supplies of alcohol and the applicant intends to provide a place for these to be consumed, for example a beer garden, he must include a description of where the place will be and its proximity to the premises.

The applicant must then specify which licensable activities he intends to carry on from the premises, and give further details of these in the appropriate boxes A–M using the 24-hour clock. Where it is intended that the supply of alcohol is to be carried on, the applicant must set out the full name, address and personal licence number of the proposed designated premises supervisor (see further **Chapter 9**).

All applicants must complete boxes N, O and P. Box N requires an applicant to highlight any adult entertainment or services, activities, other entertainment or matters ancillary to the use of the premises which may give rise to concern in respect of children. When completing this box an applicant should indicate whether there are any gaming machines on the premises. (Applications for a permit for 'amusement with prizes' machines are now made to the relevant licensing authority; see the Gaming Act 1968, s.34 and the Guidance, paras. 5.119–5.126.)

Details of the hours during which the premises will be open to the public must be stated in box O, together with any seasonal variation or non-standard timings. A difference is therefore drawn between the hours during which the licensable activities will take place and the hours during which the public will be permitted to be on the premises. Reference should be made to the statement of licensing policy of the relevant licensing authority for any requirements as to how long customers should be allowed to remain on the premises after the cessation of licensable activities. Finally box P requires an applicant to list the steps which he will take to promote the four licensing objectives (see **2.3**).

Further guidance on completing the operating schedule can be found in **Chapter 8**.

There is then a checklist, together with a warning that it is an offence, liable on conviction to a fine up to level 5 on the standard scale, under s.158 to make a false statement in or in connection with the application.

Part 4

The application form must be signed by the applicant. It can also be signed by the applicant's solicitor or other duly authorised agent; anyone signing on behalf of the applicant must state in what capacity they sign. Where there are joint applicants, both applicants or their respective agents must sign the application form. If the application is made by a limited company, partnership or unincorporated association, someone who has the capacity to bind the applicant should sign.

7.5.2 Obtaining an application form

A relevant licensing authority must provide an applicant on request with a printed application form; however an electronic version may be provided by a licensing authority on its website which a prospective applicant can download, print off and complete. An electronic copy is also provided on the DCMS website.

Table 7.1 Checklist for a premises licence application

	Original to relevant licensing authority	Copy to the police	Copy to responsible authorities
Completed application form			
Form of consent from the proposed designated premises supervisor where sale of alcohol is to take place at the premises			
Plan of the premises			
Payment of the fee			
Confirmation that the application has been advertised on the premises and that this will be maintained for 28 days			
Has the application been advertised in a local newspaper?	Name of newspaper:		Date:

7.5.3 Making an application

Regulation 21 of the Premises Licences Regulations provides that an application must be made in writing. However, notwithstanding this requirement, an application can also be made electronically; for details and requirements see **6.5.3**.

7.6 THE PLAN

Regulation 23 of the Premises Licences Regulations provides that an application for a premises licence must be accompanied by a scale plan of the premises. The plan must be of a scale of 1 to 100, unless the relevant licensing authority has previously agreed with the applicant, following a request by the applicant, that an alternative scale is acceptable. For example this scale may be impractical for large or small premises and so the applicant may ask the licensing authority to agree that a smaller-scale plan may be used.

The plan must show:

- the extent of the boundary of the building, if relevant, and any external and internal walls of the building and, if different, the perimeter of the premises;
- the location of points of access to and egress from the premises and, if different, the location of escape routes from the premises;
- if the premises are to be used for more than one licensable activity, the area within the premises used for each activity;
- fixed structures (including furniture) or similar objects temporarily in a fixed location (but not furniture) which may affect the ability of individuals on the premises to use exits or escape routes without impediment;
- if the premises include a stage or raised area, the location and height of each stage or area relative to the floor;
- if the premises include any steps, stairs, elevators or lifts, the location of the steps, stairs, elevators or lifts;
- if the premises include any room or rooms containing public conveniences, the location of the room or rooms;
- the location and type of any fire safety and any other safety equipment including, if applicable, marine safety equipment; and
- the location of a kitchen, if any, on the premises.

The plan may also include a legend so that the above can be sufficiently illustrated by using symbols on the plan.

There is no requirement to have a plan professionally drawn provided it meets the above requirements.

The plan does not need to show any areas which are not part of the premises where the licensable activities will take place, for example a beer garden where alcohol is consumed. Such areas must however be described as part of the general description of the premises which must be given in part 3 of the application form.

Providing facilities for the public to dance is a licensable activity. It is not necessary to show the precise location of any dance floor in the premises on the plan. It will be sufficient to clearly mark the relevant part of the premises or room where the dancing will take place.

The plan will form part of the licence (s.24). The licensing authority will need to make a copy of the plan to attach to the premises licence. Alternatively, a licensing authority may request an applicant to provide an additional copy of the plan with his application. There is, however, no legal requirement for an applicant to submit an additional plan.

7.7   FEES PAYABLE

7.7.1   Introduction

The fees payable both on the grant of a premises licence and annually are prescribed by the Fees Regulations (as amended by the Licensing Act 2003 (Fees) (Amendment) Regulations 2005, SI 2005/357). These fees are based on the rateable value of the premises. The fees have been set centrally by the DCMS with the intention that they will recover the licensing authorities' costs of administrating, inspecting and enforcing the new regime. The Government hope is that centrally set fees will remove the inconsistencies in fee levels that existed under the old licensing regime.

The rateable value of the premises is defined as 'the value for the time being in force for the premises entered in the local non-domestic rating list for the purposes of Part III of the Local Government Finance Act 1988' (Fees Regulations, reg. 2(1)). This is commonly called the non-domestic rateable value and new non-domestic rateable values for all premises came into force on 1 April 2005.

Where the premises form only part of a building which has a non-domestic rateable value, the premises are treated as having a non-domestic rateable value equal to the non-domestic rateable value for the whole building (Fees Regulations, reg. 3(3)).

Where the premises comprise two or more buildings, the premises are treated as having a non-domestic rateable value equal to the non-domestic rateable value for the building with the highest non-domestic rateable value (Fees Regulations, reg. 3(4)).

Premises are allocated to a fee band according to rateable value as shown in Table 7.2. Premises which do not have a non-domestic rateable value, for example parks and vehicles, will be treated as falling into band A for fee purposes.

Table 7.2   Premises fee bands

Rateable value	Band
No rateable value to £4,300	A
£4,301 to £33,000	B
£33,001 to £87,000	C
£87,001 to £125,000	D
£125,001 and above	E

Where premises are in the course of construction, the premises are allocated to band C (Fees Regulations, reg. 2(2)).

7.7.2   Application fees

Each rateable band attracts a different level of application fee, as set out in Table 7.3. Where premises fall into bands D and E and are used exclusively or primarily for the carrying on on the premises of the supply of alcohol for consumption on the premises an increased fee is payable (Fees Regulations, reg. 4(2) as substituted by reg. 2(2) of the Licensing Act 2003 (Fees) (Amendment) Regulations). These increased fees are calculated using a multiplier of twice the fee for such premises in band D and three times the fee for such premises in band E, i.e. the increased fees will be £900 and £1,905 respectively. The rationale behind these increased fees is to require those premises which are likely to need the deployment of more resources in order to promote the four licensing objectives to pay more.

Table 7.3   Fees for different premises bands

Band	A	B	C	D	E
Fee	£100	£190	£315	£450	£635

7.7.3   Annual fee

An annual fee is payable each year on the anniversary of the date of the grant of the premises licence (Fees Regulations, reg. 5(6)), as shown in Table 7.4. Where premises fall into bands D and E and are used exclusively or primarily

Table 7.4   Renewal fees for premises licenses

Band	A	B	C	D	E
Fee	£70	£180	£295	£320	£350

for the supply of alcohol for consumption on the premises an increased annual fee is payable. As with application fees these increased fees are calculated using a multiplier of twice the fee for such premises in band D and three times the fee for such premises in band E, i.e. the increased fees will be £640 and £1,050 respectively.

Where a licensee fails to pay his annual fee then it will be recoverable as a debt by the licensing authority.

7.7.4   Additional fees

An additional fee is payable where 5,000 or more people are allowed on the premises at the same time when licensable activities are taking place (Fees Regulations, reg. 4(4)).

No additional fee is payable under the Fees Regulations, reg. 4(5) where the premises consist of a structure which is not a vehicle, vessel or moveable structure, and have been constructed or structurally altered for the purpose, or for purposes which include the purpose, of enabling:

- the premises to be used for the licensable activities the applicant proposes the licence should authorise;
- the premises to be modified temporarily from time to time, if relevant, for the premises to be used for the licensable activities referred to in the application;
- at least the number of persons the applicant proposes should, during the times when the licence authorises licensable activities to take place on the premises, be allowed on the premises, to be allowed on the premises at such times; or
- the premises to be used in a manner which is not inconsistent with the operating schedule accompanying the application.

The additional fees payable are set out in Table 7.5.

Table 7.5   Additional fees

Number of persons in attendance at any one time	Additional fee
5,000 to 9,999	£1,000
10,000 to 14,999	£2,000
15,000 to 19,999	£4,000
20,000 to 29,999	£8,000
30,000 to 39,999	£16,000
40,000 to 49,999	£24,000
50,000 to 59,999	£32,000
60,000 to 69,999	£40,000
70,000 to 79,999	£48,000
80,000 to 89,999	£56,000
90,000 and over	£64,000

7.7.5 Exemptions

Where an application for a premises licence relates to the provision of regulated entertainment only, the Fees Regulations, reg. 9 provide that no fee is payable if:

- in the case of an application by a proprietor of an educational institution in respect of premises that are or form part of an educational institution, the educational institution is a school or a college, and the provision of regulated entertainment on the premises is carried on by the educational institution for and on behalf of the purposes of the educational institution; or
- the application is in respect of premises that are or form part of a church hall, chapel hall or other similar building or a village hall, parish hall or community hall or other similar building.

Thus no fee is payable by church halls, chapel halls, village halls, parish halls, community halls or other similar buildings, or schools or sixth form colleges where the premises licence only authorises the provision of regulated entertainment.

In addition, there is an exemption under the Fees Regulations, reg. 10 for such premises from the payment of an annual fee. The requirements which must be satisfied for this exemption are that the premises licence authorises the provision of regulated entertainment only, and either:

- the holder of the premises licence is the proprietor of an educational institution which is a school or college, the licence has effect in respect of premises that are or form part of the educational institution, and the provision of regulated entertainment on the premises is carried on by the educational institution for and on behalf of the purposes of the educational institution; or
- the premises licence has effect in respect of premises that are or form part of a church hall, chapel hall or other similar building or a village hall, parish hall or community hall or other similar building.

7.8 ADVERTISING THE APPLICATION

An application for a premises licence must be advertised in the prescribed form and in the manner which is prescribed and is likely to bring the application to the attention of the interested parties likely to be affected by it (s.17(5)(a)). Regulation 25 of the Premises Licences Regulations provides that a notice must be displayed at or on the premises and published in a local newspaper. Regulation 26 of the Premises Licences Regulations sets out the prescribed information which both notices must contain (see **7.8.3**).

A licensing authority may provide a specimen form of notice for an applicant to use. A suggested form of notice can be found at Box 7.1.

7.8.1   Notice to be displayed at or on the premises

An applicant must advertise his application for a premises licence by prominently displaying a notice containing prescribed information at or on the premises to which the application relates for a period of not less than 28 consecutive days starting on the day after the day on which the application was given to the relevant licensing authority.

The notice must be:

- of a size equal to or larger than A4;
- of a pale blue colour; and
- printed legibly in black ink or typed in black in a font of a size equal to or larger than 16 points.

It must be displayed prominently at or on the premises to which the application relates where it can be conveniently read from the exterior of the premises. Where the premises cover an area of more than 50 metres square, further notices in the same form and subject to the same requirements must be displayed every 50 metres along the external perimeter of the premises abutting any highway (50 metres square is not the same as 50 square metres and a common mistake, even in guidelines issued by some licensing authorities, is to interpret this requirement as applying to premises exceeding 50 square metres in area, which is not correct).

7.8.2   Notice published in a local newspaper

An applicant must also publish a notice containing prescribed information in a local newspaper or, if there is none, in a local newsletter, circular or similar document, circulating in the vicinity of the premises on at least one occasion during the 10 working days starting on the day after the day on which the application was given to the relevant licensing authority.

It is important that the notice is published in a local newspaper and an applicant should check with the relevant licensing authority to find out which newspapers are acceptable, for example in London a London-wide newspaper such as the *Evening Standard* may not be acceptable. An advertising paper may only be used if there is no local newspaper.

7.8.3   Contents of the notice

The notices to be displayed at or on the premises and to be published in a local newspaper must:

- contain a statement of the relevant licensable activities which it is proposed will be carried out on or from the premises;
- state the name of the applicant;
- state the postal address of the premises, if any, or if there is no postal

address for the premises a description of those premises sufficient to enable the location and extent of the premises to be identified;

- state the postal address and, where applicable, the worldwide web address where the register of the relevant licensing authority is kept and where and when the record of the application may be inspected;
- state the date by which an interested party or a responsible authority may make representations to the relevant licensing authority;
- state that representations shall be made in writing; and
- state that it is an offence knowingly or recklessly to make a false statement in connection with an application and the maximum fine for which a person is liable on summary conviction for the offence.

BOX 7.1 SUGGESTED FORM OF NOTICE OF AN APPLICATION FOR A PREMISES LICENCE

Licensing Act 2003

Notice of application for the Grant of a Premises Licence

Notice is hereby given that [insert the full name of the applicant] has applied to the [insert the full name of the licensing authority] on [insert the date of application to the licensing authority] for the grant of a premises licence to use the premises [insert name of premises] at [insert the name and full postal address of the premises] for the following licensable activities:

[insert details of each licensable activity including days and hours]

The register of licensing applications can be inspected at [insert details].

Any person who wishes to make a representation in relation to this application must give notice in writing to [insert name and address of the licensing authority], giving in detail the grounds of objection by [insert the date by which all relevant representations must be received by the licensing authority, i.e. 28 consecutive days starting on the day after the day on which the application is given to the licensing authority]. The Licensing Authority must receive representations by the date given above. The Licensing Authority will have regard to any such representation in considering the application.

It is an offence under Section 158 of the Licensing Act 2003 to knowingly or recklessly make a false statement in connection with this application and the maximum fine for which a person is liable on summary conviction for the offence is up to level 5 on the standard scale (£5000).

7.9 NOTICE TO RESPONSIBLE AUTHORITIES

An applicant must also give notice of his application for a premises licence to each responsible authority by giving each such authority a copy of his application together with its accompanying documents (s.17(5) and Premises

Licences Regulations, reg. 27). Notice is to be given on the same day as the day on which the application is given to the relevant licensing authority. A responsible authority may then make representations to the relevant licensing authority about the application within 28 consecutive days.

Responsible authorities are listed in s.13(4) as being:

- the chief officer of police for any police area in which the premises are situated;
- the fire and rescue authority for any area in which the premises are situated;
- the enforcing authority within the meaning given by the Health and Safety at Work etc. Act 1974, s.18 for any area in which the premises are situated;
- the local planning authority within the meaning of the Town and Country Planning Act 1990 for any area in which the premises are situated;
- the local authority which exercises the statutory functions in any area in which the premises are situated in relation to minimising or preventing the risk of pollution of the environment or of harm to human health;
- a body which represents those who, in relation to any such area, are responsible for or interested in matters relating to the protection of children from harm, and is recognised by the licensing authority for that area for the purposes of this section as being competent to advise it on such matters;
- any licensing authority (other than the relevant licensing authority) in whose area part of the premises is situated;
- in relation to a vessel, a navigation authority (within the meaning of the Water Resources Act 1991, s.221(1)) having functions in relation to the waters where the vessel is usually moored or berthed or any waters where it is, or is proposed to be, navigated at a time when it is used for licensable activities, the Environment Agency, the British Waterways Board, or the Secretary of State; and
- a person prescribed for these purposes.

The Premises Licences Regulations prescribe that the local weights and measures authority within the meaning of the Weights and Measures Act 1985, s.69 for any area in which the premises are situated is a responsible authority. This will be the local authority trading standards department.

A licensing authority may have drawn up a list of the relevant responsible authorities for its area and their contact details. An applicant should therefore contact the relevant licensing authority to obtain such a list.

7.10   INSPECTION OF PREMISES

A constable or an authorised person may, at any reasonable time before the determination of an application for a premises licence, enter the premises to which the application relates to assess the likely effect of the grant of the application on the promotion of the licensing objectives (s.59).

The following are designated by s.13(2) as authorised persons:

- an officer of a licensing authority in whose area the premises are situated who is authorised by that authority for the purposes of the Act;
- an inspector appointed under the Fire Precautions Act 1971, s.18 (from 1 April 2006 this will be an inspector appointed by the fire and rescue authority for the area in which the premises are situated (Regulatory Reform (Fire Safety) Order 2005, SI 2005/1541));
- an inspector appointed under the Health and Safety at Work etc. Act 1974, s.19;
- an officer of a local authority in whose area the premises are situated, who is authorised by that authority for the purposes of exercising one or more of its statutory functions in relation to minimising or preventing the risk of pollution of the environment or of harm to human health;
- in relation to a vessel, an inspector, or a surveyor of ships, appointed under the Merchant Shipping Act 1995, s.256; and
- a person prescribed for these purposes.

An authorised person who is exercising the power to enter the premises must, if so requested, produce evidence of his authority to exercise the power (s.59(3)). A constable or an authorised person may, if necessary, use reasonable force to obtain entry (s.59(4)). Anyone who intentionally obstructs an authorised person exercising the power of entry commits an offence, and is liable on summary conviction to a fine not exceeding level 2 on the standard scale (s.59(5) and (6)). Obstruction of a constable will constitute an offence of obstructing a constable in the execution of his duty under the Police Act 1996, s.89(2), and a person will be liable on summary conviction to imprisonment for a term not exceeding one month (this will increase to 51 weeks when the Criminal Justice Act 2003 takes effect) or to a fine not exceeding level 3 on the standard scale, or to both.

7.11 DETERMINATION OF THE APPLICATION

7.11.1 Preliminary determination

When a licensing authority receives an application for a premises licence, it must initially determine whether the application has been made properly in accordance with s.17 and with the Premises Licences Regulations. An incomplete application is invalid and will be returned to the applicant. Any failure to observe the notice requirements will also render the application invalid.

7.11.2 Unopposed applications

Where no relevant representations have been made, and the applicant has complied with all statutory requirements, s.18 provides that the licensing authority must grant the licence in the terms sought, subject only to such conditions as are consistent with the operating schedule and any conditions which must be imposed under the Act (*British Beer and Pub Association* v. *Canterbury City Council* [2005] EWHC 1318; *The Times*, 11 July 2005).

In discharging its duty, a licensing authority may grant a licence subject to different conditions in respect of either different parts of the premises, or different licensable activities (s.18(10)).

The Guidance recommends that unopposed applications should be delegated to an officer (para. 3.63), and states that this process will usually just be a simple administrative one undertaken by the licensing authority's officials who will translate the applicant's proposals in the operating schedule to promote the licensing objectives into clear and understandable conditions consistent with such proposals (para. 5.67).

7.11.3 Applications where representations have been made

If relevant representations have been made by a responsible authority or an interested party, s.18(3)(a) provides that the licensing authority must hold a hearing to consider them. The meaning of relevant representations and interested party are considered further in **Chapter 10**. The Hearings Regulations regulate hearings under the Act (see **Chapter 24**).

The hearing must be held within a period of 20 working days beginning with the day after the end of the period during which representations may be made (Hearings Regulations, reg. 5 and Sched. 5, para. 1). The period during which representations may be made is 28 consecutive days after the day on which the application is given to the authority. Notice of the hearing must be given to the applicant and persons who made relevant representations no later than 10 working days before the day or the first day on which the hearing is to be held (Hearings Regulations, reg. 6(4) and Sched. 2, para. 1). The applicant must be given the relevant representations with the notice of the hearing (Hearings Regulations, reg. 7(2) and Sched. 3, para. 1).

A hearing may be dispensed with if the licensing authority, the applicant and each person who made representations agree that it is unnecessary. This may be because they have reached agreement following mediation or negotiation.

Following the hearing, the licensing authority must, having regard to the representations, then take such of the following steps, if any, as it considers necessary to promote the licensing objectives:

- grant the licence subject to conditions that are consistent with the applicant's operating schedule modified to the extent the licensing authority considers necessary for the promotion of the licensing objectives, and any mandatory condition which must be included in the licence under the Act. For these purposes conditions are modified if any of them is altered or omitted or any new condition is added;

- exclude from the scope of the licence any of the licensable activities to which the application relates; for example, a licensing authority might decide to remove the playing of amplified recorded music after 11 pm from the scope of the licence applied for by a tenant of a pub in the middle of a quiet residential area, or it might prohibit the admittance of under-18s to premises where adult entertainment is provided;

- refuse to specify a person in the licence as the premises supervisor, for example following a police objection where the proposed premises supervisor has been removed as premises supervisor for other premises following review; or

- reject the application. The licensing authority can only reject an application where it considers that taking any of the other steps mentioned above will not be sufficient to promote the licensing objectives. In practice a rejection is likely to be rare.

The licensing authority must 'have regard' to the representations before taking any of the above steps. There is nothing to indicate that it may not take into account other matters not included in the representations.

There is no requirement for a licensing authority to notify the applicant and anyone who made representations of its reasons for any decision it makes as to whether or not to take any of the above steps. In practice reasons will usually be given as the licensing authority will need to comply with art. 6(1) of the European Convention on Human Rights providing the right to a fair trial, which includes giving reasons. These reasons need not be elaborate or lengthy but should tell the parties in broad terms the reason for the decision.

A licensing authority does not have to take any of the above steps. If it does not consider any of them necessary for the promotion of the licensing objectives, it can grant the licence in the terms sought by the applicant, subject only to such conditions as are consistent with the operating schedule and any conditions which must be imposed under the Act.

In discharging its duty a licensing authority may grant a licence subject to different conditions in respect of either different parts of the premises or different licensable activities (s.18(10)).

7.12 CONDITIONS

7.12.1 Introduction

When a licensing authority grants a premises licence it may impose conditions on the licence where they are necessary for the promotion of one or more of the licensing objectives. The types of conditions which may be imposed are considered further in **Chapter 11**.

In addition, certain conditions must be attached to a premises licence which authorises the supply of alcohol, a premises licence which authorises the exhibition of films and a premises licence which contains a condition that door supervisors must be at the premises.

7.12.2   Mandatory conditions – premises licensed to supply alcohol

Where a premises licence authorises the supply of alcohol, s.19 provides that the licence must include the following conditions:

- that no supply of alcohol may be made under the premises licence at a time when there is no designated premises supervisor in respect of the premises licence;
- that no supply of alcohol may be made under the premises licence at a time when the designated premises supervisor does not hold a personal licence or his personal licence is suspended; and
- that every supply of alcohol under the premises licence must be made or authorised by a person who holds a personal licence.

The Guidance, para. 7.67 provides:

> This does not mean that the condition should require the presence on the premises at all material times of the designated premises supervisor. Similarly, the fact that every supply of alcohol must be made under the authority of a personal licence holder does not mean that only personal licence holders can make such sales or that they must be personally present at every transaction. A personal licence holder may authorise members of staff to make sales of alcohol during the course of an evening, but may be absent at times from the premises when a transaction takes place. However, the personal licence holder will not be able to escape responsibility for the actions of those he authorises to make such sales.

7.12.3   Mandatory condition – exhibition of films

Where a premises licence authorises the exhibition of films, s.20 provides that the licence must include a condition requiring the admission of children to the exhibition of any film to be restricted as follows:

- where the film classification body is specified in the licence, then unless the provision below applies, admission of children must be restricted in accordance with any recommendation made by that body; or
- where the film classification body is not specified in the licence, or the relevant licensing authority has notified the holder of the licence that this subsection applies to the film in question, admission of children must be

restricted in accordance with any recommendation made by that licensing authority.

For these purposes, 'children' means persons aged under 18, and 'film classification body' means the person or persons designated as the authority under the Video Recordings Act 1984, s.4 which will be either the British Board of Film Classification or the licensing authority if it operates its own classification system.

7.12.4 Mandatory condition – door supervision

Where a premises licence includes a condition that at specified times one or more individuals must be at the premises to carry out a security activity, i.e. door supervisors, s.21 provides that the licence must include a condition that each such individual must be licensed by the Security Industry Authority. It is not mandatory to include a condition that door supervisors must be employed but if one is included it must state that the persons employed are licensed.

The requirement that individuals must be licensed does not however apply to:

* premises within the Private Security Industry Act 2001, Sched. 2, para. 8(3)(a), i.e. premises with a premises licence authorising plays or films;
* premises on any occasion mentioned in the Private Security Industry Act 2001, Sched. 2, para. 8(3)(b) or (c), i.e. premises being used exclusively by a club with a club premises certificate, under a temporary event notice authorising plays or films, or under a gaming licence; or
* premises on any occasion within the Private Security Industry Act 2001, Sched. 2, para. 8(3)(d), i.e. occasions prescribed by regulations under that Act.

Unless an exemption has been given, it is a criminal offence to work as a door supervisor without a licence from the Security Industry Authority. A person guilty of this offence is liable on conviction to a fine of up to £5,000 or six months' imprisonment or both.

7.12.5 Prohibited conditions

In relation to a premises licence which authorises the performance of plays, s.22 provides that a licensing authority cannot attach a condition to the licence as to the nature of the plays which may be performed, or the manner of performing plays, under the licence. However this does not prevent a licensing authority imposing any condition which it considers necessary on the grounds of public safety.

101

7.12.6 Discretionary conditions

A licensing authority may attach conditions to a licence other than the mandatory ones, but these must be necessary for the promotion of the licensing objectives (these are discussed further in **Chapter 11**). Conditions cannot be imposed for any other reason. The conditions that are necessary for the promotion of the licensing objectives should initially emerge from the applicant's risk assessment undertaken before the application for a premises licence was made.

Where the responsible authorities and interested parties do not raise any representations about an application for a premises licence, the licensing authority must grant the licence subject only to conditions that are consistent with the operating schedule and any mandatory conditions prescribed in the Act. The licensing authority may not therefore impose any conditions unless its discretion has been engaged following the making of relevant representations and it has been satisfied at a hearing of the necessity to impose conditions due to the representations raised. It may then only impose such conditions as are necessary to promote the licensing objectives arising out of the consideration of the representations. It is suggested that it might be sensible for an applicant to consult with the responsible authorities when preparing his operating schedule so that there can be proper liaison before representations prove necessary. It is clear that the conditions should not duplicate areas covered by other legislation, for example, employers and self-employed persons are required by the Management of Health and Safety at Work Regulations 1999, SI 1999/3242 to assess the risks to their workers and any others (for example, members of the public visiting the premises) who may be affected by their business so as to identify what measures are needed to avoid or control risks.

The Act provides that where an operating schedule has been submitted with an application and no relevant representations made by responsible authorities or interested parties, the licence must be granted subject only to such conditions as are consistent with the schedule accompanying the application and any mandatory conditions required by the Act itself. This means that the effect of any condition which is imposed should be substantially the same as that intended by the terms of the operating schedule. The Guidance recommends that conditions must be clear to the licence holder, to enforcement officers and to the courts.

By providing that only necessary conditions may be imposed, the Act requires that licensing conditions should be tailored to the size, style, characteristics and activities taking place at the premises concerned. This effectively rules out standardised conditions which ignore these individual matters.

The Guidance contains a pool of model conditions in respect of each of the licensing objectives and licensing authorities may use these where necessary and appropriate.

7.13 NOTIFICATION OF THE GRANT OR REFUSAL OF AN APPLICATION

Where an application for a premises licence is granted, s.23 provides that the relevant licensing authority must forthwith (see **2.9**) give a notice to that effect to:

- the applicant;
- any person who made relevant representations in respect of the application; and
- the chief officer of police for the police area (or each police area) in which the premises are situated.

It must also issue the applicant with the licence and a summary of it.

If relevant representations were made in respect of the application, the notice must state the authority's reasons for its decision as to the steps, if any, which must be taken for the promotion of the licensing objectives.

Where an application is rejected, the relevant licensing authority must forthwith give a notice to that effect, stating its reasons for the decision, to:

- the applicant;
- any person who made relevant representations in respect of the application; and
- the chief officer of police for the police area (or each police area) in which the premises are situated.

7.14 FORM OF LICENCE AND SUMMARY

Section 24 provides that a premises licence and the summary of a premises licence must be in the prescribed form, and that regulations must, in particular, provide for the licence to:

- specify the name and address of the holder;
- include a plan of the premises to which the licence relates;
- if the licence has effect for a limited period, specify that period;
- specify the licensable activities for which the premises may be used;
- if the licensable activities include the supply of alcohol, specify the name and address of the individual (if any) who is the premises supervisor in respect of the licence; and
- specify the conditions subject to which the licence has effect.

The form of both a premises licence and its summary are prescribed by the Premises Licences Regulations, reg. 33. A premises licence must be in the form set out in the Premises Licences Regulations, Sched. 12, part A. It must identify the relevant licensing authority, include the premises licence number and contain the information required by the prescribed form. This information includes the information required by s.24 together with additional details such as the designated premises supervisor's telephone number, personal licence number and the name of the issuing authority, the times at which licensable activities may take place and whether alcohol is supplied for consumption on and off or just on the premises.

Regulation 34 of the Premises Licences Regulations provides that a summary of a premises licence must be in the form and contain the information set out in the Premises Licences Regulations, Sched. 12, part B and must identify the relevant licensing authority, include the premises licence number, and be printed on paper of a size equal to or larger than A4.

7.15   THEFT OR LOSS OF A LICENCE

Where a premises licence or summary is lost, stolen, damaged or destroyed, the licence holder may apply to the relevant licensing authority for a copy of the licence or summary. The fee of £10.50 must accompany the application. There is no prescribed form of application. Where such an application is made, the relevant licensing authority must issue the licence holder with a certified copy of the licence or summary provided it is satisfied that the licence or summary has been lost, stolen, damaged or destroyed, and where it has been lost or stolen, the holder has reported that loss or theft to the police. A copy issued by the licensing authority must be a copy of the premises licence or summary in the form in which it existed immediately before it was lost, stolen, damaged or destroyed. The Act applies in relation to a copy as it applies in relation to an original licence or summary.

Should the lost or stolen licence or summary be returned to the licence holder, there is no requirement that he must return either the original document or the copy to the licensing authority.

7.16   DURATION OF A PREMISES LICENCE

A premises licence does not need to be renewed and once granted will continue in effect until it is revoked, is suspended by a licensing authority when it determines an application for review, or lapses either due to the incapacity of the licence holder or because it is surrendered. If it was originally granted for a limited period, it will cease to have effect once that period has expired.

7.17   LAPSE OF A LICENCE

A premises licence will lapse under s.27 if the holder of the licence:

- dies;
- becomes mentally incapable within the meaning of the Enduring Powers of Attorney Act 1985, s.13(1), i.e. he becomes incapable by reason of mental disorder of managing and administering his property and affairs;
- becomes insolvent;
- is dissolved; or
- if it is a club, ceases to be a recognised club.

An individual becomes insolvent on:

- the approval of a voluntary arrangement proposed by him;
- being adjudged bankrupt or having his estate sequestrated; or
- entering into a deed of arrangement made for the benefit of his creditors or a trust deed for his creditors.

A company becomes insolvent on:

- the approval of a voluntary arrangement proposed by its directors;
- the appointment of an administrator in respect of the company;
- the appointment of an administrative receiver in respect of the company; or
- going into liquidation.

It may be possible to reinstate a licence which has lapsed (see **12.6**).

7.18   SURRENDER

The holder of a premises licence may surrender his licence under s.28 by giving notice to the relevant licensing authority together with the premises licence or, if that is not practicable, for example where it has been lost, by a statement of the reasons for the failure to provide the licence. The premises licence will then lapse when the licensing authority receives the notice. In certain circumstances a licence which has been surrendered can be reinstated (see **Chapter 12**).

There is no requirement to give notice to the designated premises supervisor or the owner of the premises.

7.19 UPDATING A PREMISES LICENCE

7.19.1 Notification of change of name or address

Following the grant of a premises licence, s.33 puts the licence holder under a duty, as soon as is reasonably practicable, to notify the relevant licensing authority of any change in his name or address, and the name or address of the designated premises supervisor, unless the supervisor has already notified the authority. The notice must be accompanied by the fee of £10.50 and the premises licence, or the appropriate part of the licence or, if that is not practicable, by a statement of the reasons for the failure to produce the licence, or part.

Where the designated premises supervisor under a premises licence is not the holder of the licence, he may notify the relevant licensing authority of any change in his name or address. If he does so, he must, as soon as is reasonably practicable, give the holder of the premises licence a copy of his notice.

A person commits an offence if he fails, without reasonable excuse, to comply with these requirements, and a person guilty of such an offence is liable on summary conviction to a fine not exceeding level 2 on the standard scale.

7.19.2 A licensing authority's duty to update a premises licence

Where a premises licence is modified, lapses or an appeal is determined, the relevant licensing authority must under s.56 make any appropriate amendments to the licence and, if necessary, issue a new summary of it.

Where the licensing authority is not in possession of the licence or the appropriate part of it, it may require the licence holder to produce the licence or the appropriate part within 14 days from the date on which he was notified of the requirement. A person commits an offence if he fails, without reasonable excuse, to comply with such a requirement and a person guilty of such an offence is liable on summary conviction to a fine not exceeding level 2 on the standard scale.

7.20 DUTY TO KEEP AND PRODUCE A PREMISES LICENCE

Section 57 provides that a licence holder is under a duty to keep the premises licence or a certified copy of it at the premises. It must be kept in the custody or under the control of either the licence holder, or a person who works at the premises and whom the licence holder has nominated in writing. A summary of the licence or a certified copy of that summary, and a notice specifying the position held at the premises by any person nominated by the licence holder, must be prominently displayed at the premises.

A licence holder will commit an offence if he fails, without reasonable excuse, to comply with these requirements, and a person guilty of such an offence is liable on summary conviction to a fine not exceeding level 2 on the standard scale.

A constable or an authorised person may require the person who has custody or control of the premises licence, or a certified copy of it to produce the licence or such a copy for examination. An authorised person exercising this power must, if so requested, produce evidence of his authority to exercise the power. Any certified copy which is produced must be a copy of the document in the form in which it exists at the time. A person will commit an offence if he fails, without reasonable excuse, to produce a premises licence or a certified copy of a premises licence. A person guilty of such an offence is liable on summary conviction to a fine not exceeding level 2 on the standard scale.

References to a certified copy of any document are references to a copy of that document which is certified to be a true copy by the relevant licensing authority, a solicitor or notary, or a person of a prescribed description. A document which purports to be a certified copy of a document is to be taken to be such a copy and to be a copy of the document in the form in which it exists at the time unless the contrary is shown.

CHAPTER 8

The operating schedule

8.1 INTRODUCTION

An application for a premises licence or a club premises certificate must be accompanied by an operating schedule (s.17(3)). An operating schedule details how the applicant proposes to operate the premises when carrying out the relevant licensable activities and needs to set out all the relevant information which a responsible authority or interested party needs in order to assess whether the steps which the applicant proposes to take in order to promote the licensing objectives are satisfactory. In this way it is the applicant who initially determines the nature and extent of the activities and the conditions relating to carrying them out.

In practice the operating schedule forms part of the prescribed application form and, if the application is successful, it will be incorporated into the licence or certificate itself so that it is clear which activities are permitted on the licensed premises and any limitations on them.

8.2 CONTENTS OF THE OPERATING SCHEDULE

Section 17(4) provides that an operating schedule must state:

- the relevant licensable activities;
- the times during which it is proposed that the relevant licensable activities are to take place;
- any other times during which it is proposed that the premises are to be open to the public;
- where the applicant wishes the licence to have effect for a limited period, that period;
- where the relevant licensable activities include the supply of alcohol, prescribed information in respect of the individual whom the applicant wishes to have specified in the premises licence as the premises supervisor;
- where the relevant licensable activities include the supply of alcohol,

whether the supplies are proposed to be for consumption on the premises or off the premises or both;

- the steps which it is proposed to take to promote the licensing objectives; and
- such other matters as may be prescribed.

While the Act prescribes that the operating schedule must include the above information, the Guidance, para. 5.46 specifies other information which should be included in an operating schedule so that responsible authorities and interested parties can form a proper view as to what measures may be necessary to ensure public safety and prevent public nuisance. The matters specified in para. 5.46 include:

- a description of the style and character of the business which is to be carried out on the premises, for example, a supermarket, a restaurant or a public house with two bars and a garden open to customer;
- where alcohol is being sold for consumption on the premises in public houses, bars and night clubs, the extent to which seating is to be provided as research has shown that the amount of seating can be relevant to the prevention of crime and disorder;
- an indication of the type of activities available on the premises, whether licensable under the Act or not;
- where dancing is to take place, a description of the type of dancing in broad terms and whether the dancing involves striptease or lap-dancing, whether it would involve dancing by members of the public or by professional performers or both and in what setting;
- if music is to be provided, a clear indication of the type of music to be provided; and
- in the case of passenger vessels, a description of the area within the vessel where licensable activities will be taking place.

8.3 COMPLETING THE STANDARD FORM OF OPERATING SCHEDULE

8.3.1 Licensed activities and opening times

An applicant must tick what licensable activities he intends to provide and complete the relevant boxes. Times must be given in the 24-hour clock format.

8.3.2 Indoors or outdoors

If licensed activities will take place in a building or similar structure, an applicant will need to tick 'indoors'. If activities are to take place in the open air then he will tick 'outdoors'. If for example the premises are a pub with a garden and the applicant would like activities to take place in the garden, he would tick the 'both' box.

8.3.3 Further details

An applicant should state the type of activity to be authorised and the frequency of these activities. Examples are as follows.

Plays

If the premises licence is for a one-off event, an applicant should give the play title. Otherwise an applicant should state, for example, whether the plays are for children only, a mixed audience, for an amateur dramatics association, etc. An applicant should also set out how often he is likely to use the licence, e.g. 'Plays will only be held once a month for no more than three days at a time.'

Film exhibitions

If the premises are a cinema, an applicant should say here how many screens there are, and describe the type of films it is intended to show, e.g. art films, mixed films for all age ranges, etc.

Indoor sporting events

An applicant should describe the type of sports he intends to provide.

Boxing and wrestling entertainments

The category of fights an applicant may wish to provide should be described, how often he is likely to use the licence, and whether the events will be professional or amateur.

Performance of live music

An applicant should state how many musicians he intends to have performing, what type of music will they play and whether the music will be amplified.

Playing of recorded music

An applicant should describe what sort of recorded music will be played. Will it be a DJ or a sound system? What is the power output of any sound system to be used? Will he be providing karaoke?

Performance of dance

An applicant should describe what type of dancing will be performed. Will there be a stage or will it be roaming dancers? Will it involve strippers?

Entertainment of a similar description

The type of entertainment should be described, e.g. comedy shows, hypnotism performances, etc.

Provision of facilities for making music

The provision should be described, e.g. a piano, guitars, etc. Describe how the facilities will be used, e.g. by a folk club.

Provision of facilities for dancing

An applicant should describe where the dance floor will be, what size it is, etc.

Provision of facilities for entertainment of a similar description

An applicant should describe what the facilities are and what they might be used for.

Late night refreshment

An applicant should set out what he intends to do, e.g. selling food for take-away purposes only, selling food for consumption on the premises, the type of food he will sell, etc.

8.3.4   Seasonal variations

This would allow an applicant to open later on Christmas Eve for example or during the summer months (specifying which months). An applicant would also need to state when he wanted to open and for how long.

8.3.5   Non-standard timings

This relates to such occasions as special events or bank holidays. For example, premises may normally open until 11 pm on a Monday but on the first Monday of every month the applicant may wish to have a disco and would like to provide alcohol and regulated entertainment until midnight.

8.3.6 Activities that may give rise to concern regarding children

This would include activities which involved semi-nudity or the presence of gaming machines.

8.3.7 Hours premises are open to the public

An applicant should state the earliest the premises or club would be open to members of the public and the latest time they will leave (i.e. drinking up time).

8.3.8 Licensing objectives

This section will need to be completed carefully as it is here that an applicant will need to satisfy the responsible authorities and any interested parties that he can run the premises in accordance with the licensing objectives. The more information which can be provided in demonstrating how these licensing objectives will be met will mean that there will be less chance of the responsible authorities and interested parties objecting to the application. An applicant is not expected to address issues already covered by existing legislation. Anything which is put in this section will become a condition on the licence and an applicant should not therefore volunteer to do anything that he is not able or not prepared to do if the application is granted. Examples of conditions which an applicant may wish to consider are discussed in **Chapter 11**.

8.4 OPENING HOURS

When completing the operating schedule the applicant must specify the times on each day of the week when he intends to use the premises for each licensable activity. These times may not be the same as the hours when the premises are open to the public. This may well be the case in relation to the sale or supply of alcohol for consumption on the premises. The Guidance, para. 6.13 provides:

> It is important to note that 'opening hours', the times when premises are open to the public, are not necessarily identical to the hours during which licensable activities may take place. In the case of the sale by retail of alcohol (or supply of alcohol by or on behalf of a club to, or to the order of, a member of a club) for consumption on the premises, it must also be noted that 'consumption' of alcohol is not a licensable activity. Accordingly, the authorised period specified in the premises licence, club premises certificate or temporary event notice relates to the period during which alcohol may be sold or supplied. It is therefore permissible for premises to allow the consumption of previously purchased alcohol, within the authorisation, outside the hours authorised for the sale or supply of alcohol.

While there is no provision in the operating schedule to specify 'drinking up time', an applicant should take into account any 'drinking up time' he wishes to allow his customers when specifying the hours which the premises will be open to the public.

8.5   PREPARING AN OPERATING SCHEDULE

When preparing an operating schedule an applicant needs to be aware of the expectations of the licensing authority and the responsible authorities about the steps that are necessary in order to promote the licensing objectives (Guidance, para. 5.47). This will involve carrying out a risk assessment and liaising with the responsible authorities. Where an operating schedule meets the requirements of a responsible authority it is unlikely that the authority will make a representation about the application and so the need for a hearing will be avoided.

An applicant does not have to check his operating schedule with the responsible authorities before submitting it, but when an applicant is uncertain about something the responsible authorities can provide expert advice on matters relating to the licensing objectives. For example, advice on crime prevention should be sought from the local police. An applicant will find it useful to discuss his operating schedule with the responsible authorities prior to submitting his application. The contact details of the responsible authorities can usually be obtained from the relevant licensing authority.

The operating schedule will allow the responsible authorities to evaluate the application and to decide whether they should make a representation about it or not. If no representations are made about an application, the licensing authority will grant the licence and attach to it only conditions relating to the operating schedule and any mandatory conditions required by the Act. For example, if the operating schedule were to state that windows of the premises would be kept closed when live music was being played, this could be made a condition of the licence. However, unless there was a representation from a responsible authority, a condition could not be made that the windows should be double-glazed. If a representation were to be made by a responsible authority, unless it was subsequently withdrawn a hearing would be held to consider the representation. After the licensing authority had listened to both the applicant and the responsible authority that made the representation, the licensing authority would decide whether to grant the licence or not and what if any conditions it should apply.

In preparing an operating schedule, the Guidance at para. 5.47 recommends that an applicant should have regard to statements of licensing policy published by the relevant licensing authority, and all parties are expected to work together in partnership to ensure that the licensing objectives are promoted collectively. In straightforward cases, it is expected that the steps that an applicant proposes to take to promote the licensing objectives that he has set out in the operating schedule will very often translate directly into conditions that will be attached to the premises licence.

A guide to preparing an operating schedule may be available from the relevant licensing authority, and this should be obtained early in the process. This will assist an applicant to become aware of the likely requirements of the responsible authorities. These can be further clarified by consultation on individual applications. With this knowledge an applicant will be able to decide whether it is possible for him to meet the requirements of the responsible authorities and so avoid a hearing. As a licensing authority will keep such a guide under review it is important for an applicant to make sure that he has the most up-to-date version of the guide.

8.6   RISK ASSESSMENT

Before preparing an operating schedule an applicant should carry out a risk assessment in order to identify actual or potential risks associated with the proposed use and design of the premises. He can then identify measures which will either eliminate or minimise those risks. These measures should then be included in the operating schedule and may subsequently be converted into conditions on the premises licence. The relevant licensing authority may be able to provide an applicant with guidance on how to meet its policy requirements and promoting the licensing objectives. A number of licensing authorities have produced a 'tool-kit' which an applicant can use to identify the measures he will need to include in his operating schedule (see **Appendix A** for an example of such a 'tool-kit').

Once carried out the risk assessment should be dated and a note made of the details of the person who carried it out. An applicant may wish to submit a copy of the risk assessment with his application.

8.7   PREVENTION OF CRIME AND DISORDER

The prevention of crime and disorder will be a central feature of a licensing authority's policy. An applicant will need to set out in his operating schedule the steps which he intends to take to promote this objective. An applicant should obtain details of the issues which the relevant licensing authority expects an applicant to consider. Enquiry should also be made with the police to obtain any guidance which it has issued; for example some police forces have a code of practice which they expect licensees to adhere to.

While each licensing authority will have its own issues which it will expect an applicant to consider, the following should be considered as useful when preparing an operating schedule:

- membership of a local pubwatch scheme where a communication link is set up between the police and other members of the scheme to alert them to the fact that there are potential trouble makers or individuals suspected of criminal behaviour in a particular area;
- the provision of door supervisors registered by the Security Industry Authority. The number of door supervisors required would depend on the type of clientele, the capacity of the venue and the type of activity taking place;
- the provision of staff training in crime prevention measures appropriate to the premises;
- implementing effective customer search policies for drugs and weapons;
- development of clear procedures to deal with violence and antisocial behaviour on the premises including instances relating to drunken customers and those under the influence of illegal drugs;
- operation of a responsible drinks promotion practice;
- devising procedures for risk assessing promotions such as 'happy hours' which may contribute to the impact on crime and disorder, and plans for minimising such risks;
- raising awareness of safer drinking, date-rape drug issues, safe travel at night including the display of telephone numbers for certified licensed taxi and minicab companies, etc.;
- the use of plastic bottles and glasses or toughened glass to prevent glass bottles and drinking glasses being used as weapons;
- the installation of CCTV cameras;
- restriction on the areas where alcohol may be consumed after it has been purchased at the bar, e.g. in areas such as the terracing of sports grounds during sporting events;
- setting a capacity limit to prevent overcrowding;
- having a policy to prevent under-age sales, e.g. the production of 'proof of age' cards;
- displaying notices to warn customers of pickpockets or bag snatchers; and
- providing an appropriate ratio of tables and chairs to customers based on the capacity of the premises in order to prevent high volume vertical drinking and reduce over-consumption of alcohol and aggressive behaviour.

An applicant should ascertain whether the premises are in an area which has been designated as a saturation area. Details of areas which have been designated as saturated with licensed premises may be obtained from the relevant licensing authority. An applicant should be prepared for the police to object to a new application in any area that has been so declared.

8.8 PUBLIC SAFETY

The public safety objective is primarily focused on physical safety rather than public health matters. A licensing authority will therefore expect licensed premises to be constructed, maintained and managed so that people can work in and visit the premises safely. An applicant will be expected to detail in his operating schedule the measures identified to promote this objective and how they will be implemented and maintained to ensure public safety.

A fire risk assessment of the premises should be carried out, and the fire and rescue authority may in any event require one. An applicant should contact the local fire and rescue authority for advice. The relevant licensing authority will be able to provide the contact details. This should consider the adequacy of the means of escape, fire safety signs and notices, emergency lighting, fire warning systems, fire-fighting equipment and training. The significant outcomes of this risk assessment, including occupancy figures, designated escape routes, evacuation procedures, etc. should be included in the operating schedule accompanying the application to facilitate an evaluation as to their suitability. Further guidance can be found in *Fire Safety: An Employer's Guide* (ISBN 0-11-341229-0) and *Guide to Fire Precautions in Existing Places of Entertainment and Like Premises* (ISBN 0-11-340907-9), both published by The Stationery Office.

For certain premises, the Health and Safety Executive may also be a responsible authority for public safety.

The type of measures which a licensing authority might expect to see in an operating schedule, where relevant, to promote this objective would include:

- describing arrangements in place for the safe evacuation of disabled people and ensuring that the disabled people on the premises are aware of those arrangements;
- specifying the measures in place to maintain escape routes and exits; this may include ensuring that:
  - all exit doors are easily openable without the use of a key, card, code or similar means;
  - doors at such exits are regularly checked to ensure that they function satisfactorily and that a record of the check is kept;
  - any removable security fastenings are removed whenever the premises are open to members of the public or staff;
  - all fire doors are maintained effectively self-closing and are not held open other than by approved devices (e.g. electromagnetic releases operated by smoke detectors);
  - fire resisting doors to ducts, service shafts and cupboards are kept locked shut;
  - the edges of the treads of steps and stairways are maintained so as to be conspicuous; and

- all customers, especially those that may not be able to hear or see the fire alarm or may be unable to move easily when evacuating a building, are aware of the evacuation procedures;

- safety checks are carried out and recorded prior to the admission of the public;
- hangings, curtains and temporary decorations are maintained in a flame retardant condition;
- a capacity limit is set and controlled;
- notices are displayed detailing the action to be taken in the event of a fire or an emergency;
- access for emergency vehicles is kept clear and free from obstruction;
- adequate supply of first aid material is available on site and, where appropriate, a suitably trained first aider;
- the provision of adequate lighting, including fire safety signs and emergency lighting;
- the safety of the electrical installation is maintained;
- if an indoor sporting event is included, extra provisions are made, e.g. for a qualified medical practitioner to be present, for distances to be maintained between the ring and the audience, etc.;
- the detailing of special effects that may be used in the premises such as dry ice machines and cryogenic fog; smoke machines and fog generators; pyrotechnics, including fireworks; real flame; firearms; motor vehicles; strobe lighting; lasers; explosives and highly flammable substances. In certain circumstances it may be necessary to require that certain special effects are only used with the prior notification of the licensing authority;
- the provision of attendants for closely seated audiences, such as in theatres or cinemas; and
- the measures employed to ensure that the scenery, safety curtain, ceilings and seating are safe are recorded.

8.9 THE PREVENTION OF PUBLIC NUISANCE

The type of steps which a licensing authority might expect to see in an operating schedule, where applicable, to promote the objective of preventing public nuisance might include:

- the control of the level of music and other entertainments so that it is contained within the structure of the premises and does not give rise to a nuisance to neighbours;
- doors and windows being kept closed to ensure that noise from music and other entertainments does not break out and disturb neighbours;
- noisy activities being restricted to areas of the premises that are best able

to contain noise, with outside areas such as forecourts and beer gardens not being used for music and entertainment;

- any noise limiter device fitted within the premises being set at an agreed level and access to the controls restricted to prevent it being tampered with;
- noise levels being reduced before doors are opened and customers leaving in numbers;
- liaison meetings with residents to discuss any problems they may be experiencing as a result of noise or other nuisances arising from activities at the premises;
- stewarding or supervising of customers queuing to enter the premises;
- stewarding or supervising customers as they leave the premises, especially at the end of the evening when the premises close;
- signs displayed requesting customers to respect the neighbourhood when leaving the premises;
- appropriate security and advertising lighting installed so as to ensure that light overspill does not adversely affect neighbours;
- litter caused by customers being considered and addressed through the provision of bins and litter patrols as necessary;
- the timing of deliveries, refuse and in particular bottle collections being arranged so as to cause the minimum disturbance to neighbours; and
- all plant and equipment utilised at the premises being correctly installed and maintained to ensure that it operates without causing nuisance to neighbours from odours or noise.

All licensed premises that have the potential to generate noise from within the premises or from their customers in the immediate vicinity of the premises must take steps to prevent public nuisance. These steps should be determined by carrying out a noise impact assessment from which a strategy for noise management can be developed, and this should then be included in the operating schedule. The first step is for an applicant to carry out a noise impact assessment, as follows:

1. A list of the sources of noise likely to be generated by the premises should be drawn up. Examples include:

   (a) amplified music (pre-recorded or live);
   (b) amplified voices (karaoke, DJ or announcements);
   (c) noise from patrons using the premises (pub gardens, play areas);
   (d) plant noise (refrigeration units, air conditioning units, etc.);
   (e) noise from patrons leaving the premises.

2. The applicant should then determine how, and from where, each of these noises could be emitted from the premises. For all internal noises the doors, windows and ventilation openings through which they could

escape should be determined, and for external noises, the areas of the premises where they will be created should be determined.

3. The nature of the surrounding community and where the nearest persons who will be affected by noise from the premises live should then be established.

4. The whereabouts of other local premises that may encourage street activity should be established, in particular fast food outlets, for these may encourage customers leaving a licensed premises to remain in the area longer than would otherwise be the case.

5. The likelihood that most customers leaving the premises at closing time will pass through a residential area, and how the effects on the community could be minimised, should be considered. Any other local licensed premises which will also contribute to this should also be identified.

All of this information should then be used to establish what local properties are at greatest risk of being affected by noise from the premises. If the answer is that there are no local residential properties likely to be affected, then there is no need for the applicant to develop a noise management strategy. It is important that the reasons for this decision are justified in the operating schedule.

Once an applicant has identified potential problems by carrying out a noise impact assessment, consideration should then be given to the possible solutions to these potential problems. Measures to protect immediate neighbours will differ from those protecting residents living further away. The method of controlling noise is a matter for the licensee, but his goal should be for noise from the premises not to exceed the background noise at the boundary of the nearest residential property. The following steps should be considered as part of developing a noise management strategy:

1. If the volume of music needs to be controlled, a noise-limiting device should be used. Once set this should be inaccessible to the licensee or his staff. Access to the device should only be available to an appropriate 'noise engineer'.

2. Emergency exits should be fitted with acoustic doors to prevent noise breaking through.

3. Windows in noisy rooms should be double-glazed or acoustically sealed.

4. Rowdy behaviour of patrons in beer gardens and outdoor areas should be controlled by premises managers.

5. The use of any garden located near to noise sensitive premises should be limited to daytime and early evening, with access prevented after a specified time (perhaps 9.30 pm or 10.00 pm) where practical.

6. Children's play equipment must be located away from boundaries shared with noise sensitive premises, with hours limited as for gardens and other outdoor areas.

7. Appropriate lighting of car parks will discourage noisy behaviour, as well as improving security.
8. Deliveries and collections, particularly bottle and waste collections, should be carried out at reasonable hours of the day.

8.10 THE PROTECTION OF CHILDREN FROM HARM

The type of steps which a licensing authority might expect to see in an operating schedule, where applicable, to promote the objective of the protection of children from harm might include:

- age restrictions all or part of the time that the premises are open; this might include times at which there was adult entertainment, events for young age groups, drink promotion nights such as happy hours, etc.;
- films being classified by the British Board of Film Classification;
- notices being displayed both inside and outside the premises so that persons entering can readily be made aware of the classification of a film;
- a minimum number of attendants with seated audiences or door supervisors registered with the Security Industry Authority;
- risk assessment of any particular risks to children taking part in performances where particular attention is paid to the venue, fire safety, special effects and the general care of the child, etc.;
- compliance with the Portman Group's Code of Practice on the naming, packaging and promotion of alcoholic drinks; and
- compliance with the guidelines issued by the National Association of Cigarette Machine Operators (NACMO).

CHAPTER 9

Designated premises supervisor

9.1 INTRODUCTION

Where a premises licence authorises the supply of alcohol, the licence must include a condition that alcohol cannot be supplied at any time when there is no designated premises supervisor in respect of the premises licence, or at a time when the designated premises supervisor does not hold a personal licence or his personal licence is suspended.

This means that there must always be a designated premises supervisor in respect of all premises licensed to supply alcohol and that that person must hold a valid personal licence.

The main purpose of having a designated premises supervisor is to ensure that there is always one specified individual who can be readily identified for the premises where a premises licence is in force. If the designated premises supervisor is not also the premises licence holder he will usually be given day-to-day responsibility for running the premises by the premises licence holder.

9.2 WHO IS THE DESIGNATED PREMISES SUPERVISOR?

A designated premises supervisor is the individual for the time being specified in the licence as the premises supervisor (s.15(1)). Only an individual can be a designated premises supervisor. It is not possible for a corporate body to be one. There is nothing to prevent the person who holds the premises licence being the designated premises supervisor (s.15(2)). But only one person at any point in time can be the designated premises supervisor. This is reinforced by the Guidance, para. 4.19 which states that 'It is stressed that only one designated premises supervisor may be specified in a single premises licence'.

There does not appear to be an absolute prohibition on a person being the designated premises supervisor for more than one premises. However, in practice it is suggested that this would be unusual. The Guidance, para. 4.18 states that the main purpose of the designated premises supervisor is to ensure that there is always one specified individual, among these personal licence holders, who can be readily identified for the premises where a premises licence is in force. That person will normally have been given day to day responsibility for running the premises by the premises licence holder.

While the Guidance does not actually state that the designated premises supervisor must be an individual who can be readily identified at the premises, it is suggested that it is implicit that this must be the case.

In addition para 4.19 states:

> By specifying the premises supervisor in the premises licence, it will usually be clear who is in day to day charge of the premises. The Government considers it to be essential that police officers, fire officers or officers of the licensing authority can identify immediately the designated premises supervisor as a person in a position of authority at any premises selling or supplying alcohol. They can do that because a copy of the licence must be held at the premises and a summary displayed. The premises licence will specify the name of the designated premises supervisor who is also a personal licence holder. This should ensure that any problems can be dealt with swiftly by engaging with this key individual.

It is therefore suggested that a person cannot be a designated premises supervisor in respect of more than one premises, though exceptionally this may be possible where premises are in close proximity.

9.3   INITIAL APPOINTMENT OF A DESIGNATED PREMISES SUPERVISOR

Where the relevant licensable activities include the supply of alcohol, the operating schedule accompanying an application for a premises licence must specify the name and address of the individual whom the applicant wishes to have specified in the premises licence as the designated supervisor, together with that person's personal licence number, if known, and the name of the licensing authority which issued the personal licence, if known.

The application must also be accompanied by the written consent of the proposed designated premises supervisor in the prescribed form, which is found in the Premises Licences Regulations, Sched. 11.

The chief officer of police can object to the designation of a new premises supervisor in exceptional circumstances (see **9.5**).

9.4   CHANGE OF DESIGNATED PREMISES SUPERVISOR

9.4.1   Introduction

The holder of a premises licence which authorises the supply of alcohol may apply under s.37 to change the person named in the licence as the designated premises supervisor.

An applicant must submit the following to the relevant licensing authority:

- a completed application form. The application form is prescribed and is set out in the Premises Licences Regulations, Sched. 5;
- the consent of the person proposed as the premises supervisor. The consent form is prescribed and is set out in the Premises Licences Regulations, Sched. 11, part A;
- the premises licence (or the appropriate part of it), or if that is not practicable, a statement of the reasons why it cannot be provided; and
- the fee of £23.

9.4.2   The application form

The form should be completed as set out in **6.5.2**.

In the opening statement, the name of the applicant or applicants applying to vary the premises licence to specify a new premises supervisor should be inserted, together with the premises licence number.

The application form is then divided into three parts.

Part 1

The applicant must set out the following details of the premises:

- the postal address; and
- the telephone number at the premises, if any.

If the premises have no postal address, the location of the premises should be described or the Ordnance Survey map reference should be given.

A description of the premises must also be given, for example the type of premises and the trading name.

Part 2

Part 2 of the form asks for the full name and personal licence number of the proposed designated premises supervisor together with its issuing authority. The full name of the existing designated premises supervisor must also be given.

The applicant must indicate whether he would like the application to have immediate effect. He must confirm that he has enclosed the premises licence or relevant part of it. If the premises licence, or relevant part, cannot be enclosed with the application, an explanation must be given. Finally there is a checklist for the applicant to complete so that nothing is overlooked, together with a warning that it is an offence, liable on conviction to a fine up to level 5 on the standard scale, under s.158 to make a false statement in or in connection with the application.

Part 3

Part 3 provides for the applicant to sign the form. The form can also be signed by the applicant's solicitor or other duly authorised agent, and someone signing on behalf of the applicant must state in what capacity they sign. Where there are joint applicants, both applicants or their respective agents must sign the application form.

9.4.3 Obtaining an application form

A relevant licensing authority must provide an applicant on request with a printed application form; however an electronic version may be provided by a licensing authority on its website which a prospective applicant can download, print off and complete. An electronic copy is also provided on the DCMS website.

9.4.4 Making an application

The requirements of reg. 21 of the Premises Licences Regulations concerning the making of an application are the same as those outlined in **6.5.3**.

9.4.5 Notice to other persons

A copy of the application together with its accompanying documents, if any, must also be given on the same day as the day on which the application is given to the relevant licensing authority to the chief officer of police for the area in which the premises are situated, and to the designated premises supervisor, if there is one, and the notice must state whether the application is for the variation to be given immediate effect.

9.4.6 Objections

The chief officer of police can object to the designation of a new premises supervisor in exceptional circumstances (see **9.5**). The existing designated premises supervisor cannot object. He is only notified of the application so that he knows that he will no longer be responsible for the premises.

9.4.7 Immediate effect

Where an application includes a request under s.38(1) that the variation applied for should have immediate effect, the premises licence has effect during the application period as if it had been varied in the manner set out in the application. This will allow for a situation where emergency cover is required, for example where the designated premises supervisor has died or is unable to work.

'The application period' is the period which begins when the application is received by the relevant licensing authority, and ends:

- if the application is granted, when the variation takes effect;
- if the application is rejected, at the time the rejection is notified to the applicant; or
- if the application is withdrawn before it is determined, at the time of the withdrawal.

9.4.8 Determination of the application

Section 39 provides that the application must be granted if it has been made in accordance with the statutory requirements, and the chief officer of police has not objected or has objected but has withdrawn the objection.

If the chief officer of police has given a notice objecting, and has not withdrawn it, the licensing authority must hold a hearing to consider it, unless the authority, the applicant and the chief officer of police who gave the notice agree that a hearing is unnecessary. A hearing must be held within 20 working days beginning with the day after the end of the period within which a chief officer of police may object (Hearings Regulations, reg. 5 and Sched. 1, para. 4). Notice of the hearing must be given to the applicant, the chief officer of police and the person who is proposed as the new designated premises supervisor no later than 10 working days before the day or the first day on which the hearing is to be held (Hearings Regulations, reg. 6(4) and Sched. 2, para. 4). The applicant must be given the notice of objection with the notice of the hearing (Hearings Regulations, reg. 7(2) and Sched. 3, para. 4).

The licensing authority must reject the application if, having regard to the notice of objection, it considers that it is necessary to do so for the promotion of the crime prevention objective.

9.4.9 Notification of the decision

Whether an application is granted or rejected, the relevant licensing authority must forthwith (see **2.9**) give a notice of the decision to:

- the applicant;
- the individual who is proposed as the new designated premises supervisor; and
- the chief officer of police for the police area (or each police area) in which the premises are situated.

The notice must be accompanied by information regarding the right of a party to appeal against the decision.

This notice must, if the chief officer of police gave a notice of objection and did not withdraw it, state the reasons why the licensing authority has granted or rejected the application. In addition, where the application is granted, the notice must specify the time when the variation takes effect. This will either be the time specified in the application or, if the applicant is given the notice after that time, such later time as the relevant licensing authority specifies in the notice.

When the holder of a premises licence is notified by the licensing authority that his application has been granted, he must forthwith notify the person, if any, who has been replaced as the designated premises supervisor. If his application has been rejected, he must forthwith (see **2.9**) give the designated premises supervisor, if any, notice to that effect. An offence will be committed by the licence holder if he fails, without reasonable excuse, to give the appropriate notice and he will be liable on summary conviction to a fine not exceeding level 3 on the standard scale.

9.5 POLICE OBJECTIONS

The chief officer of police can object to the designation of a new premises supervisor under s.37(5) where, in exceptional circumstances, he believes that the appointment would undermine the crime prevention objective. The police might object where the presence of a particular designated premises supervisor would give rise to exceptional concerns, for example, where a personal licence holder has been allowed by the courts to retain his licence despite convictions for selling alcohol to minors and he then moves to premises which suffer from some degree of notoriety for under-age drinking. Where the police object, the licensing authority must arrange for a hearing at which the issue can be considered and both parties can put their arguments (see **9.4.8**). If the chief officer of police is satisfied that the exceptional circumstances of the case are such that if the application was granted it would undermine the crime prevention objective, he must give the relevant licensing authority a notice of the reasons why he is so satisfied within 14 days beginning with the day on which he is notified of the application (s.37(6)).

In respect of police objections, the Guidance provides at para. 4.22:

The portability of personal licences from one premises to another is an important concept within the 2003 Act. The Secretary of State expects that objections by the police on the specification of the designated premises supervisor would arise in only genuinely exceptional circumstances. An objection made routinely in individual circumstances that could not be regarded as exceptional would not be in accordance with the 2003 Act. If a licensing authority believes that the police are routinely objecting on unexceptional grounds, they should raise the matter with the chief officer of police as a matter of urgency. The 2003 Act provides for the suspension and forfeiture of personal licences by the courts following convictions for relevant offences, including breaches of licensing law. The police can at any stage after the appointment of a designated premises supervisor seek a review of a premises licence on any grounds relating to the licensing objectives if anxieties arise about the performance of such a supervisor. The portability of personal licences is also important to industry because of the frequency with which some businesses move managers from premises to premises. It is therefore not expected that licensing authorities or the police should seek to use the power of intervention as a routine mechanism for hindering the portability of a licence or use hearings of this kind as a fishing expedition to test out the individual's background and character. The Secretary of State therefore expects that such hearings should be rare and genuinely exceptional.

9.6   REQUEST TO BE REMOVED AS DESIGNATED PREMISES SUPERVISOR

Section 41 provides that where a designated premises supervisor decides that he no longer wishes to carry on in that role, he may give the relevant licensing authority a notice to that effect. The notice must be in the prescribed form but at the time of writing no form had been prescribed. Presumably the notice must be in writing and may be given electronically (see the Premises Licences Regulations, reg. 21).

Where the designated premises supervisor is also the holder of the premises licence, the notice must be accompanied by the premises licence, or the appropriate part of the licence or, if that is not practicable, by a statement of the reasons for the failure to provide the licence, or that part.

In all other situations, the designated premises supervisor must within 48 hours after giving the notice to the relevant licensing authority give the holder of the premises licence a copy of the notice, and a notice directing the licence holder to send to the relevant licensing authority within 14 days of receiving the notice either the premises licence, or the appropriate part of the licence, or if that is not practicable, a statement of the reasons for the failure to provide the licence, or that part. A licence holder will commit an offence if he fails, without reasonable excuse, to comply with such a direction given to him and he will be liable on summary conviction to a fine not exceeding level 3 on the standard scale.

Where a designated premises supervisor has complied with these provisions, he is treated as if, from the relevant time, he were not the designated premises supervisor. For this purpose 'the relevant time' means either the time the designated premises supervisor's notice is received by the relevant licensing authority or, if later, the time specified in the notice.

CHAPTER 10

Relevant representations

10.1 INTRODUCTION

Following the making of certain applications under the Act, objections in the form of representations may be made by a responsible authority or an interested party. If these amount to 'relevant representations' they can lead to a hearing to consider them. Where a representation is made, the licensing authority must initially decide whether it is relevant which will involve deciding:

- that it relates to a licensing objective;
- whether it has been made by an interested party or a responsible authority; and
- whether it is vexatious or frivolous.

10.2 RELEVANT REPRESENTATIONS – GENERAL

10.2.1 A representation must be made by an interested party or a responsible authority

A representation must be made by either an 'interested party' or a 'responsible authority' (s.18(7)(a)).

Interested party

Certain persons and bodies referred to as 'interested parties' have the right to make representations in respect of certain applications relating to a premises licence or a club premises certificate. They are also entitled to receive certain notices and be advised of determinations made by the relevant licensing authority.

The following are designated in s.13(3) as interested parties:

- a person living in the vicinity of the premises;
- a body representing persons who live in that vicinity;

- a person involved in a business in that vicinity; and
- a body representing persons involved in such businesses.

A licensing authority may notify an applicant of the interested parties it will advise of the application.

The term 'in the vicinity' is not defined in the Act and its meaning will be a question of fact for a licensing authority to determine. Ultimately it will be question for the courts. The Guidance at para. 5.33 provides:

> Whether or not an individual resides 'in the vicinity of' the licensed premises is ultimately a matter of fact to be decided by the courts, but initially licensing authorities must decide if the individual or body making a representation qualifies as an interested party. In making their initial decision, licensing authorities should consider, for example, whether the individual's residence or business is likely to be directly affected by disorder and disturbance occurring or potentially occurring on those premises or immediately outside the premises. Where a representation concerns 'cumulative impact', the licensing authority may be unable to consider this factor and would probably need to examine issues such as the proximity of the residence or business. In essence, it is expected that the decision will be approached with common sense and individuals living and working in the neighbourhood or area immediately surrounding the premises will be able to make representations.

When making a decision as to whether individuals or bodies are in the 'vicinity' a licensing authority should consider, for example, whether their home or business is likely to be directly affected by disorder and disturbance occurring or potentially occurring from either inside or immediately outside the premises. Each case should be looked at on its merits and, while people who live or work within a few hundred yards of a premises are likely to be deemed to be 'in the vicinity', those who live several miles away should only be deemed to be so in exceptional circumstances such as with licence applications for outdoor pop festivals.

A licensing authority may give an indication in its statement of licensing policy as to how it will interpret 'vicinity'; so for example a licensing authority may state that it will only consider representations from interested parties within say a 100-metre radius of the premises (though this could be a lesser or greater distance should the circumstances of an individual case warrant it).

An interested party must either live in the vicinity of the premises or be involved in a business in that vicinity or be a body representing such persons.

While a licensing authority cannot be an interested party, a parish or town council can be, as it is a body representing persons who live in the vicinity.

Responsible authority

Responsible authorities are listed in s.13(4) (see **7.9**).

10.2.2   A representation must be made within the prescribed period

The Act provides that the Secretary of State must by regulations prescribe the period during which representation may be made. Regulation 22 of the Premises Licences Regulations provides that an interested party or responsible authority may make representations at any time during the period of 28 consecutive days starting on the day after the day on which the application to which it relates was given to the authority by the applicant.

It would appear that there is nothing to prevent a representation being made outside the prescribed period. But both the Act and the Premises Licences Regulations are silent on whether a licensing authority may take late representations into account. It could be argued that the use of the word 'may' gives a discretion to an interested party or responsible authority to make late representations. There is no discretion though for a licensing authority to accept them outside the prescribed period. Indeed, a licensing authority may state in its licensing policy that it will not entertain late representations. It could be argued that this might conflict with the duty of the licensing authority under s.4(1) to carry out its licensing functions with a view to promoting the licensing objectives. However accepting late representations may cause procedural difficulties for a licensing authority. A hearing must be commenced within 20 working days beginning with the day after the end of the period during which representations may be made. Notice of the hearing must be given no later than 10 working days before the day or the first day on which the hearing is to be held. If a licensing authority accepts a late representation, it may have difficulty keeping to these time limits with the result that other persons who have made representations within the prescribed time limit may be prejudiced.

10.2.3   A representation must not be withdrawn

A representation must not have been withdrawn (s.18(7)(b)). Regulation 10 of the Hearings Regulations provides that a party who wishes to withdraw any representations they have made may do so by giving notice to the authority no later than 24 hours before the day or the first day on which the hearing is to be held, or orally at the hearing.

10.2.4   A representation must not be frivolous or vexatious

A representation is only relevant if it relates to the likely effect of the application on the promotion of at least one of the four licensing objectives. A representation which does not do this is not relevant. The Guidance at para. 5.73 provides that:

> It is not intended, for example, that the consideration of the application should be a re-run of the planning application which would have considered a wider range of

matters. Premises licences authorise the activities within the scope of the 2003 Act that it is proposed should take place on the premises. For example, a representation from a local businessman which argued that his business would be commercially damaged by the new business for which an application is being made under Part 3 of the 2003 Act would not be relevant. On the other hand, a representation to the effect that nuisance caused by the new business would deter customers from entering the local area and the steps proposed by the applicant to control that nuisance are inadequate would amount to relevant representations and must be considered provided the other conditions necessary to be a relevant representation were fulfilled.

A licensing authority must decide whether any representation by an interested party is frivolous or vexatious and it must reach its decision on the basis of what might ordinarily be considered to be vexatious or frivolous. Vexation may arise because of disputes between rival businesses and local knowledge will therefore be invaluable in considering such matters. Frivolous representations would be essentially categorised by a lack of seriousness. A trivial complaint may not always be frivolous, but it would have to be pertinent in order to be relevant. An interested party aggrieved by a rejection of his representations on these grounds may challenge the authority's decision by way of judicial review.

The Guidance recommends that the decision should be delegated to an officer and para. 5.76 provides:

> Decisions as to whether representations are relevant should not be made on the basis of any political judgement which would undermine a natural approach to the issue. This may be difficult for ward councillors receiving complaints from residents within their own wards. If consideration is not to be delegated, contrary to the recommendation in this Guidance, an assessment should be prepared by officials for consideration by the sub-committee before any decision is taken that necessitates a hearing; i.e. the decision would be that the representations are relevant. Any ward councillor who considers that his own interests are such that he is unable to consider the matter independently should disqualify himself.

The Guidance also recommends that in borderline cases, the benefit of the doubt should be given to the interested party making the representation. The subsequent hearing would then provide an opportunity for the person or body making the representation to amplify and clarify it. If it then emerged for example that the representation should not be supported, the licensing authority could decide not to take any action in respect of the application for the grant or variation of a premises licence (para. 5.77).

Where a licensing authority decides that a representation is frivolous or vexatious, it must notify the person who made it of the reasons for the decision (s.18(8)). This notification must be given in writing and as soon as is reasonably practicable and in any event before the determination of the application to which the representation relates (Premises Licences Regulations, reg. 31). There is no right of appeal but it may be possible to resubmit an amended representation if there is time.

10.3 RELEVANT REPRESENTATIONS – SPECIFIC APPLICATIONS UNDER THE ACT

10.3.1 Application for a premises licence

In respect of an application for a premises licence, s.18(6) and (7) provides that a representation is a 'relevant representation' if it:

- is about the likely effect of the grant of the premises licence on the promotion of the licensing objectives;
- has been made by an interested party or a responsible authority within the prescribed time limit of 28 days starting on the day after the day on which the application for a premises licence was given to the licensing authority by the applicant;
- has not been withdrawn;
- is made by an interested party who is not also a responsible authority and it is not, in the opinion of the relevant licensing authority, frivolous or vexatious;
- relates to the identity of the person named in the application as the proposed premises supervisor, it has been made by a chief officer of police for a police area in which the premises are situated, and includes a statement that, due to the exceptional circumstances of the case, he is satisfied that the designation of the person concerned as the premises supervisor under the premises licence would undermine the crime prevention objective; and
- is not an excluded representation by virtue of s.32 which restricts the making of representations following the issue of a provisional statement.

10.3.2 Application for a provisional statement

In respect of an application for a provisional statement, s.31(5) and (6) provides that a representation is a 'relevant representation' if it:

- is about the likely effect on the licensing objectives of the grant of a premises licence in the form described in the provisional statement application, if the work at the premises was satisfactorily completed;
- has been made by an interested party or a responsible authority at any time during a period of 28 days starting on the day after the day on which the application for a provisional statement was given to the licensing authority by the applicant;
- has not been withdrawn; and

- is made by an interested party who is not also a responsible authority, it is not, in the opinion of the relevant licensing authority, frivolous or vexatious (see **10.2.4**).

Section 32 contains restrictions on making representations following the issue of a provisional statement.

10.3.3 Application for a variation of a premises licence

In respect of an application for a variation of a premises licence, s.35(5) and (6) provides that a representation is a 'relevant representation' if it:

- is about the likely effect of the grant of the application on the promotion of the licensing objectives;
- has been made by an interested party or a responsible authority at any time during a period of 28 days starting on the day after the day on which the application for a variation was given to the licensing authority by the applicant;
- has not been withdrawn; and
- is made by an interested party who is not also a responsible authority and it is not, in the opinion of the relevant licensing authority, frivolous or vexatious (see **10.2.4**).

10.3.4 Application for a review of a premises licence

In respect of an application for a review of a premises licence, s.52(7) and (8) provides that a representation is a 'relevant representation' if it:

- is relevant to one or more of the licensing objectives;
- has been made by the holder of the premises licence, a responsible authority or an interested party at any time during a period of 28 days starting on the day after the day on which the application for a review was given to the licensing authority by the applicant;
- has not been withdrawn; and
- is made by an interested party who is not also a responsible authority and it is not, in the opinion of the relevant licensing authority, frivolous or vexatious (see **10.2.4**).

10.3.5 Application for a review of a premises licence following a closure order

In respect of an application for a review of a premises licence following a closure order, s.167(9) and (10) provides that a representation is a 'relevant representation' if it:

- is relevant to one or more of the licensing objectives;

- has been made by the holder of the premises licence, a responsible authority or an interested party at any time up to and including seven days starting on the day after the day on which the licensing authority received the notice of the magistrates' court determination and extension to it;
- has not been withdrawn; and
- is made by an interested party who is not also a responsible authority and it is not, in the opinion of the relevant licensing authority, frivolous or vexatious (see **10.2.4**).

10.3.6   Application for a club premises certificate

In respect of an application for a club premises certificate, s.72(7) and (8) provides that a representation is a 'relevant representation' if it:

- is about the likely effect of the grant of the club premises certificate on the promotion of the licensing objectives;
- has been made by an interested party or a responsible authority at any time during a period of 28 days starting on the day after the day on which the application for a club premises certificate was given to the licensing authority by the applicant;
- has not been withdrawn; and
- is made by an interested party who is not also a responsible authority and it is not, in the opinion of the relevant licensing authority, frivolous or vexatious (see **10.2.4**).

10.3.7   Application for a variation of a club premises certificate

In respect of an application for a variation of a club premises certificate, s.85(5) and (6) provides that a representation is a 'relevant representation' if it:

- is about the likely effect of the grant of the application on the promotion of the licensing objectives;
- has been made by an interested party or a responsible authority at any time during a period of 28 days starting on the day after the day on which the application for a variation was given to the licensing authority by the applicant;
- has not been withdrawn; and
- is made by an interested party who is not also a responsible authority and it is not, in the opinion of the relevant licensing authority, frivolous or vexatious (see **10.2.4**).

10.3.8 Application for a review of a club premises certificate

In respect of an application for a review of a club premises certificate, s.88(7) and (8) provides that a representation is a 'relevant representation' if it:

- is relevant to one or more of the licensing objectives;
- has been made by the holder of the club, a responsible authority or an interested party at any time during a period of 28 days starting on the day after the day on which the application for a review was given to the licensing authority by the applicant;
- has not been withdrawn; and
- is made by an interested party who is not also a responsible authority and it is not, in the opinion of the relevant licensing authority, frivolous or vexatious (see **10.2.4**).

10.4 MAKING A REPRESENTATION

A representation must relate to one or more of the four licensing objectives. It should not relate to other matters such as planning permission, trade competition or the effect on house prices.

10.4.1 How does someone know that an application has been made?

Applications can be viewed at the licensing authority offices. In addition, a person will know if an application has been made if he sees:

- a notice displayed on the premises;
- an official notice in the notices section of a local newspaper; or
- a statement on the licensing authority's website.

A licensing authority might also write to people and businesses in the immediate vicinity advising them of the application.

10.4.2 Representations to be in writing

Regulation 21 of the Premises Licences Regulations provides that a representation must be made in writing. However, notwithstanding this requirement, a representation can also be made electronically provided:

- the text of the representation is transmitted by electronic means, is capable of being accessed by the recipient, is legible in all material respects (i.e. the information contained in the representation is available to the recipient to no lesser extent than it would be if given by means of a written document), and is capable of being read and reproduced in written form and used for subsequent reference;

- the person to whom the representation is to be given has agreed in advance that a representation may be given by electronic means; and
- forthwith (see **2.9**) on sending the text of the representation by electronic means, the representation is given to the recipient in writing.

Where the text of the representation is transmitted by electronic means, the giving of the representation shall be effected at the time the first set of above requirements is satisfied, provided that where a representation is required to be accompanied by a fee, plan or other document or information that representation shall not be treated as given until the fee, plan or other document or information has been received by the relevant licensing authority. This means that where additional documentation is required the electronic transmission is not effective until that additional documentation is received by the licensing authority.

10.4.3 Advice and standard forms of representation

A person wishing to make a representation should first consult the relevant licensing authority to see what advice it can provide. The Guidance, para. 5.34 states: 'Licensing authorities should consider providing advice on their websites about how any interested party can make representations to them.' A licensing authority may provide a standard form for use when making a representation. Some may even provide an on-line form which can be used to submit a representation. **Appendix B** contains a suggested form for use when making a representation. The representation must include the name and address of the person making the representation. These will be disclosed to the applicant and will be included in the report to the licensing committee which is a public document. If a person does not want his details to be made public in this way he should inform the licensing authority.

10.4.4 Evidence in support of a representation

A person making a representation should provide evidence to support his representation. Possible ways of doing this include using:

- a diary/record of events or incidents;
- photographs;
- video evidence;
- sound recordings;
- a record of complaints made to appropriate authorities; and
- supporting statements from neighbours/witnesses.

It will be essential that a written note or a diary is kept so that the date, the time and a brief description of any incidents that take place can be recorded. In addition, this should be supplemented with photographs, a video recording or a sound recording. It will also help if other people in the vicinity can also make notes about what happened (or keeps happening). If an incident prompted an official response, for example a noise complaint is logged or the police arrive, then details of this should be kept.

Where noise is a problem, a noise diary should be kept. The local environmental health authority may be able to provide a standard form of noise diary. Otherwise a noise diary should set out:

- the date the noise happens;
- the time the noise started and finished;
- where the person completing the diary was when he heard the noise;
- the address of the premises where the noise is coming from;
- a description of the noise, e.g. loud music, people shouting, etc.;
- the level of the noise and the disturbance it caused;
- the name of the person causing the noise, if known; and
- the name and address of any witnesses (who should also keep their own noise diary).

Records should be kept over a period of time so as to prevent a licensee from arguing that something was just a one-off problem.

It may also be useful to check whether:

- council records confirm that the premises have the right planning consent for what is going on;
- there are records of any other complaints;
- the local crime and disorder partnership can assist;
- there have been articles in the local press about nuisance or trouble on the premises; and
- any of the relevant authorities support the representation.

A petition may be used to support a representation. Care must be taken with this as a representation must be from persons in the vicinity of the premises. It could be argued that a petition containing signatures from people outside the vicinity should not be admitted.

Difficulties may arise in the preparation of a case against an application for a proposed variation or provisional statement as this will have to include the fears of what may happen in the event that the application is granted. It may be easy for the applicant to deny that any problems will arise. It is important to include points that suggest whether:

- there has been a previous licence;
- there have been problems in the past;
- if the premises are part of a chain, there have been similar problems at other branches;
- similar premises in the area have shown similar problems; and
- the applicant has thought through how the premises will be operated in order to avoid problems.

CHAPTER 11

Conditions

11.1 INTRODUCTION

A licensing authority may impose conditions when granting a premises licence or a club premises certificate. These may be imposed because it is mandatory to do so or they may be imposed at the discretion of the licensing authority. Where no relevant representations have been made in respect of an application for a premises licence, no conditions can be imposed beyond those consistent with the operating schedule and any mandatory conditions (*British Beer and Pub Association* v. *Canterbury City Council* [2005] EWHC 1318; *The Times*, 11 July 2005).

Conditions cannot be attached to a personal licence and may only be attached to a temporary event notice where the licensable activities include the supply of alcohol when a condition must be attached under s.100(6) that all supplies of alcohol must be made or authorised by the premises user (see **20.5**).

In certain circumstances mandatory conditions must be attached to a premises licence or a club premises certificate (see **7.12** and **17.11**). There are also certain conditions which are prohibited from being included (see **7.12.5**, **17.11.3** and **17.11.4**). A licensing authority may also impose conditions at its discretion. Where no relevant representations have been made, a licensing authority may only attach such conditions as are consistent with the operating schedule (ss.18(2)(a) and 72(2)(a)). Where relevant representations have been made a licensing authority can impose such conditions as are consistent with the operating schedule modified to the extent it considers necessary for the promotion of the licensing objectives (ss.18(4)(a)(i) and 72(4)(a)(i)).

11.2 GENERAL REQUIREMENTS FOR CONDITIONS

Conditions may only be imposed in a premises licence or a club premises certificate where they are necessary for the promotion of one or more of the four licensing objectives. Conditions may not be imposed for other purposes. Conditions must only apply while the licensable activities are taking place and so for example conditions relating to night café and take-away outlets operating from 11.00 pm must relate to the night-time operation of the premises and must not be used to impose conditions which relate to day-time operation. A condition must not duplicate something which is already imposed by the existing law (Guidance, para. 7.13).

The Act requires that licensing conditions should be tailored to the size, style, characteristics and activities taking place at the premises concerned, which effectively rules out standardised conditions which ignore these individual aspects (Guidance, para. 7.17). There are however certain conditions which will be attached to most licences. As the Guidance considers that these should be formulated consistently it sets out examples of such conditions in annexes, as follows:

- Annex D – crime and disorder;
- Annex E – public safety;
- Annex F – theatres, cinemas, concert halls and similar places – protection of children from harm;
- Annex G – public nuisance; and
- Annex H – protection of children from harm.

These conditions can be used where necessary and appropriate to the particular circumstances of any individual premises. Accordingly, they should be treated as a pool of conditions from which the necessary conditions for premises licences and club premises certificates may be drawn to tailor a licence or certificate to particular premises. It is important that they should not be applied universally irrespective of circumstances.

Any conditions which are imposed must be proportionate and recognise that there are significant differences between venues (Guidance, para. 7.17). In addition, the Guidance at para. 7.19 states that licensing authorities and responsible authorities should also have proper regard for the history of certain events and activities.

11.3 HOURS OF TRADING

The hours during which licensable activities can take place can be regulated by conditions on a premises licence or club premises certificate. Clearly such conditions can only be imposed if they are necessary for the promotion of the licensing objectives, particularly the prevention of crime and disorder and the prevention of public nuisance. The Guidance promotes flexibility in closing hours.

Where premises supply alcohol for consumption off the premises, for example shops, stores and supermarkets, it is recommended that they should generally be permitted to match the hours during which they may sell alcohol with their normal trading hours during which other sales take place, unless there are exceptional reasons relating to the licensing objectives, in particular the prevention of crime and disorder and public nuisance (Guidance, para. 6.2). This means that a shop with 24-hour opening should be allowed to sell alcohol during those hours unless there are very good reasons as to why it is necessary for it not to do so. However restrictions on hours may be required in respect of certain premises, as the Guidance, para. 6.3 provides:

> Some shops may however be known to be a focus for disturbance because youths congregate there and engage in nuisance and anti-social behaviour, including trying to pressurise shop staff to make unlawful sales of alcohol. Where relevant representations are made by an interested party or a responsible authority (particularly, the police) concerning applications for premises licences for such places, or in connection with existing licences, licensing authorities should consider a restriction on opening hours as one mechanism of combating such problems if this would be necessary.

Where alcohol is supplied for consumption on the premises, there should be flexibility in closing hours. The Guidance, para. 6.5 provides:

> The Government strongly believes that fixed and artificially early closing times promote, in the case of the sale or supply of alcohol for consumption on the premises, rapid binge drinking close to closing times; and are a key cause of disorder and disturbance when large numbers of customers are required to leave premises simultaneously. This creates excessive pressures at places where fast food is sold or public or private transport is provided. This in turn produces friction and gives rise to disorder and peaks of noise and other nuisance behaviour. It is therefore important that licensing authorities recognise these problems when addressing issues such as the hours at which premises should be used to carry on the provision of licensable activities to the public.

The aim should therefore be to reduce the potential for concentrations and achieve a slower dispersal of people from licensed premises through longer opening times, and arbitrary restrictions that would undermine the principle of flexibility should be avoided (Guidance, para. 6.6). A restriction may take the form of setting fixed trading hours within a designated area, which is known as 'zoning', or the setting of quotas for particular closing times, which is known as 'staggered closing times', for example by allocating closing times of 11 pm, 12 midnight, 1 am, 2 am, 3 am, etc. to specific premises. Neither of these forms of restriction should be used (Guidance, paras. 6.9 and 6.10) as they will not make any significant improvement in preventing crime and disorder or public nuisance. Licensing authorities should not fix predetermined closing times for particular areas (Guidance, para. 6.9). The general principle should be to support later opening so that customers leave for natural reasons slowly over a longer period which will prevent any artificial concentrations (Guidance, para. 6.10).

Zoning was used in Edinburgh for an 18-month period in the early 1990s when five zones were created. However it had to be abandoned in 1993 because of the problems created for the police and significant improvements in terms of the reduction of disorder and disturbance were noted following its removal (Guidance, para. 6.9).

11.3.1   Drinking up time

The Guidance, para. 6.13 deals with drinking up time as follows:

> It is important to note that 'opening hours', the times when premises are open to the public, are not necessarily identical to the hours during which licensable activities may take place. In the case of the sale by retail of alcohol (or supply of alcohol by or on behalf of a club to, or to the order of, a member of a club) for consumption on the premises, it must also be noted that 'consumption' of alcohol is not a licensable activity. Accordingly, the authorised period specified in the premises licence, club premises certificate or temporary event notice relates to the period during which alcohol may be sold or supplied. It is therefore permissible for premises to allow the consumption of previously purchased alcohol, within the authorisation, outside the hours authorised for the sale or supply of alcohol.

A licensing authority might therefore impose a condition that alcohol must be consumed within a reasonable time after the hours authorised for the sale or supply of alcohol have ended.

11.3.2   Relaxation of opening hours for local, national and international occasions

Section 172(1) provides that where the Secretary of State considers that there is an occasion of exceptional international, national or local significance, he may relax the opening hours by making a licensing hours order. Such a period is referred to as a 'celebration period'. Before making an order, the Secretary of State must consult such persons as he considers appropriate (s.172(4)). If an order is made it will provide that during the specified relaxation period, which may be up to four days, premises licences and club premises certificates will have effect as if the times specified in the order were included in their opening hours.

A licensing hours order may relax the hours generally throughout the country or may just apply to premises in specified areas. It may also make different provision in respect of different days during the specified relaxation period, and may make different provision in respect of different licensable activities.

It is not expected that licensing hours orders would be used for bank holidays and events which might in the past have been dealt with by a special order of exemption under the Licensing Act 1964. The Guidance at para. 6.11 provides:

> It should normally be possible for applicants for premises licences and club premises certificates to anticipate special occasions which occur regularly each year –

such as bank holidays – and to incorporate appropriate opening hours for these occasions in their operating schedules. Similarly, temporary event notices – in respect of which a personal licence holder may give fifty each year – should be sufficient to cover events like Golden Wedding Anniversaries or 21st Birthday parties which take place at premises which do not have a premises licence or club premises certificate. However, with the passage of time exceptional events of local, national or international significance will arise which could not or have not been anticipated. Such events can give rise to the need to vary the conditions of large numbers of premises licences and club premises certificates. In such circumstances, it will be open to the Secretary of State to make a licensing hours order to provide for premises with a premises licence or club premises certificate to open for specified, generally extended, hours on these special occasions. Examples might include a one-off local festival, a Royal Jubilee, a World Cup or an Olympic Games.

The Secretary of State may himself decide to make a licensing hours order. Other people, for example a licensing authority, may request an order. In such a case the Guidance, para. 6.12 provides:

Licensing authorities (or any other persons) approaching the Secretary of State about the making of such an order are advised that they should give at least six months notice before the celebration in question. Before making such an order, the Secretary of State is required to consult such persons as she considers appropriate, and this would generally enable a wide-range of bodies to make representations to her for consideration. In addition, such an order will require the approval of both Houses of Parliament. Six months would be the minimum period in which such a process could be satisfactorily completed.

11.4 SMALL PREMISES PROVIDING LIVE MUSIC AND DANCE

There are special provisions in s.177 for dancing and live music in small premises which have a premises licence authorising the supply of alcohol for consumption on the premises, and the provision of music entertainment, and the premises are used primarily for the supply of alcohol for consumption on the premises and they have a permitted capacity of not more than 200 persons.

The provisions in s.177 are confusing and allow a licensing authority to put conditions on a premises licence to restrict noise but then give the holder of the premises licence permission to ignore those conditions.

'Music entertainment' is defined in s.177(8) as a performance of live music or a performance of dance, and facilities enabling people to take part in the performance of live music or the performance of a dance.

Section 177 only applies where the permitted capacity is not more than 200 people. 'Permitted capacity', in relation to any premises, is determined by reference to either a limit imposed under a fire certificate or any recommendation made by the fire and rescue authority. Section 177(8) provides that 'permitted capacity' means:

(a) where a fire certificate issued under the Fire Precautions Act 1971 is in force in respect of the premises and that certificate imposes a requirement under s.6(2)(d) of that Act, the limit on the number of persons who, in accordance with that requirement, may be on the premises at any one time; and

(b) in any other case, the limit on the number of persons who may be on the premises at any one time in accordance with a recommendation made by, or on behalf of, the fire and rescue authority for the area in which the premises are situated (or, if the premises are situated in the area of more than one fire and rescue authority, those authorities).

Very few small premises will have a fire certificate. An example of one which might would be a small hotel. It is possible that the other method involving a limit on the number of people who can use the premises as recommended by the fire and rescue authority will be more common. This is because the Guidance at para. 7.35 provides that where a fire certificate does not include a capacity or one does not exist, the fire and rescue authority must be asked to make a recommendation on the capacity of the premises. Where an applicant wishes to take advantage of the special provisions set out in s.177 he should conduct his own risk assessment as to the appropriate capacity of the premises, and then send this to the fire and rescue authority who will consider it and then decide what the 'permitted capacity' of those premises should be.

The general principle is that at any time when the premises are open for the purposes of being used for the supply of alcohol for consumption on the premises, and are being used for the provision of music entertainment, any licensing authority imposed condition of the premises licence which relates to the provision of the live music and dancing does not have effect, in relation to the provision of that entertainment, unless it relates to the prevention of crime and disorder or public safety. This means that any licensing authority imposed conditions will not have effect if they relate to prevention of public nuisance or the protection of children from harm.

In addition any licensing authority imposed conditions relating to the provision of music entertainment do not apply at any time between 8 am and midnight when the premises are being used for the provision of music entertainment which consists of the performance of unamplified live music, or facilities for enabling persons to take part in the performance of unamplified live music, but are not being used for the provision of any other description of regulated entertainment, unless it relates to the prevention of crime and disorder or public safety.

A licensing authority imposed condition will also apply to small premises if, on a review of the premises licence, it is altered so as to include a statement that s.177 does not apply to it, or it is added to the licence and includes such a statement.

A 'licensing authority imposed condition' is a condition imposed by a licensing authority for the promotion of the licensing objectives, or a mandatory condition relating to door supervision under s.21. It does not include a condition volunteered by the applicant in the operating schedule. So if conditions are suggested in an operating schedule the licensing authority must 'rubber stamp' them and they apply whatever the situation.

Section 177 applies to club premises certificates in the same way as it applies to premises licences except so far as the definition of a 'licensing authority imposed condition' is concerned. In the case of clubs 'licensing authority imposed condition' means a condition imposed by the licensing authority for the promotion of the licensing objectives. It does not include a condition volunteered by the applicant in the operating schedule, nor the mandatory conditions which must be imposed in respect of off-sales.

For the purposes of s.177 'supply of alcohol' means the sale by retail of alcohol, or the supply of alcohol by or on behalf of a club to, or to the order of, a member of the club.

CHAPTER 12

Interim authorities

12.1 INTRODUCTION

A premises licence will lapse where the licensee dies, becomes mentally incapable or becomes bankrupt. While it is possible to apply for a transfer of the licence by reinstatement (see **12.6**) this may take some time, for example because of the time before a deceased licensee's estate can be dealt with or an administrative receiver appointed. So, the Act makes provision for the licence to be reinstated for up to two months in such circumstances by allowing an interim authority notice to be given. Without this the carrying on of licensable activities would be an offence as an unauthorised licensable activity under s.136(1)(a) (see **21.2.1**). There is a 'defence of due diligence' in s.139 which may be relevant where, for example, the manager of particular premises is wholly unaware for a period of time that the premises licence holder has died. As soon as an interim authority notice is properly given, the business may continue to carry on any licensable activities permitted by the premises licence.

12.2 GIVING AN INTERIM AUTHORITY

An interim authority notice can be given under s.47 where:

- the premises licence has lapsed due to the death, incapacity or insolvency of the holder; and
- no application has been made for the reinstatement of the licence on transfer following the death, incapacity or insolvency.

An interim authority notice can be given either by a person who has a prescribed interest in the premises, or a person who is connected to the person who is the former holder of the premises licence. In respect of the first category a person who has a legal interest in the premises as freeholder or leaseholder has been prescribed for these purposes by the Premises Licences Regulations. In respect of the second category, a person is connected to the former holder of the premises licence if, and only if:

- the former holder has died and that person is his personal representative;
- the former holder has become mentally incapable and that person acts for him under a power of attorney created by an instrument registered under the Enduring Powers of Attorney Act 1985, s.6; or
- the former holder has become insolvent and that person is his insolvency practitioner.

An interim authority notice must be given to the relevant licensing authority within the period of seven days beginning with the day after the day the licence lapses. This is referred to in the Act as 'the initial seven day period'. In addition, the fee of £23 must accompany the notice. Only one interim authority notice may be given.

A copy of the notice must also be given to the chief officer of police on the same day as the day on which the notice is give to the relevant licensing authority.

Where a person becomes the holder of a premises licence by virtue of an interim authority notice, he must, unless he is the designated premises supervisor under the licence, forthwith (see **2.9**) notify the designated premises supervisor of the interim authority notice. Failure to so notify the designated premises supervisor, without reasonable excuse, is an offence and a person guilty of such an offence is liable on summary conviction to a fine not exceeding level 3 on the standard scale.

12.3   FORM OF INTERIM NOTICE

The form of an interim notice is prescribed in the Premises Licences Regulations, Sched. 7.

12.3.1   Completing the notice

The form should be completed as indicated in **6.5.2**.

In the opening statement, the name of the person or persons who are giving the interim authority notice and the premises licence number, if known, should be inserted.

The notice is then divided into four parts.

Part 1

The person giving the interim authority notice must set out the postal address of the premises, and the telephone number at the premises, if any. If the premises have no postal address, the location of the premises should be described or the Ordnance Survey map reference should be given.

147

Part 2

Part 2 deals with details of the person giving the interim authority notice. He must state in which capacity he is giving the interim authority notice and give details of when and how the licence lapsed, for example the date on which the premises licence holder died or became insolvent. He must then give details of his name and address, telephone number, e-mail address and confirmation, where relevant, that he is at least 18 years old.

Part 3

Part 3 asks whether an interim authority notice has been given previously in relation to the premises and the former premises licence holder, and if it has for the date. It also asks whether or not there has been an application to transfer the premises licence under s.50 (see **12.6**). There is a checklist for the person giving the interim authority notice so that nothing is overlooked. There are then two warnings. The first is a warning that the notice will lapse at the end of the initial seven-day period after the lapsing of the premises licence unless a copy of the notice has been given to the chief officer of police for the police area or each police area in which the premises are situated. There is also a warning that it is an offence under s.158, liable on conviction to a fine up to level 5 on the standard scale, to make a false statement in or in connection with the application

Part 4

The final part of the form makes provision for the person giving the interim authority notice to sign the form. The application form must be signed. The form can also be signed by a solicitor or other duly authorised agent, and someone signing on behalf of the person giving the interim authority notice must state in what capacity he signs. Where there are joint persons giving the interim authority notice, both of them or their respective agents must sign the application form.

12.3.2 Obtaining an interim authority notice

A relevant licensing authority must provide a printed interim authority notice on request; however an electronic version may be provided by a licensing authority on its website which can be downloaded, printed off and completed. An electronic copy is also provided on the DCMS website.

12.3.3　Giving a notice

Regulation 21 of the Premises Licences Regulations provides that an interim authority notice must be given in writing. For details of electronic submission see **6.5.3**.

On receipt of an interim authority notice, s.49 provides that the relevant licensing authority must issue to the person who gave the interim authority notice a copy of the licence and a copy of the summary of it. Each of these must be certified by the authority to be a true copy. The copies issued must be copies of the premises licence and summary in the form in which they existed immediately before the licence lapsed, except that they must specify the person who gave the interim authority notice as the person who is the holder. The Act then applies in relation to the certified copies as it applies in relation to the original licence or summary.

12.4　THE EFFECT OF AN INTERIM AUTHORITY NOTICE

The effect of an interim authority notice is that it reinstates the premises licence from the time the notice is received by the relevant licensing authority, and the person who gave the notice is from that time the holder of the premises licence (s.47(6)).

The premises licence is reinstated for a period of up to two months ('the interim authority period'), and during this period an application for a transfer of the premises licence must be made. There is no requirement that the transfer application must be made by the person who gave the interim authority notice and so it could be made by someone else. During the interim authority period the person who gave the notice can notify the relevant licensing authority that he is terminating the interim authority period and it will then come to an end (s.47(10)).

The premises licence will lapse at the end of the initial seven-day period if the person who gave the interim authority notice has not given a copy of the interim authority notice to the chief officer of police for the police area, or each police area, in which the premises are situated. It will also lapse at the end of the interim authority period unless a relevant transfer application is made during that time. If such an application is made and it is either rejected or withdrawn then the licence will lapse at the time of the rejection or the withdrawal.

12.5 CANCELLATION OF AN INTERIM AUTHORITY FOLLOWING POLICE OBJECTIONS

Where an interim authority notice has been given to the chief officer of police for the police area, or each police area in which the premises are situated before the end of the initial seven-day period, and he is satisfied that the exceptional circumstances of the case are such that a failure to cancel the interim authority notice would undermine the crime prevention objective, then he must no later than 48 hours after he receives the copy of the interim authority notice give the relevant licensing authority a notice stating why he is so satisfied (s.48).

Where such a notice is given and not withdrawn, the relevant licensing authority must then hold a hearing to consider it, unless the licensing authority, the person who gave the interim authority notice and the chief officer of police agree that a hearing is unnecessary. A hearing must be held within five working days beginning with the day after the end of the period within which the chief officer of police may give a notice (Hearings Regulations, reg. 5 and Sched. 1, para. 6). Notice of the hearing must be given to the person who gave the interim authority notice and the chief officer of police no later than two working days before the day or the first day on which the hearing is to be held (Hearings Regulations, reg. 6(2) and Sched. 2, para. 6). The person who gave the interim authority notice must be given the police notice of objection with the notice of hearing (Hearings Regulations, reg. 7(2) and Sched. 3, para. 6).

The Guidance states that it is expected that a licensing authority will be alert to the urgency of the circumstances and the need to consider the objection quickly (para. 5.97).

If, on hearing the police objection, the licensing authority considers that it is necessary for the promotion of the crime prevention objective, it must cancel the interim authority notice by giving the person who gave the interim authority notice a notice of cancellation together with the reasons for its decision. The licensing authority must also give a copy of the notice of cancellation to the chief officer of police for the police area or each police area in which the premises are situated.

The premises licence will lapse when a notice cancelling it is given; however there is a right of appeal against the cancellation. Where an appeal is lodged, the premises licence is reinstated pending the determination of the appeal by the magistrates' court. A person who gave the interim authority notice may appeal against a decision to cancel the interim authority notice, and a chief officer of police may appeal against a decision not to cancel the notice. Where an appeal is made, the magistrates' court may, on such terms as it thinks fit, order the reinstatement of the interim authority notice pending the disposal of the appeal, or the expiry of the interim authority period, whichever occurs first.

The relevant licensing authority must not cancel an interim authority notice after an application to transfer the premises licence with a request for this to have immediate effect has been made.

12.6   REINSTATEMENT OF A LAPSED LICENCE

Where a premises licence lapses either:

- due to the death, incapacity or insolvency of the holder, and no interim authority notice has been given, or one has been given but has been cancelled or withdrawn; or
- by surrender,

s.50 provides that any person who is entitled to apply for a premises licence may apply for the licence to be transferred to him, even though the licence has lapsed. If the applicant is an individual, he must be aged 18 or over. Only one application for the transfer of the premises licence may be made in these circumstances. The procedure for a transfer can be found in **Chapter 16**.

An application for transfer must be made no later than seven days after the day on which the licence lapsed and it must include a request that the transfer has immediate effect. Where such an application is made the premises licence is reinstated from the time the application is received by the relevant licensing authority, and the requirements of s.43 are disregarded. These requirements include obtaining, or taking reasonable steps to obtain, the consent of the holder of the premises licence. This may be difficult where the licence has lapsed and impossible where this is due to the death of the licence holder.

The premises licence will lapse again if and when the applicant is notified of the rejection of the application, or the application is withdrawn.

CHAPTER 13

Provisional statements

13.1 INTRODUCTION

Where premises are being or are about to be constructed, or are being or about to be extended or otherwise altered in order to be used for one or more of the licensable activities, the person proposing to carry out the work may not be able or prepared to proceed until he is assured not only that the project has appropriate planning permission but also that he has some degree of assurance that a premises licence would be granted for the premises when the works are completed. Under the Licensing Act 1964 a developer could apply for a provisional grant before the works were started and then apply for a final grant once they had been completed. The final grant could only be refused if the work had not been completed in accordance with the plans deposited with the application for the provisional grant or where the provisional licence holder had been disqualified from holding a licence or was not a 'fit and proper' person to hold a licence.

Provisional statements have now replaced the system of provisional grants. However unlike with a provisional grant there is no guarantee with a provisional statement that a premises licence will be granted once the works have been completed. All it does is describe the likely effect of the intended licensable activities and indicate what the prospects of any subsequent application for a premises licence will be. Thus there is not the assurance that a licence will be granted as there was with the previous system. Consequently, instead of applying for a provisional statement, an applicant may decide to apply for a premises licence, and there is nothing to prevent him from doing so. However the applicant would need to have clear plans of the proposed structure and would also need to prepare an operating schedule and it might not be possible to prepare these at this early stage. If the application is then granted, the licence would not have immediate effect but the licensing authority would include in the licence the date upon which it would have effect. The Guidance envisages that a provisional statement will normally only be required when an applicant is not able to provide the plan and operating schedule required to apply for a premises licence. Paragraph 5.85 provides:

It is open to any person falling within section 16 of the 2003 Act to apply for a premises licence before new premises are constructed or extended or changed. Nothing in the 2003 Act prevents such an application. This would be possible where clear plans of the proposed structure exist and an operating schedule is capable of being completed about the activities to take place there, the time at which such activities will take place, the proposed hours of opening, where the applicant wishes the licence to have effect for a limited period, that period, the steps to be taken to promote the licensing objectives, and where the sale of alcohol is involved, whether supplies are proposed to be for consumption on or off the premises (or both) and the name of the designated premises supervisor the applicant wishes to specify. On granting such an application, the authority of the licence would not have immediate effect but the licensing authority would include in the licence the date upon which it would have effect. A provisional statement will therefore normally only be required when the information described above is not available.

13.2 EXISTING PROVISIONAL GRANTS

The transitional provisions in the Act provide for the situation where a provisional grant has been made under the Licensing Act 1964 and an application for a final grant of a Justices' licence had not been made before the Act came into force. In this situation an application now has to be made for a premises licence when the premises have been completed. Paragraph 12 of Sched. 8 provides that where an application for a premises licence is made during a specified period the licensing authority must have regard to the provisional grant when determining the application for the grant of the premises licence. The Licensing Act 2003 (Transitional Provisions) Order 2005, SI 2005/40, art. 6 provides that the specified period is the period from 7 February 2005 until 24 November 2006.

The licensing authority must have regard to the provisional grant provided the premises are substantially the same, the provisional grant has not been declared final and the premises have been completed substantially in accordance with the plans deposited under the Licensing Act 1964. It would seem that if the applicant has complied with these requirements, the provisional grant would usually have been declared final in due course. The occasions when a licensing authority may refuse a premises licence would be rare and would only relate to a case where the provisional grant had been in existence for a considerable time and there had been a material change in circumstances in the vicinity of the premises. If relevant representations are received, the licensing authority may impose conditions on the premises licence which were not conditions on the original provisional grant if they are necessary to promote the licensing objectives. If no relevant representations are received or are discounted by the licensing authority, less restrictive hours are obtainable under a premises licence than the Justices' licence.

13.3 PREMISES IN RESPECT OF WHICH AN APPLICATION CAN BE MADE

A provisional statement may be applied for in respect of premises which are being or are about to be constructed, extended or otherwise altered in order to be used for one or more licensable activities (s.29(1)).

The Act does not define what is meant by 'otherwise altered'; however the Guidance at para. 5.84 states that:

> the alteration must relate to the purpose of being used for one or more licensable activities. For example, a premises licence should indicate the whole of or part of the premises which are licensed for one or more licensable activity. If the building is to be altered to allow a previously unlicensed area to be used for a licensable activity, a provisional statement may be sought in respect of the additional area.

'Premises' include a vessel, vehicle or structure. Section 189(5) provides that the provisions in the Act relating to provisional statements do not apply in relation to a vessel, vehicle or structure to which s.189 applies. Section 189 applies to vessels, vehicles or moveable structures which are not permanently located in one place. A provisional statement cannot therefore be applied for in respect of such premises. However, if the vessel, vehicle or structure is in a permanent location it would be possible to apply for a provisional statement in respect of it.

13.4 APPLICANTS FOR PROVISIONAL STATEMENTS

Any person who is interested in the premises and who, if he is an individual, is aged 18 or over, may apply to the relevant licensing authority for a provisional statement (s.29(2)).

A 'person' in this context can be either an individual or a company. The applicant could therefore be a firm of architects or a construction company or a financier. The class of potential applicants for a provisional statement is therefore wider than those who may apply for a premises licence.

An applicant must be 'interested' in the premises. There is nothing in the Act or the Guidance to indicate what is meant by this. It is suggested that some sort of proprietary interest in the premises, for example where the applicant is the owner or tenant of the premises, would suffice but there is nothing to confine the provision to such interests. Under the previous legislation (Licensing Act 1964, s.6(1)) the phrase 'interested in the premises' was construed broadly in the circumstances of each case. A person who occupied premises but who had no interest in the land and no contract with the owner was thus able to apply for a provisional grant (see *R. v. Dudley Crown Court ex p. Roger Pask* (1983) 147 JP 417 where Taylor J said: 'I see no reason why one should import automatically any requirement of an interest in property legal or equitable nor any requirement of any actual contractual right to operate on the premises').

154

13.5 APPLYING FOR A PROVISIONAL STATEMENT

In order to apply for a provisional statement, an applicant must submit the following to the relevant licensing authority:

- a completed application form;
- a schedule of works in the prescribed form (in practice this forms part of the application form) which includes:

    - a statement made by or on behalf of the applicant setting out particulars of the premises to which the application relates and of the licensable activities for which the premises are to be used;
    - plans of the work being or about to be done at the premises; and
    - such other information as may be prescribed. The prescribed form requests written details of the work being done or about to be done at the premises; and

- the fee of £315.

13.6 THE APPLICATION FORM

An application for a provisional statement must be in the prescribed form which is set out in the Premises Licences Regulations, Sched. 3.

13.6.1 Completing the application form

For guidance on completing the form see **6.5.2**.

In the opening statement, the name of the applicant or applicants who are applying for the provisional statement should be inserted.

The application form is then divided into five parts, as follows.

Part 1

The applicant must set out the following details of the premises:

- the postal address;
- the telephone number at the premises, if any; and
- the non-domestic rateable value of the premises.

If the premises have no postal address, the location of the premises should be described or the Ordnance Survey map reference should be given.

Part 2

Part 2 deals with details of the applicant. The applicant must state in which capacity he is applying for a premises licence, and if he is applying as an individual, a limited company, a partnership, an unincorporated association or a statutory corporation, he must confirm that he is carrying on or proposing to carry on a business which involves the use of the premises for licensable activities, or that he is making the application pursuant to a statutory function or a function discharged by virtue of Her Majesty's prerogative.

The applicant must then give further details such as his name and address, telephone number, e-mail address (this is optional) and confirmation, where relevant, that he is at least 18 years old.

Part 3

Part 3 contains the schedule of works. The applicant must indicate whether the premises are about to be constructed or are being extended or altered. Details must then be provided of the work and there is a reminder that a plan or plans must be attached showing the work being done or about to be done at the premises. There do not appear to be any prescribed requirements for the plans and the requirements which apply to the plan to accompany an application for a premises licence do not apply. Particulars must also be given of the premises to which the application relates, though it may be in practice that this is a repetition of the information already given in part 1. Finally, the licensable activities which the premises will be used for must be specified.

Part 4

Part 4 sets out an optional operating schedule which an applicant may choose to complete if he wishes. At this early stage it may be too soon for these details to have been finalised. See **Chapter 8** as to operating schedules.

Part 5

Part 5 provides for the applicant to sign the form. The form can also be signed by the applicant's solicitor or other duly authorised agent, and someone signing on behalf of the applicant must state in what capacity they sign. Where there are joint applicants both applicants or their respective agents must sign the application form.

13.6.2 Obtaining an application form

A relevant licensing authority must provide an applicant on request with a printed application form; however an electronic version may be provided by a licensing authority on its website which a prospective applicant can download, print off and complete. An electronic copy is also provided on the DCMS website.

13.6.3 Making an application

Regulation 21 of the Premises Licences Regulations provides that an application must be made in writing. For details on how to apply electronically see **6.5.3**.

Table 13.1 Checklist for a provisional statement application

	Original to relevant licensing authority	Copy to the police	Copy to responsible authorities
Completed application form			
Plan of the premises			
Payment of the fee			

Confirmation that the application has been advertised on the premises and that this will be maintained for 28 days		
Has the application been advertised in a local newspaper?	Name of newspaper:	Date:

13.7 ADVERTISING

The applicant must advertise his application for a provisional statement in the same way as an application for the grant of a premises licence (s.30). Thus he must display a notice at or on the premises and publish a notice in a local newspaper (see **7.8** for the specific requirements). In addition:

- the notice must state that representations are restricted after the provisional statement has been issued (see below); and
- the notice may, where they are known, contain a statement of the relevant licensable activities which it is proposed will be carried out on or from the premises.

An applicant should always check with the relevant licensing authority to see whether it provides a specimen form of notice to use. If not, a suggested form of notice is given in Box 13.1.

BOX 13.1   SUGGESTED FORM OF NOTICE OF AN APPLICATION FOR A PROVISIONAL STATEMENT

Licensing Act 2003

Notice of application for a Provisional Statement

Notice is hereby given that [insert the full name of the applicant] has applied to the [insert the full name of the licensing authority] on [insert the date of application to the licensing authority] for a provisional statement for the premises at [insert the name and full postal address of the premises, or if no address, a description of the site]. The proposed relevant licensable activities (where these are known) are: the provision of regulated entertainment / provision of late night refreshment / the sale by retail of alcohol [delete the inappropriate words]. Any person who wishes to make a representation in relation to this application must give notice in writing of his/her representation by [insert the date by which all relevant representations must be received by the licensing authority, i.e. 28 consecutive days starting on the day after the day on which the application is given to the licensing authority] stating the grounds for making a representation to [insert contact details for the licensing authority]. The public register where applications are available to be viewed by members of the public can be viewed at [insert details]. The Licensing Authority must receive representations by the date given above. The Licensing Authority will have regard to any such representation in considering the application.

Representations are restricted after the issue of a provisional statement and cannot be made to the subsequent licence application if they could have been made to the application for the provisional statement (for details see section 32 of the Licensing Act 2003).

It is an offence, under section 158 of the Licensing Act 2003, to knowingly or recklessly make a false statement in or in connection with an application for a provisional statement and the maximum fine on being convicted of such an offence is £5000.

The notice to be displayed on or at the premises must also fulfil the requirements mentioned at **7.8**.

13.8   NOTICE TO RESPONSIBLE AUTHORITIES

An applicant must give notice of his application for a provisional statement to each responsible authority (see **7.9**) by giving each responsible authority a copy of his application together with its accompanying documents. Notice is to be given on the same day as the day on which the application is given to the relevant licensing authority. A responsible authority may then make representations to the relevant licensing authority about the application.

13.9 DETERMINATION OF THE APPLICATION

13.9.1 Preliminary determination

When a licensing authority receives an application for a provisional statement, it must initially determine whether the application has been made properly in accordance with the Act and with the Premises Licences Regulations. An incomplete application is invalid and will be returned to the applicant. Any failure to observe the notice requirements will also render the application invalid.

13.9.2 Unopposed applications

Where no relevant representations have been made by either an interested party or a responsible authority the licensing authority must, provided the applicant has complied with the statutory requirements as to advertising and giving notice to each responsible authority, issue a statement confirming that no relevant representations have been made (s.31(2)). This statement will be the provisional statement (s.29(3)).

13.9.3 Applications where representations have been made

Where relevant representations have been made by an interested party or a responsible authority, the licensing authority must hold a hearing, unless it is satisfied that the applicant and each person making a representation agree that a hearing is unnecessary. The hearing must be held within 20 working days beginning with the day after the end of the period during which representations may be made (Hearings Regulations, reg. 5 and Sched. 1, para. 2). Notice of the hearing must be given to the applicant and any person who has made a relevant representation not less than 10 working days before the day or the first day on which the hearing is to be held (Hearings Regulations, reg. 6(4) and Sched. 2, para. 2). The notice to the applicant must include a copy of the relevant representations (Hearings Regulations, reg. 7(2) and Sched. 3, para. 2).

Following the hearing, the licensing authority must determine whether, on the basis of the representations and the application for a provisional statement, it would consider it necessary to take any of the following steps to promote the licensing objectives if, on the work being satisfactorily completed, it had to decide whether to grant a premises licence in the form described in the application for the provisional statement:

- to grant the premises licence subject to:

  – conditions that were consistent with the applicant's operating schedule modified to such extent as the licensing authority considered necessary for the promotion of the licensing objectives; and

- any mandatory condition which had to be included in the premises licence;

- to exclude from the scope of the licence any of the licensable activities to which the application related;
- to refuse to specify a person in the licence as the premises supervisor; or
- to reject the application.

Work is 'satisfactorily completed' when it has been completed in a manner which substantially complies with the schedule of work accompanying the application for the provisional statement.

Once it has determined the application the licensing authority must issue the applicant with a provisional statement which gives details of the determination and sets out its reasons for its decision as to the steps, if any, that it would be necessary to take in order to promote the licensing objectives (s.31(3)(c)). The Guidance, para. 5.87 states that the licensing authority should give full and comprehensive reasons for its decision. The licensing authority must send the provisional statement to the applicant forthwith (see **2.9**) on making its decision (Hearings Regulations, reg. 28(1)). The licensing authority must also give a copy of this provisional statement to anyone who made relevant representations and the chief officer of police for each police area in which the premises are situated.

For the purposes of these provisions, 'relevant representations' means representations which:

- are about the likely effect on the licensing objectives of the grant of a premises licence in the form described in the application for the provisional statement, if the work was satisfactorily completed; and
- were made at any time during the period of 28 consecutive days starting on the day after the day on which the applicant gave the application to the licensing authority by (s.31(5)).

If a licensing authority decides that a representation is frivolous or vexatious, it must notify the person who made the representation of both its decision and its reasons for reaching it (s.31(7)).

The applicant for a provisional statement or anyone who has made a relevant representation may appeal against the terms of the provisional statement.

13.10   SUBSEQUENT ACTION AND RESTRICTIONS ON REPRESENTATIONS

Once a provisional statement has been issued, the works may be carried out. Once the works have been completed an application can then be made for a premises licence. Section 32 imposes restrictions on the representations which can be made in respect of this application for a premises licence.

The application for a premises licence must be for the premises or a part of them, of for premises that are substantially the same as the premises or a part of them. This allows an application to be made for a premises licence in respect of only part of the premises for which the provisional statement was issued and the restrictions will apply. The restrictions will also apply if the application is for premises that are substantially the same as the premises for which the provisional statement was issued. There is nothing in the Act or the Guidance as to the meaning of 'substantially the same'.

The restrictions on representations will apply provided:

- the application for the premises licence is in the same form as the licence described in the provisional statement;
- the work described in the schedule of works accompanying the application for that statement has been satisfactorily completed;
- given the information provided in the application for the provisional statement, the person seeking to make a representation could have made the same, or substantially the same, representations about that application but failed, without reasonable excuse, to do so; and
- there has been no material change in circumstances relating either to the premises or to the area in the vicinity of those premises since the provisional statement was made.

It is assumed that if the application relates to different licensable activities, then it will not be in the same form as the licence described in the provisional statement. But it is not clear what the effect of a change in the details of the specified licensable activities, for example by changing the hours for the licensable activities, would be.

The Guidance at para. 5.89 provides that:

> Licensing authorities should exclude representations in these circumstances. It will be important for investment and employment opportunities in their areas for provisional statements to function properly by providing a limited assurance. But it should be recognised that a great deal of time may pass between the issue of a provisional statement and the completion of a premises in accordance with a schedule of works. Genuine and material changes in circumstances may arise during the intervening years.

These provisions therefore give some comfort to the applicant as representations to the grant of a premises licence for the same or similar premises may be excluded if he can show that the objector could have made the same, or substantially the same, representations about the application for the provisional statement but failed to do so without reasonable excuse. It will be a matter for the licensing authority to determine what would be a 'reasonable excuse' in the circumstances of each case. A person may have been in hospital during the period for making representations and therefore unable to make them, for example because he was unconscious or critically ill.

In addition, an applicant will have to show that there has been no material change in circumstances relating either to the premises or to the area in the vicinity of those premises since the provisional statement was made. So if the objector could not have raised such representations at the time of the original application or if there has been a material change to the premises or the area since the provisional statement, then the representations may be made. Whether or not there has been a material change will be a question of fact for the licensing authority to decide on the facts of each case.

A provisional statement does not have a time limit on it but the longer the delay before a premises licence is applied for the greater the potential for representations not to be excluded.

13.11 POWER TO INSPECT THE PREMISES

Section 59 provides that a constable or an authorised person may, at any reasonable time before the determination of an application for a provisional statement, enter the premises to which the application relates to assess the likely effect of the grant of the application on the promotion of the licensing objectives. Anyone who intentionally obstructs an authorised person exercising the power of entry commits an offence, and is liable on summary conviction to a fine not exceeding level 2 on the standard scale. Obstructing a constable exercising the right of entry will be an offence of obstructing a constable in the execution of his duties under the Police Act 1996, s.89(2). A person guilty of such an offence is liable on summary conviction to imprisonment for a term not exceeding one month (this will increase to 51 weeks when the Criminal Justice Act 2003 takes effect) or to a fine not exceeding level 3 on the standard scale, or to both.

CHAPTER 14

Variation of a premises licence

14.1 INTRODUCTION

It is possible for the holder of a premises licence to apply to vary his licence, for example to alter the hours of operation or the authorised licensable activities. These are referred to in the Guidance as 'new and major variations of premises licences'. The approach which the Act takes to such applications is based on the following five main policy aims as set out in the Guidance, para. 5.65:

- the main purpose of the licensing regime is to promote the licensing objectives;
- applicants for premises licences or for major variations of such licences are expected to conduct a thorough risk assessment with regard to the licensing objectives when preparing their applications. This risk assessment will inform any necessary steps to be set out in an operating schedule to promote the four licensing objectives;
- operating schedules, which form part of an application, should be considered by professional experts in the areas concerned, such as the police and environmental health officers, when applications for premises licences and club premises certificates are copied to them by applicants;
- persons living in the vicinity and businesses in the vicinity are free to raise relevant representations, which relate to the promotion of the licensing objectives, about the proposals contained in an application; and
- the role of a licensing authority is primarily to regulate the carrying on of the licensable activity when there are differing specific interests in those activities to ensure that the licensing objectives are promoted in the wider interests of the community.

The Guidance, para. 5.65 expects that when considering applications, a licensing authority will seek to uphold these policy aims.

A licensing authority may also vary a premises licence so that it has effect subject to different conditions in respect of different parts of the premises or different licensable activities. In addition there are separate procedures for changing the name or address of the holder of a premises licence and for changing the designated premises supervisor.

163

A premises licence cannot be varied so as to extend the period for which the licence has effect or to vary substantially the premises to which the licence relates. If such changes are required, an application must be made for a new premises licence.

14.2   APPLYING FOR A VARIATION

The holder of a premises licence may at any time apply to the relevant licensing authority to vary the premises licence. Section 34 provides that an applicant for a variation must submit the following to the relevant licensing authority:

- a completed application form;
- the premises licence, or the appropriate part of it, or if that is not practicable, a statement of the reasons why it cannot be provided; and
- the fee which will be the same as that payable on the grant of a premises licence (see **7.7**).

14.3   THE APPLICATION FORM

An application for a variation must be in the prescribed form which is set out in the Premises Licences Regulations, Sched. 4.

14.3.1   Completing the application form

For information on completing the form see **6.5.2**.

In the opening statement, the name of the applicant or applicants who are applying for the variation should be inserted.

The application form is then divided into five parts, as follows.

Part 1

The applicant must set out the following details of the premises:

- the postal address;
- the telephone number at the premises, if any; and
- the non-domestic rateable value of the premises.

If the premises have no postal address, the location of the premises should be described or the Ordnance Survey map reference should be given.

The non-domestic rateable value of the premises will determine the fee to be paid for the variation. The non-domestic rateable value is based on the annual rent that the premises could have been let for on the open market at a

164

particular date. It can be checked on the Valuation Office Agency website (**www.voa.gov.uk**).

Part 2

Part 2 deals with the details of the applicant. The applicant must give such details as his address, if this is not the same as the premises address, a daytime contact telephone number and an e-mail address (this is optional).

Part 3

Part 3 deals with the proposed variation. The applicant must indicate whether he wants the proposed variation to have effect as soon as possible, or if not, when he wants it to take effect from. If the variation would result in 5,000 or more people attending the premises at any one time, the applicant must state the number expected to attend. The applicant must then briefly describe the nature of the proposed variation. This description should include a description of the premises, for example the type of premises, its general situation and layout and any other information which could be relevant to the licensing objectives. Where the application includes off-supplies of alcohol and the applicant intends to provide a place for consumption of these off-supplies he must include a description of where the place will be and its proximity to the premises.

Part 4

Part 4 is the operating schedule and an applicant must complete those parts which would be subject to change if the application is successful. The applicant must also identify any existing conditions which he believes could be removed if the variation was approved. If the premises licence, or relevant part, cannot be enclosed with the application, an explanation must be given. The applicant must then describe any additional steps he intends to take to promote the four licensing objectives as a result of the proposed variation. Finally there is a checklist for the applicant to complete so that nothing is overlooked, together with a warning that it is an offence, liable on conviction to a fine up to level 5 on the standard scale, under s.158 to make a false statement in or in connection with the application.

Part 5

Part 5 provides for the applicant to sign the form. The form can also be signed by the applicant's solicitor or other duly authorised agent and someone signing on behalf of the applicant must state in what capacity they sign. Where there are joint applicants, both applicants or their respective agents must sign the application form.

14.3.2 Obtaining an application form

A relevant licensing authority must provide an applicant on request with a printed application form; however an electronic version may be provided by a licensing authority on its website which a prospective applicant can download, print off and complete. An electronic copy is also provided on the DCMS website.

14.3.3 Making an application

Regulation 21 of the Premises Licences Regulations provides that an application must be made in writing. For information on submitting the form electronically see **6.5.3**.

14.4 ADVERTISING

The application must be advertised in accordance with the Premises Licences Regulations, reg. 25 (s.17(5)) by displaying a notice at or on the premises and by publishing a notice in a local newspaper.

An applicant must advertise his application by displaying a notice containing prescribed information on the premises for a period of not less than 28 consecutive days starting on the day after the day on which the application was given to the relevant licensing authority.

The notice must be:

- of a size equal to or larger than A4;
- of a pale blue colour; and
- printed legibly in black ink or typed in black in a font of a size equal to or larger than 16 points.

The notice must be displayed prominently at or on the premises to which the application relates where it can be conveniently read from the exterior of the premises. Where the premises cover an area of more than 50 metres square, a further notice in the same form and subject to the same requirements must be displayed every 50 metres along the external perimeter of the premises abutting any highway.

An applicant must publish a notice containing prescribed information in a local newspaper or, if there is none, in a local newsletter, circular or similar document, circulating in the vicinity of the premises on at least one occasion during the 10 working days starting on the day after the day on which the application was given to the relevant licensing authority.

The notices to be displayed at or on the premises and to be published in a local newspaper must:

- briefly describe the proposed variation;
- state the name of the applicant;
- state the postal address of the premises, if any, or if there is no postal address for the premises a description of those premises sufficient to enable the location and extent of the premises to be identified;
- state the postal address and, where applicable, the worldwide web address where the register of the relevant licensing authority is kept and where and when the record of the application may be inspected;
- state the date by which an interested party or a responsible authority may make representations to the relevant licensing authority;
- state that representations shall be made in writing; and
- state that it is an offence knowingly or recklessly to make a false statement in connection with an application and the maximum fine for which a person is liable on summary conviction for the offence.

A suggested form of notice is as shown in Box 14.1.

BOX 14.1   SUGGESTED FORM OF NOTICE OF APPLICATION TO VARY A PREMISES LICENCE

Licensing Act 2003

Notice of application to vary a Premises Licence

PREMISES: [insert address of premises]
Notice is hereby given that [insert the full name of the applicant] has applied to the [insert the full name of the licensing authority] on [insert the date of application to the licensing authority] to vary a premises licence under the Licensing Act 2003.

The proposed variation is: [set out details of the proposed variation].

Any person who wishes to make a representation in relation to this application must give notice in writing of his/her representation by [insert the date by which all relevant representations must be received by the licensing authority, i.e. 28 consecutive days starting on the day after the day on which the application is given to the licensing authority] stating the grounds for making said representation to [insert contact details for the licensing authority]. The public register where applications are available to be viewed by members of the public can be viewed at [insert details]. The Licensing Authority must receive representations by the date given above. The Licensing Authority will have regard to any such representation in considering the application. It is an offence, under section 158 of the Licensing Act 2003, to knowingly or recklessly make a false statement in or in connection with an application to vary a premises licence and the maximum fine on being convicted of such an offence is £5000.

14.5   NOTICE TO RESPONSIBLE AUTHORITIES

An applicant must give notice of his application to each responsible authority by giving each responsible authority a copy of his application together with its accompanying documents, if any. Notice is to be given on the same day as the day on which the application is given to the relevant licensing authority. A responsible authority may then make representations to the relevant licensing authority about the application.

14.6   DETERMINATION OF THE APPLICATION

14.6.1   Preliminary determination

When a licensing authority receives an application for a variation, it must initially determine whether the application has been made properly in accordance with the Act and the Premises Licences Regulations. An incomplete application is invalid and will be returned to the applicant. Any failure to observe the notice requirements will also render the application invalid.

14.6.2   Unopposed applications

Where a licensing authority has received an application to vary a premises licence and is satisfied that the applicant has complied with all the procedural requirements, and no relevant representations have been received there is no need for a hearing and it must grant the application (s.35(2)).

The Guidance at para. 5.67 provides that:

> This should be undertaken as a simple administrative process by the licensing authority's officials by whom the proposals contained in the operating schedule to promote the licensing objectives should be translated into clear and understandable conditions consistent with the proposals in the operating schedule. In these circumstances, it is expected and particularly important that licensing authorities do not attempt to second-guess the views of the professional and expert consultees, for example, those of the police, the fire authority and environmental health authority. Accordingly, if operating schedules are prepared efficiently, often in consultation with responsible authorities, it is expected that the likelihood of hearings being necessary following relevant representations would be significantly reduced.

14.6.3   Applications where representations have been made

Where relevant representations are made by an interested party or a responsible authority, the licensing authority must hold a hearing to consider them, unless the licensing authority, the applicant and each person who has made such representations agree that a hearing is unnecessary (s.35(3)(a)). A hearing must be held within 20 working days beginning with the day after the end of the period during which representations may be made (Hearings Regulations, reg. 5 and Sched. 1, para. 3). Notice of the hearing must be given to the applicant and persons who have made relevant representations no later than 10 working days before the day or the first day on which the hearing is to be held (Hearings Regulations, reg. 6(4) and Sched. 2, para. 3). The applicant must be sent the relevant representations with the notice of hearing (Hearings Regulations, reg. 7(2) and Sched. 3, para. 3).

The hearing should focus only on the steps needed to promote the particular licensing objective which has given rise to the representation. Following the hearing the licensing authority may, having regard to the representations, and if it considers it necessary for the promotion of the licensing objectives, modify the conditions of the licence, or reject the whole or part of the application (s.35(4)). The conditions are treated as being modified if any of them is altered or omitted or any new condition is added. The premises licence may be varied in such a way so that it has effect subject to different conditions in respect of different parts of the premises or different licensable activities (s.36(7)). If the licensing authority does not consider that any steps are necessary, it can grant the variation in accordance with the application.

For these purposes 'relevant representations' means representations which:

- are about the likely effect of the grant of the application on the promotion of the licensing objectives;
- are made by an interested party or a responsible authority within the prescribed period for making them;
- have not been withdrawn; and
- in the case of representations made by an interested party (who is not also a responsible authority), are not, in the opinion of the relevant licensing authority, frivolous or vexatious.

When considering an application, the licensing authority must take into account the mandatory conditions which must be attached to a premises licence.

Section 36(6) prevents a licensing authority from varying a premises licence so as to extend the period of its duration or from making a substantial variation in respect of the premises to which the licence relates.

The Guidance, paras. 5.71 and 5.72 provides the following in respect of specific variations:

5.71 With regard to applications to vary the hours during which alcohol may be sold in shops, stores and supermarkets, the Secretary of State recommends that the norm should be for such premises to be free to provide sales of alcohol for consumption off the premises at any times when the retail outlet is open for shopping unless there are very good reasons for restricting those hours. Where representations are received from the police, for example, in the case of some shops known to be a focus of disorder and disturbance because youths gather there, a limitation may be necessary.

5.72 In the context of variations, which may involve structural alteration to or change of use of the building, it should be noted that the decision of the licensing authority will not exempt an applicant from the need to apply for building control where appropriate.

14.7   NOTIFICATION OF A DECISION

When an application is granted either in whole or in part, the licensing authority must forthwith give notice of this to:

- the applicant:
- any person who made relevant representations in respect of the application; and
- the chief officer of police for the police area, or each police area, in which the premises are situated (s.36(1)).

If relevant representations were made in respect of the application, the notice must state the licensing authority's reasons for its decision as to any steps to be taken for the promotion of the licensing objectives.

The notice must also specify the time when the variation is to take effect (s.36(3)). This will be the time specified in the application if this is after the date when the applicant is given the notice, otherwise it will be such later time as the relevant licensing authority specifies in the notice.

Where an application, or any part of it, is rejected, the licensing authority must forthwith (see **2.9**) give a notice stating its reasons for rejecting the application to:

- the applicant;
- any person who made relevant representations in respect of the application; and
- the chief officer of police for the police area, or each police area, in which the premises are situated (s.36(4)).

Where the licensing authority decides that any representations are frivolous or vexatious, it must notify the person who made them of the reasons for its decision.

14.8   APPEALS

An applicant for a variation may appeal against a decision to reject either the whole or part of his application, or against a decision to modify the conditions of the premises licence. A person who made relevant representations may appeal on the ground that a variation should not have been made or that the licensing authority ought not to have modified the conditions of the premises licence or should have modified them differently. Any appeal must be brought within 21 days beginning with the day on which the appellant was notified of the licensing authority of its decision.

14.9 CHANGE OF NAME OR ADDRESS

Section 33 provides that the holder of a premises licence must, as soon as is reasonably practicable, notify the relevant licensing authority of any change in either his name or address. He must also, as soon as is reasonably practicable, notify the relevant licensing authority of any change in the name or address of the designated premises supervisor unless the designated premises supervisor has already notified the authority. Where the designated premises supervisor under a premises licence is not the holder of the licence, he may notify the relevant licensing authority of any change in his name or address and, if he does, he must, as soon as is reasonably practicable, give the holder of the premises licence a copy of that notice.

In all cases the notification to the relevant licensing authority must be accompanied by the fee of £10.50 and the premises licence, or the appropriate part of the licence, or, if that is not practicable, by a statement of the reasons for the failure to produce the licence or part.

A person commits an offence if he fails, without reasonable excuse, to comply with these requirements, and a person guilty of this offence is liable on summary conviction to a fine not exceeding level 2 on the standard scale.

CHAPTER 15

Review of a premises licence

15.1 INTRODUCTION

The Act provides a procedure whereby a premises licence can be reviewed at any time on the application of an interested party, such as a resident living in the vicinity of the premises, or a responsible authority, such as the police, because of a matter arising at the premises in connection with any of the licensing objectives. This is necessary as otherwise there would be no other opportunity to deal with problems which might arise during the currency of the licence. The Guidance, para. 5.99 provides that:

> The proceedings set out in the 2003 Act for reviewing premises licences represent a key protection for the community where problems associated with crime and disorder, public safety, public nuisance or the protection of children from harm are occurring. It is the existence of these procedures which should, in general, allow licensing authorities to apply a light touch bureaucracy to the grant and variation of premises licences by providing a review mechanism when concerns relating to the licensing objectives arise later in respect of individual premises.

A review of a premises licence will also take place if the police have taken steps to close down the premises for up to 24 hours on the grounds of disorder or noise nuisance.

The Violent Crime Reduction Bill proposes to insert a new review procedure into the Act. This will allow a licensing authority to carry out an accelerated review of licensed premises, and to attach temporary conditions to a premises licence pending a full review of the licence. This procedure would be used where the premises were associated with serious crime and disorder and it is part of the Government's overall aim to reduce violent crime by contributing to changing the culture of carrying weapons – searching pubs and clubs where there is a demonstrable risk will serve as a clear deterrent to carrying knives, and reducing the risk of injury caused by glass – requiring pubs and clubs to use toughened glass where there is a demonstrable risk will help reduce the risk of injury from glassing (Explanatory Notes, para. 26).

15.2   WHO CAN APPLY FOR A REVIEW?

At any time an interested party or a responsible authority may apply to the relevant licensing authority for a review of the licence (s.51). An application for review must relate to the licensing objectives in respect of specific premises rather than general problems in a locality. However, an application for a review need not be the first step where problems arise and the Guidance at para. 5.103 recommends that:

> It would therefore be good practice for authorised persons and responsible authorities to give licence holders early warning of their concerns about problems identified at the premises concerned and of the need for improvement. It is expected that a failure to respond to such warnings would lead to a decision to request a review.

A licensing authority cannot initiate a review. However, where a local authority is both the relevant licensing authority and a responsible authority, it may, in its capacity as a responsible authority, apply for a review of a premises licence and, in its capacity as licensing authority, determine the application (s.53). For example, an environmental health officer may request a review on a matter which relates to the promotion of one or more of the licensing objectives.

15.3   WHEN CAN AN APPLICATION BE MADE?

An application for a review may be made at any time where a premises licence has effect (s.51(1)). It is clear that an application can be made at any time as the Guidance, para. 5.100 states:

> At any stage, following the grant of a premises licence, a responsible authority, such as the police or the fire authority, or an interested party, such as a resident living in the vicinity of the premises, may ask the licensing authority to review the licence because of a matter arising at the premises in connection with any of the four licensing objectives.

15.4   MAKING AN APPLICATION

An application for a review of a premises licence must be made to the relevant licensing authority (s.51(1)). There is no fee payable for a review.

A copy of the application must also be sent to the holder of the premises licence and each of the responsible authorities. The application must also be advertised (see **15.6**).

15.5   THE APPLICATION FORM

An application for a review must be in the prescribed form which is set out in the Premises Licences Regulations, Sched. 8.

15.5.1   Completing the application form

For information on completing the form see **6.5.2**.

In the opening statement, the name of the applicant or applicants who are applying for the review should be inserted.

The application form is then divided into three parts.

Part 1

The applicant must set out the postal address of the premises. If the premises have no postal address, the location of the premises should be described or the Ordnance Survey map reference should be given. The name of the premises licence holder and the number of the premises licence should then be given, if these are known.

Part 2

Part 2 deals with the details of the applicant and the reason for the review. The applicant must state whether he is an interested party or a responsible authority. In the former case he must indicate how he claims to be an interested party. He must then give such details as his name and address, telephone number and confirmation, where relevant, that he is at least 18 years old.

The applicant must then state which of the licensing objectives the application relates to, state the grounds for review and provide as much information as possible to support the application, such as details of problems which have occurred.

The form also asks whether the applicant has applied for a review in relation to the premises before and, if so, the date of that application.

If the applicant has made representations before in relation to the premises he must set them out and when they were made.

Part 2 also includes a checklist for the applicant so that nothing is overlooked, together with a warning that it is an offence, liable on conviction to a fine up to level 5 on the standard scale, under s.158 to make a false statement in or in connection with the application

Part 3

Part 3 provides for the applicant to sign the form. The form can also be signed by the applicant's solicitor or other duly authorised agent, and someone signing on behalf of the applicant must state in what capacity they sign. Where there are joint applicants, both applicants or their respective agents must sign the application form.

15.5.2   Obtaining an application form

A relevant licensing authority must provide an applicant on request with a printed application form; however an electronic version may be provided by a licensing authority on its website which a prospective applicant can download, print off and complete. An electronic copy is also provided on the DCMS website.

15.5.3   Making an application

Regulation 21 of the Premises Licences Regulations provides that an application must be made in writing. However, for information on making an electronic application see **6.5.3**.

15.5.4   Notice to other persons

The applicant must give a copy of the application form together with any accompanying documents to each responsible authority and to the holder of the premises licence on the same day as it is given to the licensing authority. It must also be advertised (see **15.6**). An interested party or a responsible authority may then make a representation to the licensing authority within the period of 28 days starting on the day after the day on which the application for review was given to the licensing authority.

15.6   ADVERTISING THE APPLICATION

Once a licensing authority has received an application for review, it must advertise the application by displaying prominently for a period of no less than 28 consecutive days starting on the day after the day on which the application was given to the licensing authority a notice which is:

- of a size equal to or larger than A4;
- of a pale blue colour; and
- printed legibly in black ink or typed in black in a font of a size equal to or larger than 16 points.

The notice must be displayed:

- at, on or near the site of the premises to which the application relates where it can conveniently be read from the exterior of the premises by the public and in the case of a premises covering an area of more than 50 metres square, one further notice in the same form and subject to the same requirements shall be displayed every 50 metres along the external perimeter of the premises abutting any highway; and
- at the offices, or the main offices, of the licensing authority in a central and conspicuous place.

If the licensing authority has a website which it uses to advertise applications it receives, then a notice of the application for review must also be published on that website.

The notices displayed on the premises and on the website must state:

- the address of the premises about which an application for a review has been made;
- the dates between which interested parties and responsible authorities may make representations to the relevant licensing authority;
- the grounds of the application for review;
- the postal address and, where relevant, the worldwide web address where the register of the relevant licensing authority is kept and where and when the grounds for the review may be inspected; and
- that it is an offence knowingly or recklessly to make a false statement in connection with an application and the maximum fine for which a person is liable on summary conviction for the offence.

15.7 REJECTION OF THE APPLICATION

A licensing authority which receives an application for a review must initially consider whether the grounds for review stated in the application are relevant to the licensing objectives. Any ground for review specified in the application may, at any time, be rejected by the licensing authority if it is satisfied that the ground is not relevant to one or more of the licensing objectives, or, in the case of an application made by an interested party, that the ground is frivolous or vexatious, or is a repetition.

A ground will not be relevant if it does not relate to one or more of the licensing objectives. Rejection of a ground because it is frivolous or vexatious will be similar to a rejection of a relevant representation by an interested party on an application for a premises licence.

A ground for review will be a repetition if:

- it is identical or substantially similar to:
  - a ground for review specified in an earlier application for review made in respect of the same premises licence which has been determined; or
  - representations considered by the relevant licensing authority before it originally granted the premises licence; or
  - representations which would have been so considered but for the fact that they were excluded as irrelevant, vexatious or frivolous; and
- a reasonable interval has not elapsed since that earlier application for review or the grant of the licence.

'Substantially similar' has not been interpreted in the Act or the Guidance. It is suggested that in order to be 'substantially similar' a ground will not only have to relate to the same licensing objective but also to the same facet of the objective, for example a public nuisance caused by noise from music played in the licensed premises. The onus is on the licensing authority to demonstrate that the ground is substantially similar.

If a ground is found to be identical or substantially similar, this does not mean that it will automatically be ruled invalid. This will only occur where a reasonable interval has not elapsed since the ground was previously considered. The Guidance indicates that there should usually be an interval of 12 months. The Guidance at para. 5.105 provides:

> Licensing authorities are expected to be aware of the need to prevent attempts to review licences merely as a second bite of the cherry following the failure of representations to persuade the licensing authority on earlier occasions. It is for licensing authorities themselves to judge what should be regarded as a reasonable interval in these circumstances. However, the Secretary of State recommends that more than one review originating from an interested party should not be permitted within a period of twelve months on similar grounds save in compelling circumstances or where it arises following a closure order.

If a licensing authority rejects a ground for review, it must notify the applicant in writing of its decision as soon as reasonably practicable. If the ground was rejected because it was frivolous or vexatious, it must include its reasons for rejecting the ground. Where an application is rejected because the ground is frivolous, vexatious or a repetition, the written notification must be given as soon as is reasonably practicable.

If an applicant has raised more than one ground for review in his application, and not all of them are rejected, then the application will be treated as only being rejected in respect of the ground which has been rejected. The application will still be valid in relation to any grounds which have not been rejected. Even though one of the grounds stated in the application may have been rejected the obligation to give notice still applies. By way of example, if a licensing authority receives an application which sets out two grounds for review and it decides that one of the grounds is frivolous it must give notice of this to the applicant together with the reasons for its decision, and then proceed to determine the application on the basis of the remaining ground.

15.8 DETERMINATION OF THE APPLICATION FOR REVIEW

Once the 28-day period in which representations can be made has come to an end, the licensing authority must hold a hearing within 20 working days beginning with the day after the end of that 28-day period to consider the application and any relevant representations (Hearings Regulations, reg. 5 and Sched. 1, para. 7). See **15.10** for when a representation will be a relevant representation. Notice of the hearing must be given to the premises licence holder, anyone who has made a relevant representation and the person who has applied for the review no later than 10 working days before the day or the first day on which the hearing is to be held (Hearings Regulations, reg. 6(4) and Sched. 2, para. 7). There is no provision for dispensing with the hearing if all the parties consider it unnecessary.

The premises licence holder must be given the relevant representations with the notice of hearing (Hearings Regulations, reg. 7(2) and Sched. 3, para. 7). The Guidance, para. 5.106 reinforces this by stating that:

> The Secretary of State considers it particularly important that the premises licence holder is fully aware of the representations made in respect of the premises, any evidence supporting the representations and that he or his legal representatives has therefore been able to prepare a response.

When determining the application, the licensing authority must have regard to the application and any relevant representations. It may decide that no action is required in order to promote the licensing objectives, or that informal action should be taken, for example by giving the holder of the premises licence an informal warning or a recommendation to improve matters within a specified period of time. The Guidance, para 5.108 expects that:

> licensing authorities will regard such warnings as an important mechanism for ensuring that the licensing objectives are effectively promoted and that warnings should be issued in writing to the holder of the licence. However, where responsible authorities like the police or environmental health officers have already issued warnings requiring improvement – either orally or in writing – that have failed as part of their own stepped approach to concerns, licensing authorities should not merely repeat that approach.

If, following the hearing, the licensing authority considers that formal action is required, it may take such of the following steps, if any, which it considers necessary for the promotion of the licensing objectives:

- to modify the conditions of the licence. This will involve any of the conditions of the licence being altered or omitted or the addition of a new condition, for example, by reducing the hours of opening or by requiring door supervisors at particular times;
- to exclude a licensable activity from the scope of the licence, for example, by excluding the playing of live music;
- to remove the designated premises supervisor, for example, because the licensing authority considers that the problems are due to poor management;
- to suspend the licence for a period not exceeding three months; or
- to revoke the licence.

When reaching its decision, the licensing authority must have regard to the requirements in the Act to include mandatory conditions in the licence.

If a licensing authority decides that none of these steps is necessary, then it need take no action.

Where a licensing authority takes one of the above steps its decision will not take effect until the end of the period for appealing against the decision, or if the decision is appealed against, until the appeal is disposed of. An appeal may be made by the holder of the licence, the applicant or any person who made relevant representations within 21 days.

If a licensing authority decides to modify the conditions of the premises licence or to exclude a licensable activity from the scope of the licence, it may provide that the modification or exclusion is to have temporary effect for a period not exceeding three months, as it may specify.

In deciding which of its powers to invoke, the Guidance, para. 5.110 states that:

> it is expected that licensing authorities should so far as possible seek to establish the cause or causes of the concerns which the representations identify. The remedial action taken should generally be directed at these causes and should always be no more than a necessary and proportionate response. For example, licensing authorities should be alive to the possibility that the removal and replacement of the designated premises supervisor may be sufficient to remedy a problem where the cause of the identified problem directly relates to poor management decisions made by that individual. Equally, it may emerge that poor management is a direct reflection of poor company practice or policy and the mere removal of the designated premises supervisor may be an inadequate response to the problems presented. Indeed, where subsequent review hearings are generated by representations, it should be rare merely to remove a succession of designated premises supervisors as this would be a clear indication of deeper problems which impact upon the licensing objectives.

Where the licensing authority is conducting a review on the ground that the premises have been used for criminal purposes, the Guidance at para. 5.113 makes it clear that only steps necessary in connection with the premises licence for the promotion of the crime prevention objective should be taken. It goes on to state:

It is important to recognise that certain criminal activity or associated problems may be taking place or have taken place despite the best efforts of the licensee and the staff working at the premises and despite full compliance with the conditions attached to the licence. In such circumstances, the licensing authority is still empowered to take any necessary steps to remedy the problems. The licensing authority's duty is to take steps with a view to the promotion of the licensing objectives in the interests of the wider community and not those of the individual holder of the premises licence.

There are certain criminal activities that may arise in connection with licensed premises, which the Guidance considers should be treated particularly seriously. These are set out in para. 5.115 and are where the licensed premises are used:

- for the sale and distribution of Class A drugs and the laundering of the proceeds of drugs crime;
- for the sale and distribution of illegal firearms;
- for the evasion of copyright in respect of pirated or unlicensed films and music, which does considerable damage to the industries affected;
- for the purchase and consumption of alcohol by minors which impacts on the health, educational attainment, employment prospects and propensity for crime of young people;
- for prostitution or the sale of unlawful pornography;
- by organised groups of paedophiles to groom children;
- as the base for the organisation of criminal activity, particularly by gangs;
- for the organisation of racist activity or the promotion of racist attacks;
- for unlawful gaming and gambling;
- for the sale of smuggled tobacco and alcohol.

Paragraph 5.116 goes on to state:

It is envisaged that licensing authorities, the police and other law enforcement agencies, which are responsible authorities, will use the review procedures effectively to deter such activities and crime. Where reviews arise and the licensing authority determines that the crime prevention objective is being undermined through the premises being used to further crimes, it is expected that revocation of the licence – even in the first instance – should be seriously considered. We would also encourage liaison with the local Crime and Disorder Reduction Partnership.

Finally in para. 5.117 it provides that:

It should be noted that it is unlawful to discriminate or to refuse service on grounds of race or by displaying racially discriminatory signs on the premises. Representations made about such activity from responsible authorities or interested parties would be relevant to the promotion of the crime prevention objective and justifiably give rise to a review.

15.9   NOTIFICATION OF THE DECISION

Once an application for a review has been determined, the licensing authority must notify the following of its decision and its reasons:

- the premises licence holder;
- the applicant;
- any person who made relevant representations; and
- the chief officer of police for the police area (or each police area) in which the premises are situated.

15.10   RELEVANT REPRESENTATIONS

For the purposes of a review, s. 52(7) and (8) provide that representations are relevant if they:

- are relevant to one or more of the licensing objectives;
- are made by the holder of the premises licence, a responsible authority or an interested party within the 28-day period prescribed for making representations;
- have not been withdrawn; and
- if they are made by an interested party, who is not also a responsible authority, are not, in the opinion of the relevant licensing authority, frivolous or vexatious.

Where the licensing authority decides that a representation is frivolous or vexatious, it must notify the person who made it of its reasons for its decision.

Thus, for the purposes of a review, a representation must be relevant to one or more of the licensing objectives. This is different from representations made in respect of the grant or variation of a premises licence. In those situations a representation must be 'about the likely effect of the grant . . . on the promotion of the licensing objectives'. Thus it would seem that the requirement on review is less onerous than those on a grant or variation.

15.11   INSPECTION OF PREMISES

Section 59 provides that a constable or an authorised person may, at any reasonable time before the determination of an application for review, enter the premises to which the application relates to assess the effect of the activities authorised by the premises licence on the promotion of the licensing objectives.

An authorised person who is exercising the power to enter the premises must, if so requested, produce evidence of his authority to exercise the power (s.59(3)). Anyone who intentionally obstructs an authorised person exercising the power of entry commits an offence, and is liable on summary conviction to a fine not exceeding level 2 on the standard scale (s.59(5) and (6)).

CHAPTER 16

Transfer of a premises licence

16.1 INTRODUCTION

Where a business involving licensable activities is sold, the new owner will need to apply to have the premises licence transferred to him. A transfer of the licence will only change the identity of the holder of the licence and will not alter the licence in any way, and it is expected that most applications will be dealt with by a very simple administrative process.

16.2 WHO CAN APPLY FOR A TRANSFER?

Under s.42 any person who is eligible to apply for a premises licence (see **7.3**) may apply to have the licence transferred to him. Where an applicant is an individual he must be aged 18 or over.

16.3 APPLYING FOR A TRANSFER

In order to apply for a transfer, an applicant must submit the following to the relevant licensing authority:

- a completed application form. The application form is prescribed and is set out in the Premises Licences Regulations, Sched. 6;
- the premises licence, or if that is not practicable, a statement of the reasons why it cannot be provided;
- the consent of the current licence holder, or if not available, a statement of the reasons why it cannot be provided and of the steps taken to try and obtain it. The consent must be in the prescribed form and is set out in the Premises Licences Regulations, Sched. 11, part B; and
- the fee of £23.

16.3.1   Completing the application form

For information on completing the form see **6.5.2**. Care must be taken when completing the application form as any mistakes will be built into the new licence.

In the opening statement, the name of the applicant or applicants who are applying to transfer the premises licence should be inserted together with the premises licence number.

The application form is then divided into four parts.

Part 1

The applicant must set out the postal address of the premises, the telephone number at the premises, if any, and a brief description of the premises. If the premises have no postal address, the location of the premises should be described or the Ordnance Survey map reference should be given. The name of the current premises licence holder must also be given.

Part 2

Part 2 deals with details of the applicant. The applicant must state in which capacity he is applying for the premises licence to be transferred to him, and if he is applying as an individual, a limited company, a partnership, an unincorporated association or a statutory corporation, he must confirm that he is carrying on or proposing to carry on a business which involves the use of the premises for licensable activities, or that he is making the application pursuant to a statutory function or a function discharged by virtue of Her Majesty's prerogative.

The applicant must then give further details such as his name and address, telephone number, e-mail address (this is optional) and confirmation, where relevant, that he is at least 18 years old. Where the applicant is not an individual it must give details of its name, address, registered number, telephone number, e-mail address (this is optional) and a description of itself, for example whether it is a limited company, partnership or unincorporated association.

Part 3

Part 3 asks whether the applicant is the holder of the premises licence under an interim authority notice, whether the applicant wishes the transfer to have immediate effect and if not when he would like the transfer to take effect. It asks for the consent form signed by the existing premises licence holder, and if this is not available a statement of the reasons why it is not enclosed must be given together with details of the steps the applicant has taken to try and obtain the consent. The applicant must confirm that if the licence is transferred he would be able to use the premises during the application period for the licensable activities authorised by the licence. The applicant must enclose the premises licence and if he cannot do this must set out the reasons why it is not enclosed. The form also includes a checklist for the applicant to complete so that nothing is overlooked, together with a warning that it is an offence, liable on conviction to a fine up to level 5 on the standard scale, under s.158 to make a false statement in or in connection with the application.

Part 4

The final part of the form makes provision for the applicant to sign the form. The application form must be signed. The form can also be signed by the applicant's solicitor or other duly authorised agent, and someone signing on behalf of the applicant must state in what capacity they sign. Where there are joint applicants, both applicants or their respective agents must sign the application form.

16.3.2   Obtaining an application form

A relevant licensing authority must provide an applicant on request with a printed application form; however an electronic version may be provided by a licensing authority on its website which a prospective applicant can download, print off and complete. An electronic copy is also provided on the DCMS website.

16.3.3   Making an application

For details on making the application electronically see **6.5.3**.

16.3.4   Notice to the police

An applicant must give notice of his application to the chief officer of police for the police area, or each police area, in which the premises are situated by giving the chief officer of police a copy of the application together with its accompanying documents, if any, on the same day as the day on which the application is given to the relevant licensing authority.

16.3.5   Police objections

If the chief officer of police is satisfied that the exceptional circumstances of the case are such that granting the application would undermine the crime prevention objective, he must give notice of objection to the relevant licensing authority. This notice must set out the reasons why he has decided to object. It must be given within 14 days beginning with the day on which the chief officer of police is notified of the transfer application.

The Guidance anticipates that such objections are expected to be rare and will arise where the police have evidence that the business or individuals seeking to hold the licence or business or individuals linked to such persons are involved in crime (or disorder); for example, the police might seek to prevent a company having a licence transferred to it in respect of licensed premises if they had evidence that the premises might be used for money laundering (para. 5.80).

Objections should not be used routinely to vet applicants and para. 5.81 of the Guidance states:

> It is stressed that such objections (and therefore ... hearings) should only arise in truly exceptional circumstances. If the licensing authority believes that the police are using this mechanism to vet transfer applicants routinely and to seek hearings as a fishing expedition to inquire into applicants' backgrounds, it is expected that they would raise the matter immediately with the chief officer of police.

16.4 INTERIM EFFECT

It is possible under s.43 for an applicant to request that his application for a transfer is given immediate effect. This will then allow the business carried on at the premises to continue during the period beginning with when the application is received by the relevant licensing authority, and ending either when the licence is transferred following the grant of the application, or if the application is rejected when the applicant is notified of the rejection, or when the application is withdrawn. Licensable activities can thus be carried on pending the determination of the transfer application.

Where a request has been made for the transfer to have immediate effect the applicant must forthwith (see **2.9**) notify any designated premises supervisor of the application (unless the applicant is the designated premises supervisor). He must also notify the designated premises supervisor if the application for transfer is subsequently granted.

An application for a transfer to have immediate effect may usually be made only with the consent of the holder of the premises licence. The form of consent is prescribed and is set out in the Premises Licences Regulations, Sched. 11, part B. Consent is not required where the applicant is the holder of the premises licence by virtue of an interim authority notice. If the consent of the holder of the premises licence is not available then the relevant licensing authority must exempt the applicant from the requirement to obtain the holder's consent if the applicant shows to the authority's satisfaction:

- that he has taken all reasonable steps to obtain that consent; and
- that, if the application were treated as though the transfer had interim effect, he would be in a position to use the premises during the application period for the licensable activity or activities authorised by the premises licence.

Where the relevant licensing authority refuses to exempt an applicant from having to obtain the consent of the holder of the premises licence, it must notify the applicant of its reasons for that decision. In this situation, the applicant ceases to be treated as the holder of the licence and the licence reverts to the person who held it before the application was made.

16.5   DETERMINATION OF THE APPLICATION

If an application has been made in accordance with the statutory provisions, it will be granted (s.44). The Guidance, para. 5.79 states that 'In the vast majority of cases, it is expected that a transfer will be a very simple administrative process . . .'.

However, if the application for transfer includes a request for it to be given immediate effect, the licensing authority must reject the application unless the holder of the premises licence gives his consent to the transfer or the relevant licensing authority has exempted the applicant from having to obtain the consent.

The licensing authority must exempt the applicant from the requirement to obtain the consent of the holder of the premises licence if the applicant shows to the authority's satisfaction:

- that he has taken all reasonable steps to obtain that consent; and
- that, if the application were granted, he would be in a position to use the premises during the application period for the licensable activity or activities authorised by the premises licence.

If the relevant licensing authority refuses to exempt an applicant, it must notify the applicant of its reasons for that decision.

Where a notice is given by the chief officer of police that the crime prevention objective would be undermined if the application were granted, the licensing authority must hold a hearing to consider it, unless the authority, the applicant and the chief officer of police who gave the notice agree that a hearing is unnecessary. The hearing must be held within 20 working days beginning with the day after the end of the 14-day period within which the chief officer of police may object (Hearings Regulations, reg. 5 and Sched. 1, para. 5). Notice of the hearing must be given to the applicant for the transfer,

187

the chief officer of police and the premises licence holder no later than 10 working days before the day or the first day on which the hearing is to be held (Hearings Regulations, reg. 6(4) and Sched. 2, para. 5). Both the applicant and the holder of the premises licence must be given a copy of the police notice of objection with the notice of the hearing (Hearings Regulations, reg. 7(2) and Sched. 3, para. 5).

At the hearing, the licensing authority can only consider the issue of the crime prevention objective. The burden is on the police to show that there are good grounds for believing that the transfer of the licence would undermine this. The licensing authority must reject the application if it considers it necessary to do so for the promotion of the crime prevention objective. An applicant may appeal against the rejection to the magistrates' court. The chief officer of police may also appeal if the transfer is granted despite his objection.

16.6   NOTIFICATION OF THE DETERMINATION

Once an application for a transfer has been determined by being either granted or rejected, the relevant licensing authority must forthwith (see **2.9**) notify the applicant, and the chief officer of police for the police area, or each police area, in which the premises are situated. The notice must be accompanied by information regarding the right of a party to appeal against the decision.

If the chief officer of police gave notice that the crime prevention objective would be undermined if the application were granted and this notice has not been withdrawn, the notice given by the licensing authority must state the licensing authority's reasons for granting or rejecting the application.

If the application has been granted, the notice must specify the time when the transfer is to take effect, and this must be either the time specified in the application or, if that time is before the applicant is given that notice, such later time as the relevant licensing authority specifies in the notice. So by way of example, if the applicant states that the transfer is to take effect on 1 September and the notice is not given until 5 September, the licensing authority must specify the date on which the transfer is to become effective.

If the application is granted, the licensing authority must also give a copy of the notice:

- to the holder of the licence immediately before the application was granted; or
- if the application was one which has been given interim effect, to the holder of the licence immediately before the application was made (if any).

If the application is rejected, the licensing authority must also give a copy of the notice to the holder of the premises licence, if there is one.

In addition, if the applicant is not the designated premises supervisor, the applicant must notify the designated premises supervisor of the application. If the application is granted, the applicant must notify the designated premises supervisor of the transfer. An applicant will commit an offence if he fails, without reasonable excuse, to comply with these requirements and a person guilty of such an offence will be liable on summary conviction to a fine not exceeding level 3 on the standard scale.

CHAPTER 17

Clubs

17.1 INTRODUCTION

Club premises to which the public have restricted access and where alcohol is supplied other than for profit are treated differently under the Act from other licensed premises. In essence the Act preserves the position under the Licensing Act 1964 as it applied to 'registered members clubs'. These clubs are organisations where members have joined together for particular social, sporting or political purposes and then combined to buy alcohol in bulk as members of the organisation for supply in that context. Examples include Labour, Conservative and Liberal Clubs, the Royal British Legion and other ex-services clubs, working men's clubs, miners' welfare institutes and social and sports clubs, such as rugby and cricket clubs.

There are technically no sales by retail of alcohol by the club at such premises except to a guest when he purchases alcohol. Where a member purchases alcohol, there can be no sale by retail as each member owns part of the alcohol stock, and so the money passing across the bar is merely a mechanism to preserve equity between members where one may consume more than another (*Graff* v. *Evans* (1882) 9 QBD 373).

Under the Act members' clubs must satisfy certain conditions in order to be a qualifying club so that they can then apply to the licensing authority for a club premises certificate. A club premises certificate means that a qualifying club is entitled to benefits including:

- the authority to supply alcohol to members and to sell it to members' guests on the premises to which the certificate relates without the need for any member or employee to hold a personal licence;
- no requirement to specify a designated premises supervisor;
- more limited rights of entry for the police and authorised persons as club premises are private and not generally open to the public;
- the premises not being subject to police powers of instant closure on grounds of disorder and noise nuisance (except when being used under the authority of a temporary event notice or premises licence) because they operate under their own codes of discipline and rules which are rigorously enforced; and

190

- not being subject to potential orders of the magistrates' court for the closure of all licensed premises in an area when disorder is happening or expected.

It is important to distinguish between a qualifying club and a proprietary club. The latter is a commercially run club and so will require a premises licence. The distinction was summarised in the *Report of the Departmental Committee on Liquor Licensing* Cmnd 5154, 1972, para. 1.30 as follows:

> Proprietary clubs are clubs in which the premises and stock belong to a proprietor or group of proprietors. If the stock of liquor belongs to the proprietor, a 'sale' takes place when a member orders and pays for a drink ... In the case of 'members' clubs, all the property, including the stock of liquor, belongs to the members jointly, and when a member obtains liquor, even on payment, the position is that a 'supply' rather than a sale takes place.

A qualifying club can always apply for a premises licence if it decides that it wishes to offer its facilities commercially to members of the general public, including the sale of alcohol to them. However this would not be necessary if the club wished to sell alcohol on a temporary basis to the general public. An individual on behalf of a club may give temporary event notices in respect of the premises to cover a period of up to 96 hours on up to 12 occasions each calendar year so long as no more than 499 people attend the event and subject to an overall maximum duration in the year of 15 days. On such occasions the club may then sell alcohol to the public or hire out its premises for use by the public.

Under the Licensing Act 1964 registered members clubs were allowed to sell alcohol to minors and allow them to consume it on the club premises. The Act now prohibits this and the sale or supply of alcohol to children in such clubs is now unlawful.

17.2 CLUB PREMISES CERTIFICATE

A club premises certificate is defined in s.60 as a certificate granted by the relevant licensing authority under part 4 of the Act in respect of premises occupied by, and habitually used for the purposes of, a club and which certifies:

- that the premises may be used by the club for one or more qualifying club activities specified in the certificate; and
- that the club is a qualifying club in relation to each of those activities.

The qualifying club activities are set out in s.1(2) as follows:

- the supply of alcohol by or on behalf of a club to, or to the order of, a member of the club;

- the sale by retail of alcohol by or on behalf of a club to a guest of a member of the club for consumption on the premises where the sale takes place; and
- the provision of regulated entertainment where that provision is by or on behalf of a club for members of the club or members of the club and their guests.

The certificate will specify which of these qualifying club activities can be carried out. These will also be specified in the club rules.

17.3 QUALIFYING CLUBS

Section 61 provides that a club will be a qualifying club in relation to the provision of regulated entertainment if it satisfies the conditions in s.62. A club that wishes to be a qualifying club in relation to the supply of alcohol to members or guests must also satisfy the conditions in s.64 in addition to those in s.62.

17.3.1 The general conditions for a qualifying club

Section 62 sets out five general conditions which a club must satisfy in order to be a qualifying club as follows:

- the club rules provide that persons may not be admitted to membership, or be admitted as candidates for membership to any of the privileges of membership, without an interval of at least two days between their nomination or application for membership and their admission;
- the club rules provide that persons becoming members without prior nomination or application may not be admitted to the privileges of membership without an interval of at least two days between their becoming members and their admission;
- the club is established and conducted in good faith as a club (see **17.5**);
- the club has at least 25 members; and
- alcohol is not supplied, or intended to be supplied, to members on the premises otherwise than by or on behalf of the club, i.e. the bar is operated by the club rather than by a third party under a franchise or similar arrangement.

17.3.2 Additional conditions for the supply of alcohol

Section 64 sets out the following additional conditions which need to met by a club which intends to supply alcohol to its members and guests:

- so far as it is not managed by the club in general meeting or otherwise by the general body of members, the purchase of alcohol for the club, and the supply of alcohol by the club, are managed by a committee whose members are members of the club who have attained the age of 18 years, and who are elected by the members of the club (this condition does not apply to industrial and provident societies, friendly societies, etc. – see **17.6**);

- no arrangements are, or are intended to be, made for any person to receive at the expense of the club any commission, percentage or similar payment on, or with reference to, purchases of alcohol by the club; and
- no arrangements are, or are intended to be, made for any person directly or indirectly to derive any pecuniary benefit from the supply of alcohol by or on behalf of the club to members or guests, apart from a benefit accruing to the club as a whole, or any benefit which a person derives indirectly by reason of the supply giving rise or contributing to a general gain from the carrying on of the club.

17.4 ASSOCIATE MEMBERS

In addition to admitting its own members and their guests, a qualifying club can admit an associate member and his guests. This reflects the traditional arrangements whereby a club makes its facilities available to members of other clubs on a reciprocal basis, for example, where clubs are part of the Club and Institute Union. A person is an associate member of a club if in accordance with the club rules, he is admitted to its premises as being a member of another club which is a recognised club (s.67).

A recognised club is defined in s.193 as a club where:

- the club rules provide that persons may not be admitted to membership, or be admitted, as candidates for membership, to any of the privileges of membership, without an interval of at least two days between their nomination or application for membership and their admission;
- the club rules provide that persons becoming members without prior nomination or application may not be admitted to the privileges of membership without an interval of at least two days between their becoming members and their admission; and
- the club is established and conducted in good faith as a club (see **17.5**).

The supply and sale of alcohol under a club premises certificate can therefore be made to club members and guests, and to associate members and guests. It would seem that it cannot be supplied to anyone else who might be 'visiting' the club, for example a member of the public paying a green fee to a golf club in order to play a round of golf who wishes to buy a drink at the bar after he has played his round, though the Government's view is that such 'visitors' would be allowed to purchase alcohol (see HC Deb, vol. 423, col. 3, 28 June 2004). A solution might be to make such a person a 'temporary member' of the club but as at least two days must elapse between nomination and admission of members this would not be practical for the golfer who turned up on the day to play his round and enjoy a drink afterwards.

17.5   THE ESTABLISHMENT AND CONDUCT OF A CLUB IN GOOD FAITH

The third requirement for a qualifying club is that it is established and conducted in good faith as a club. In determining whether this is the case, a licensing authority must under s.63 take into account:

- any arrangements restricting the club's freedom of purchase of alcohol;
- any provision in the rules, or arrangements, under which money or property of the club, or any gain arising from the carrying on of the club, is or may be applied otherwise than for the benefit of the club as a whole or for charitable, benevolent or political purposes;
- the arrangements for giving members information about the finances of the club;
- the books of account and other records kept to ensure the accuracy of the financial information given to members; and
- the nature of the premises occupied by the club.

If a licensing authority decides that a club does not satisfy the requirement that it is established and conducted in good faith, the authority must give the club notice of its decision and its reasons for it (s.63(3)). There are no provisions about the form of this notice but presumably it must be in writing.

17.6   INDUSTRIAL AND PROVIDENT SOCIETIES

Special provision is made for clubs which are registered societies within the meaning of the Industrial and Provident Societies Act 1965, registered societies within the meaning of the Friendly Societies Act 1974, and registered friendly societies within the meaning of the Friendly Societies Act 1992. These clubs are mainly working men's clubs.

Such clubs will be taken to satisfy the condition in s.64 that the purchase and supply of alcohol are managed by a committee elected by the members of the club if the purchase and supply are under the control of the members or of a committee appointed by the members (s.65(2)). Thus where the committee is appointed rather than elected such a club is eligible to apply for a club premises certificate.

The Act also applies to an incorporated friendly society as it applies to a club (s.65(4)). An 'incorporated friendly society' has the same meaning as in the Friendly Societies Act 1992. A friendly society is a voluntary mutual organisation whose main purpose is to assist members, usually financially, during sickness, unemployment or retirement and to provide life assurance. This means that the premises of the society are treated as the premises of a club, the members of the society are treated as the members of the club and anything done by or on behalf of the society is treated as done by or on behalf of the club. When deciding whether an incorporated friendly society is a qualifying club in relation to a qualifying club activity, the society is to be taken to satisfy the conditions in s.62 that it is established and conducted in good faith, and that alcohol is not supplied, or intended to be supplied, to members on the premises otherwise than by or on behalf of the club, together with the additional conditions in s.64.

17.7 MINERS' WELFARE INSTITUTES

Special provision is made for miners' welfare institutes. The Act applies to a miners' welfare institute as it applies to a club. This means that the premises of the institute are treated as the premises of a club, the persons enrolled as members of the institute are treated as the members of the club, and anything done by or on behalf of the trustees or managers in carrying on the institute is treated as done by or on behalf of the club (s.66(1)). When deciding whether a miners' welfare institute is a qualifying club in relation to a qualifying club activity, the institute is to be taken to satisfy the conditions in s.62 that it is established and conducted in good faith, that it has at least 25 members and that alcohol is not supplied, or intended to be supplied, to members on the premises otherwise than by or on behalf of the club, together with the additional conditions in s.64 (s.66(2)).

For the purposes of these provisions 'miners' welfare institute' means an association organised for the social well-being and recreation of persons employed in or about coalmines, or of such persons in particular, and the Act will apply to a miners' welfare institute if the institute satisfies one of the following conditions:

- the institute is managed by a committee or board, and at least two-thirds of the committee or board consists partly of persons appointed or nominated, or appointed or elected from among persons nominated, by one or more licensed operators within the meaning of the Coal Industry Act 1994, and partly of persons appointed or nominated, or appointed or elected from among persons nominated, by one or more organisations representing persons employed in or about coal mines;
- the institute is managed by a committee or board, but the appointment or nomination of board members as provided for in the previous condition is not practicable or would not be appropriate, and at least two-thirds of the committee or board consists partly of persons employed, or formerly employed, in or about coal mines, and partly of persons appointed by the

Coal Industry Social Welfare Organisation or a body or person to which the functions of that Organisation have been transferred under the Miners' Welfare Act 1952, s.12(3); or

- the premises of the institute are held on trusts to which the Recreational Charities Act 1958, s.2 applies.

17.8 APPLICATION FOR A CLUB PREMISES CERTIFICATE

A club may apply for a club premises certificate in respect of any premises which are occupied by, and habitually used for the purposes of, the club (s.71(1)). This seems to mean that a club may apply for a club premises certificate for more than one premises, which was possible under the Licensing Act 1964.

An application for a club premises certificate must be made to the relevant licensing authority (s.71(2)). This will be the licensing authority within whose area the club premises are situated. In addition, a copy of the application must be sent to each of the appropriate responsible authorities (see **7.9**).

The procedure for applying for a club premises certificate is very similar to that for a premises licence, and the Guidance, para. 9.11 states:

> The arrangements for applying for or seeking to vary club premises certificates are extremely similar to those in respect of a premises licence. Licensing authorities should therefore look to Chapter 5 of this Guidance on the handling of such applications and to Chapter 6 in respect of hours of opening. In those Chapters most of the references to the premises licence, premises licence holders and applicants can be read for the purposes of this Chapter as club premises certificates, qualifying clubs and club applicants.

However it is not possible to apply for a provisional statement in respect of club premises that are being or are about to be constructed, altered or extended.

A club applying for a club premises certificate must submit the following to the relevant licensing authority:

- a completed application form;
- a club operating schedule;
- a plan of the club premises in the prescribed form;
- a copy of the club rules; and
- the fee.

The application fee for a club premises certificate is the same as for a premises licence (see **7.7**). There are however no increased fees or additional fees in respect of either the application fee or the annual fee for club premises which fall within the two higher non-domestic rateable value bands. The annual fee is due and payable each year on the anniversary of the date of the grant of the club premises certificate and the responsibility to discharge the duty to pay the annual fee is placed on the club secretary.

In addition a declaration as to qualifying club status must be submitted to the licensing authority either on or before an application is made for a club premises certificate. In practice, this will usually be submitted at the same time as the application for the club premises certificate. The prescribed form of declaration is set out in the Premises Licences Regulations, Sched. 9, part A.

The application must also be advertised (see **17.8.5**).

17.8.1 The application form

An application for a club premises certificate must be made using the prescribed form. This is set out in the Premises Licences Regulations, Sched. 9, part B.

For completing the application form see **6.5.2**. Care must be taken when completing the application form as any mistakes will be built into the new licence.

In the opening statement, the name of club which is applying for the club premises certificate should be inserted.

The application form is divided into three parts.

Part 1 – club premises details

Part 1 asks for the name of the club, its postal address, or if none, the ordnance survey map reference or description, and the telephone number, if any, at the premises. It also asks for the name and address of the club secretary, together with his daytime telephone number, if any.

It also asks for the non-domestic rateable value of the premises. The non-domestic rateable value of the premises will determine the fee to be paid both for the initial application and annually. The non-domestic rateable value is based on the annual rent that the premises could have been let for on the open market at a particular date. It can be checked on the Valuation Office Agency website (**www.voa.gov.uk**).

The applicant club must confirm whether or not the club premises are occupied and habitually used by the club.

Part 2 – club operating schedule

Part 2 sets out the club operating schedule (see **17.8.4**). It starts by asking the club to specify when it wants the club premises certificate to start and if it wishes the certificate to be valid for a limited period only, to specify a date when it is to end.

Where 5,000 or more people are expected to attend the premises at any one time, the number expected to attend must be stated. This figure relates to the

197

maximum number of people on the club premises at any one time and must include employees. The additional fee payable under the Fees Regulations for large events does not apply to licensable activities being carried on under a club premises certificate.

A general description of the club must then be given, for example the type of premises, its general situation, layout and any other information which could be relevant to the licensing objectives. Where the application includes off-supplies of alcohol and the club intends to provide a place where these can be consumed, it must include a description of where that place will be and its proximity to the club premises.

The club must then specify which qualifying club activities it intends to conduct on the club premises, and give further details of these in the appropriate boxes A–L using the 24-hour clock. All applicants must complete boxes M, N and O. Box N requires an applicant to highlight any adult entertainment or services, activities, other entertainment or matters ancillary to the use of the club premises which may give rise to concern in respect of children. Details of the hours when the club premises will be open to members and guests must be stated in box M, together with any seasonal variation or non-standard timings. A distinction is therefore made between the hours during which the licensable activities will take place and the hours during which members and guests will be permitted to be on the club premises. Reference should be made to the statement of licensing policy of the relevant licensing authority for any requirements as to how long members and guests should be allowed to remain on the premises after the cessation of licensable activities. Finally, box O requires an applicant to list the steps which he will take to promote the four licensing objectives.

There is a checklist for the club to complete so that nothing is overlooked, together with a warning that it is an offence, liable on conviction to a fine up to level 5 on the standard scale, under s.158 to make a false statement in or in connection with the application.

Part 3

Part 3 provides for the form to be signed on behalf of the club. The signatory must confirm that he is making the application on behalf of the club and has authority to bind the club. He must indicate the capacity in which he signs the form, for example as club secretary. The form can also be signed by the applicant's solicitor or other duly authorised agent, and someone signing on behalf of the applicant must state in what capacity they sign. Where there are joint applicants, both applicants or their respective agents must sign the application form. There is also space for an address to be given for all correspondence associated with this application.

17.8.2   Obtaining an application form

For details on obtaining a form see **6.5.1**.

17.8.3   Making an application

For details on making an electronic application see **6.5.3**.

17.8.4   The club operating schedule

An application for a club premises certificate must be accompanied by a club operating schedule (s.71(4)). This forms part of the prescribed application form and, if the application is successful, it will be incorporated into the club premises certificate itself so that it is clear which activities are permitted on the club premises and any limitations on them.

A club operating schedule must state:

- the qualifying club activities;
- the times during which it is proposed that the qualifying club activities are to take place;
- any other times during which it is proposed that the premises are to be open to the members and their guests;
- where the relevant licensable activities include the supply of alcohol, whether the supplies are proposed to be for consumption on the premises or off the premises, or both;
- the steps which it is proposed to take to promote the licensing objectives; and
- such other matters as may be prescribed (s.71(5)).

There is no requirement to specify a designated premises supervisor.

The contents of an operating schedule are discussed further in **Chapter 8** and the conditions in **Chapter 11**.

17.8.5   Advertising and notification of applications

An application for a club premises certificate must be advertised (s.71(6)(a)). The requirements are the same as those for advertising an application for a premises licence (see **7.8**). A licensing authority may provide a specimen form of notice for a club to use. A suggested form of notice is set out in Box 17.1.

Notice of an application must also be given to each responsible authority by giving to each of them a copy of the application together with its accompanying documents on the same day as the day on which the application is given to the relevant licensing authority (s.71(6)(b)).

BOX 17.1   SUGGESTED FORM OF NOTICE OF AN APPLICATION FOR A CLUB PREMISES CERTIFICATE

Licensing Act 2003

Notice of application for the Grant of a Club Premises Certificate

Notice is hereby given that [insert the full name of the applicant] has applied to the [insert the full name of the licensing authority] on [insert the date of application to the licensing authority] for the grant of a club premises certificate to use the premises [insert name of premises] at [insert the name and full postal address of the premises] for the following licensable activities:

[insert details of each licensable activity including days and hours]

The register of licensing applications can be inspected at [insert details].

Any person who wishes to make a representation in relation to this application must give notice in writing to [insert name and address of the licensing authority], giving in detail the grounds of objection by [insert the date by which all relevant representations must be received by the licensing authority, i.e. 28 consecutive days starting on the day after the day on which the application is given to the licensing authority]. The Licensing Authority must receive representations by the date given above. The Licensing Authority will have regard to any such representation in considering the application.

It is an offence under Section 158 of the Licensing Act 2003 to knowingly or recklessly make a false statement in connection with this application and the maximum fine for which a person is liable on summary conviction for the offence is up to level 5 on the standard scale (£5000).

17.8.6   Inspection of premises

A constable or an authorised person may, at any reasonable time before the determination of an application for a club premises certificate, enter the club premises to which the application relates to inspect them.

The following are designated by s.13(2) as authorised persons:

- an officer of a licensing authority in whose area the premises are situated who is authorised by that authority for the purposes of the Act;
- an inspector appointed under the Fire Precautions Act 1971, s.18 (from 1 April 2006 this will be an inspector appointed by the fire and rescue authority for the area in which the premises are situated (Regulatory Reform (Fire Safety) Order 2005, SI 2005/1541));
- an inspector appointed under the Health and Safety at Work etc. Act 1974, s.19;
- an officer of a local authority, in whose area the premises are situated, who is authorised by that authority for the purposes of exercising one or more of its statutory functions in relation to minimising or preventing the risk of pollution of the environment or of harm to human health;

- in relation to a vessel, an inspector, or a surveyor of ships, appointed under the Merchant Shipping Act 1995, s.256; and
- a person prescribed for these purposes.

A constable or an authorised person who is exercising the power to enter the premises must, if so requested, produce evidence of his authority to exercise the power (s.96(2)). Before an authorised person or constable can enter and inspect any premises, at least 48 hours' notice must be given to the club (s.96(3)). The entry and inspection must take place at a reasonable time on a day which is not more than 14 days after the application for the club premises certificate was made, and the date of the inspection must be in the notice (s.96(3)). Anyone who intentionally obstructs an authorised person exercising the power of entry commits an offence, and is liable on summary conviction to a fine not exceeding level 2 on the standard scale (s.96(5) and (6)). Obstruction of a constable will constitute an offence of obstructing a constable in the execution of his duty under the Police Act 1996, s.89(2), and a person will be liable on summary conviction to imprisonment for a term not exceeding one month (this will increase to 51 weeks when the Criminal Justice Act 2003 takes effect) or to a fine not exceeding level 3 on the standard scale, or to both.

The relevant licensing authority may, on the application of a responsible authority, extend by not more than seven days the time allowed for carrying out an entry and inspection (s.96(7)). The relevant licensing authority may

Table 17.1 Checklist for a club premises certificate application

	Original to relevant licensing authority	Copy to the police	Copy to responsible authorities
Completed application form			
Completed declaration form			
Copy of the club rules			
Plan of the premises			
Payment of the fee			
Confirmation that the application has been advertised on the premises and that this will be maintained for 28 days			
Has the application been advertised in a local newspaper?	Name of newspaper:		Date:

allow such an extension of time only if it appears that reasonable steps had been taken for an authorised person or constable authorised by the applicant to inspect the premises in good time, but it was not possible for the inspection to take place within the time allowed (s.96(8)).

17.9 DETERMINATION OF THE APPLICATION

17.9.1 Preliminary determination

When a licensing authority receives an application for a club premises certificate, it must initially determine whether the application has been made properly in accordance with s.71 and with the Premises Licences Regulations. An incomplete application is invalid and will be returned to the applicant. Any failure to observe the notice requirements will also render the application invalid.

17.9.2 Unopposed applications

When no relevant representations have been made and the relevant licensing authority is satisfied that the applicant has complied with all the application requirements, it must grant the club premises certificate in accordance with the application subject only to such conditions as are consistent with the club operating schedule accompanying the application, and any mandatory conditions (see **17.11**) which must be included in the certificate (s.72(2)).

17.9.3 Applications where representations have been made

If relevant representations have been made by an interested party or a responsible authority, s.72(3)(a) provides that the licensing authority must hold a hearing to consider them (see **Chapter 10**).

The hearing must be held within a period of 20 working days beginning with the day after the end of the period during which representations may be made, which is 28 consecutive days starting on the day after the day on which the application is given to the relevant licensing authority (Hearings Regulations, reg. 5 and Sched. 1, para. 8). Notice of the hearing must be given to the club and persons who made relevant representations no later than 10 working days before the day or the first day on which the hearing is to be held (Hearings Regulations, reg. 6(4) and Sched. 2, para. 8). The club must be given the relevant representations with the notice of the hearing (Hearings Regulations, reg. 7(2) and Sched. 3, para. 8). A hearing may be dispensed with if the licensing authority, the club and each person who made representations agree that a hearing is unnecessary.

Following the hearing and having regard to the representations, the licensing authority must then take such of the following steps, if any, as it considers necessary for the promotion of the licensing objectives:

- to grant the certificate subject to such conditions as are consistent with the club operating schedule accompanying the application modified to such extent as the authority considers necessary for the promotion of the licensing objectives, and any mandatory conditions which must be included in the certificate. For these purposes conditions are modified if any of them is altered or omitted or any new condition is added (s.72(6));
- to exclude from the scope of the certificate any of the qualifying club activities to which the application relates; or
- to reject the application (s.72(4)).

The licensing authority must 'have regard' to the representations before taking any of the above steps. This would appear to imply that it can also take into account other matters not included in the representations. A licensing authority does not have to take any of the above steps. So if it does not consider any of them necessary for the promotion of the licensing objectives, it can grant the certificate in the terms sought by the applicant subject only to such conditions as are consistent with the operating schedule and any conditions which must be imposed under the Act.

Any conditions which are included in a club premises certificate must take account of s.73(1) which provides that a certificate can only authorise off-supplies if it also authorises supplies for consumption on the premises (s.72(5)).

A licensing authority may grant a club premises certificate subject to different conditions in respect of different parts of the premises concerned, or different qualifying club activities (s.72(10)).

It would appear that licensing authorities should not attach conditions to a club premises certificate unless they are 'strictly necessary' (Guidance, para. 9.13).

Conditions relating to sex equality should not be attached as the Guidance, para. 9.14 provides that equal treatment on these grounds is not a licensing objective.

17.9.4 Relevant representations

The position regarding relevant representations is the same as in respect of premises licences (see **Chapter 10** as to representations generally).

'Relevant representations' are defined in s.72(7) and (8) and mean representations which:

- are about the likely effect of the grant of the certificate on the promotion of the licensing objectives;

- were made by an interested party or a responsible authority within the prescribed period;
- have not been withdrawn; and
- in the case of representations made by an interested party (who is not also a responsible authority), are not, in the opinion of the relevant licensing authority, frivolous or vexatious.

The prescribed period for making representations is 28 consecutive days starting on the day after the day on which the application is given to the relevant licensing authority.

Where the licensing authority determines that any representations are frivolous or vexatious, it must notify the person who made them of the reasons for its determination (s.72(9)).

17.10   ACTION FOLLOWING THE GRANT OR REJECTION OF AN APPLICATION

17.10.1   The grant of an application

Once an application for a club premises certificate has been granted, the licensing authority must forthwith (see **2.9**) give notice that it has been granted to:

- the applicant;
- any person who made relevant representations in respect of the application; and
- the chief officer of police for the police area, or each police area, in which the premises are situated.

In addition, if relevant representations were made, the notice must set out the authority's reasons for its decision to take any steps to promote the licensing objectives.

The licensing authority must also issue the club with the club premises certificate and a summary of it (see **17.12**).

17.10.2   The rejection of an application

If an application is rejected, the licensing authority must forthwith (see **2.9**) give notice that it has been rejected, stating its reasons for that decision, to:

- the applicant;
- any person who made relevant representations in respect of the application; and
- the chief officer of police for the police area, or each police area, in which the premises are situated.

17.11   MANDATORY AND PROHIBITED CONDITIONS

17.11.1   Supply of alcohol for consumption off the premises

A club premises certificate may not authorise the supply of alcohol for consumption off the premises unless it also authorises the supply of alcohol to a member of the club for consumption on those premises (s.73(1)). A club premises certificate which authorises the supply of alcohol for consumption off the premises must include the following conditions (s.73(2)–(5)):

- the supply must only be made at a time when the premises are open for the purposes of supplying alcohol, in accordance with the club premises certificate, to members of the club for consumption on the premises;
- any alcohol supplied for consumption off the premises must be in a sealed container;
- any supply of alcohol for consumption off the premises must be made to a member of the club in person.

There is no requirement that the alcohol supplied to a member for consumption off the premises must only be consumed by that member. Thus a member could purchase alcohol in the club which is then consumed off the premises by someone else.

17.11.2   Exhibition of films

Section 74 provides that where a club premises certificate authorises the exhibition of films, the certificate must include a condition requiring the admission of children to the exhibition of any film to be restricted in accordance with film classification recommendations. Such recommendations can be made either by the British Board of Film Classification or the relevant licensing authority if it operates its own film classification certificate.

17.11.3   Prohibited conditions: associate members and their guests

A licensing authority is prohibited, where the rules of a club provide for the sale by retail of alcohol on any premises by or on behalf of the club to, or to a guest of, an associate member of the club, from attaching a condition to a club premises certificate in respect of the sale by retail of alcohol on those premises by or on behalf of the club which would prevent the sale by retail of alcohol to any such associate member or guest (s.75(1)). In addition where the rules of a club provide for the provision of any regulated entertainment on any premises by or on behalf of the club to, or to a guest of, an associate member of the club, no condition may be attached to a club premises certificate in respect of the provision of any such regulated entertainment on those premises by or on behalf of the club so as to prevent its provision to any such associate member or guest (s.75(2)).

17.11.4   Prohibited conditions: plays

Where a club premises certificate authorises the performance of plays, no condition may be attached to the certificate as to the nature of the plays which may be performed, or the manner of performing plays, under the certificate (s.76). This prohibition does not, however, prevent a licensing authority imposing any condition which it considers necessary on the grounds of public safety.

17.12   THE FORM OF THE CERTIFICATE AND SUMMARY

17.12.1   Club premises certificate

A club premises certificate must be in the prescribed form (s.78). This is set out in the Premises Licences Regulations, Sched. 13, part A.

A club premises certificate must:

- identify the relevant licensing authority;
- include the certificate number;
- specify the name of the club and the address which is to be its relevant registered address which is defined in s.184(7) as the address given for the holder of the certificate recorded in the licensing authority's register;
- specify the address of the premises to which the certificate relates;
- include a plan of those premises;
- specify the qualifying club activities for which the premises may be used; and
- specify the conditions subject to which the certificate has effect.

17.12.2   Summary of a club premises certificate

A summary of a club premises certificate must be in the prescribed form (s.78(1)). This is set out in the Premises Licences Regulations, Sched. 13, part B.

A summary must:

- identify the relevant licensing authority;
- include the certificate number;
- specify all matters mentioned in the certificate, except for a plan; and
- be printed on paper of at least A4 size.

17.13   THEFT OR LOSS

If a club premises certificate or summary is lost, stolen, damaged or destroyed, the club may apply to the relevant licensing authority for a copy (s.79). Presumably an application will be made by the club secretary or some other club official. The fee of £10.50 must accompany the application.

Where an application for a copy is made, the relevant licensing authority must issue the club with a copy of the certificate or summary if it is satisfied that the certificate or summary has been lost, stolen, damaged or destroyed, and if it has been lost or stolen, that the club has reported the loss or theft to the police. The copy must be certified by the authority to be a true copy of the original. It must be a copy of the club premises certificate or summary in the form in which it existed immediately before it was lost, stolen, damaged or destroyed. Once a copy has been issued, the Act will apply to the copy as it applies to an original club premises certificate or summary.

17.14 PERIOD OF VALIDITY OF A CLUB PREMISES CERTIFICATE

Once granted a club premises certificate does not need to be renewed. Section 80 provides that a club premises certificate has effect until either it is withdrawn by the licensing authority or it lapses by the club surrendering it. A club premises certificate does not have effect during any period when it is suspended.

17.15 SURRENDER OF A CLUB PREMISES CERTIFICATE

A club which holds a club premises certificate may decide it no longer requires the certificate. Presumably the club committee would reach such a decision. It should therefore surrender it back to the relevant licensing authority (s.81). This is done by giving the relevant licensing authority a notice to that effect. The notice must be accompanied by the club premises certificate or, if that is not practicable, by a statement of the reasons for the failure to produce the certificate. No fee is payable, nor need notice be given to anyone other than the relevant licensing authority.

Where a certificate is surrendered, it will lapse when the notice surrendering it is received by the relevant licensing authority.

There is no provision for a certificate which has been surrendered to be reinstated.

17.16 CHANGE OF CLUB NAME OR ALTERATION OF CLUB RULES

If a club decides to change its name, or alter its rules, the club secretary must notify the relevant licensing authority of the change or alteration (s.81). This requirement applies to a club which holds a club premises certificate, and to a club which has made an application for a club premises certificate which has not yet been determined by the relevant licensing authority. The notification must be accompanied by the prescribed fee of £10.50, and the club premises certificate or, if that is not practicable, by a statement of the reasons for the failure to produce the certificate.

When a licensing authority receives notification of a change in the name, or alteration to the rules, of a club it must amend the club premises certificate accordingly. However this obligation to amend the certificate does not apply to any amendment which would change the premises to which the certificate relates. A club that wishes to change its premises must make an application to vary its club premises certificate.

Notification to the licensing authority must be given within 28 days following the day on which the change of name or alteration to the rules is made, otherwise the secretary of the club commits an offence. A person guilty of such an offence is liable on summary conviction to a fine not exceeding level 2 on the standard scale.

17.17 CHANGE OF RELEVANT REGISTERED ADDRESS OF A CLUB

If a club changes its relevant registered address (i.e. the address in the record for the certificate in the register kept by the licensing authority which granted the certificate), the club may give the relevant licensing authority notice of the change so that it can be recorded in the licensing register (s.83(1)). If a club ceases to have authority to use the address which is its relevant registered address, it must as soon as reasonably practicable give notice of this to the relevant licensing authority together with details of the new address that is to be its relevant registered address (s.83(2)).

Both of these applications must be accompanied by the prescribed fee of £10.50 and the club premises certificate or, if that is not practicable, by a statement of the reasons for the failure to produce the certificate.

A licensing authority which is notified of a change to be made in the relevant registered address of a club must amend the club premises certificate accordingly.

If a club fails, without reasonable excuse, where it ceases to have authority to use the address which is its relevant registered address, to give notice of this to the relevant licensing authority together with details of the new address that is to be its relevant registered address, the secretary commits an offence. A person guilty of such an offence is liable on summary conviction to a fine not exceeding level 2 on the standard scale.

17.18   WITHDRAWAL OF A CLUB PREMISES CERTIFICATE

17.18.1   Withdrawal on review

A club premises certificate can be withdrawn under s.88 following an application for review.

17.18.2   Withdrawal by the licensing authority

A club premises certificate may be withdrawn under s.90 if the club ceases to be a qualifying club. If it appears to the relevant licensing authority that a club does not satisfy the conditions for being a qualifying club in relation to a qualifying club activity to which the certificate relates, the authority must give the club a notice withdrawing the certificate so far as it relates to that activity. It does not seem that a licensing authority must be satisfied that a club does not satisfy the qualifying conditions. It must just 'appear' that the club does not do so. Section 90 is silent on when the withdrawal takes place. It is assumed that this will be the date the notice of withdrawal is given, particularly in view of the three-month requirement in s.90(2)).

Where the only reason that the club does not satisfy qualifying club conditions in relation to the activity in question is because it has fewer than the required 25 members, s.90(2) provides that the notice withdrawing the certificate must state that the withdrawal:

- does not take effect until immediately after the end of the period of three months following the date of the notice; and
- will not take effect if, at the end of that period, the club again has at least the required number of members.

A licensing authority can give a further notice of withdrawal at any time (s.90(4)). This would allow an authority which has given a notice under s.90(2) which then discovers during the three-month duration of the notice that the club does not satisfy another of the qualifying condition to give a further notice which would then have immediate effect.

A club which wishes to challenge a notice withdrawing its club premises certificate may appeal to the magistrates' court against the decision to withdraw the certificate (Sched. 5, para. 14). There is no other way of challenging a notice.

17.18.3   Entry and search of club premises

In order to obtain evidence that a club no longer satisfies the qualifying club conditions, an application may be made for a warrant to enter and search the club premises (s.90(5) and (6)).

Where a Justice of the Peace is satisfied, on information on oath, that there are reasonable grounds for believing:

- that a club which holds a club premises certificate does not satisfy the conditions for being a qualifying club in relation to a qualifying club activity to which the certificate relates; and
- that evidence of that fact is to be obtained at the premises to which the certificate relates,

he may issue a warrant authorising a constable to enter the premises, if necessary by force, at any time within one month from the time of the issue of the warrant, and search them. A person who enters premises under the authority of such a warrant may seize and remove any documents relating to the club's business.

17.19 DUTIES IN RELATION TO A CLUB PREMISES CERTIFICATE

17.19.1 A licensing authority's duty to update a club premises certificate

If a licensing authority makes a determination or receives a notice under the Act in respect of a club, or an appeal against a decision is disposed of, it must make any appropriate amendments to the certificate and, if necessary, issue a new summary of the certificate (s.93(1)).

Where a licensing authority is not in possession of the club premises certificate, it may, in order to make any amendments, require the secretary of the club to produce the certificate within 14 days of being notified of this requirement (s.93(2)). A person commits an offence if he fails, without reasonable excuse, to comply with this requirement. A person guilty of such an offence is liable on summary conviction to a fine not exceeding level 2 on the standard scale.

17.19.2 Duty to keep and produce a club premises certificate

Where club premises are being used for one or more qualifying club activities authorised by the club premises certificate, s.91 provides that the club secretary must ensure that the certificate, or a certified copy of it, is kept at the premises in the custody or under the control of a nominated person who:

- is either the secretary of the club, a member of the club, or a person who works at the premises for the purposes of the club;
- has been nominated for the purpose by the secretary in writing; and
- has been identified to the relevant licensing authority in a notice given by the secretary.

The nominated person must make sure that the summary of the certificate or a certified copy of that summary, and a notice specifying the position which he holds at the premises, are prominently displayed at the premises. There is no requirement that the summary and notice be displayed in the same place in the premises, though obviously this would be desirable.

Both the club secretary and the nominated person will commit an offence if they fail, without reasonable excuse, to comply with their obligations. A person guilty of such an offence is liable on summary conviction to a fine not exceeding level 2 on the standard scale.

A constable or an authorised person may require the nominated person to produce the club premises certificate, or certified copy, for examination. An authorised person exercising this power must, if so requested, produce evidence of his authority to exercise the power. A person commits an offence if he fails, without reasonable excuse, to produce a club premises certificate or certified copy of a club premises certificate when required to do so, and a person guilty of such an offence is liable on summary conviction to a fine not exceeding level 2 on the standard scale.

Under s.94 the reference above to a certified copy is a reference to a copy of the document which is certified to be a true copy by:

- the relevant licensing authority:
- a solicitor or notary; or
- a person of a prescribed description.

Any certified copy which is produced to a constable or an authorised person must be a copy of the document in the form in which it exists at the time. A document which purports to be a certified copy of a document is to be taken to be such a copy, and to comply with the above requirements, unless the contrary is shown.

17.20   POLICE POWERS TO ENTER AND SEARCH CLUB PREMISES

Section 97 provides that a constable may enter and search premises which have a club premises certificate if he has reasonable cause to believe:

- that an offence of supplying or offering to supply, or being concerned in supplying or making an offer to supply, a controlled drug under the Misuse of Drugs Act 1971, s.4(3)(a), (b) or (c) has been, is being, or is about to be, committed there; or
- that there is likely to be a breach of the peace there.

A constable exercising this power may, if necessary, use reasonable force.

CHAPTER 18

Variation of a club premises certificate

18.1 INTRODUCTION

Section 84 provides that a club which holds a club premises certificate may apply to the relevant licensing authority to vary its certificate. The variation could relate to the conditions attached to the certificate or a change in the licensable activities. A club premises certificate may not be varied so as to vary substantially the premises to which it relates. A licensing authority may vary a club premises certificate so that it has effect subject to different conditions in respect of different parts of the premises concerned or different qualifying club activities.

Under previous legislation a club which provided entertainment for its members and their guests did not need any authorisation for this. A club certificate only authorised the supply of alcohol to members and their guests. The position is different under the Act and on conversion of their club certificate to a club premises certificate many clubs will have applied as part of the conversion application for a variation to allow them to provide regulated entertainment. However some clubs may not have done this and if they subsequently wish to provide regulated entertainment they will need to apply for a variation under s.84.

The provisions in s.84 are comparable to those for the variation of a premises licence.

18.2 APPLYING FOR A VARIATION

A club which holds a club premises certificate may at any time apply to the relevant licensing authority to vary the premises licence.

A club seeking a variation must submit the following to the relevant licensing authority:

- a completed application form;
- the club premises certificate or, if that is not practicable, a statement of the reasons for the failure to provide the certificate; and

- the fee which will be the same as that payable on the grant of a club premises certificate (see **7.7**).

18.3   THE APPLICATION FORM

An application for a variation must be in the prescribed form which is set out in the Premises Licences Regulations, Sched. 10.

18.3.1   Completing the application form

For guidance in completing the application form see **6.5.2**.

In the opening statement, the name of the club which is applying for the variation should be inserted together with the number of its club premises certificate.

The application form is then divided into five parts, as follows.

Part 1

The applicant must set out the postal address or, if none, the ordnance survey map reference or a description of the premises, and its telephone number, if any. An e-mail address can also be given though this is optional. The following details of the club secretary must also be given:

- the name of the club secretary;
- the address of the club secretary;
- a daytime contact telephone number, if any; and
- an e-mail address (optional).

Part 2

Part 2 deals with the details of the applicant. The applicant must give such information as his address, if this is not the same as the club premises and daytime telephone number. An e-mail address can also be given though this is optional.

Part 3

Part 3 deals with the proposed variation. The applicant must indicate whether the proposed variation is to have effect as soon as possible, or if not, when it is to take effect from. If the variation would result in 5,000 or more people attending the premises at any one time, the number expected to attend must be stated.

The nature of the proposed variation must be briefly described. This

213

description should include a description of the premises, for example the type of premises, their general situation and layout and any other information which could be relevant to the licensing objectives. Where the application includes off-supplies of alcohol and it is intended to provide a place for consumption of these off-supplies, a description of where the place will be and its proximity to the premises must be included.

Part 4

Part 4 is the club operating schedule. Those parts which would be subject to change if the application is successful must be completed. The club must indicate the qualifying activities which it is intended to conduct on the club premises that will be affected by the application. It must also identify any existing conditions which it believes could be removed if the variation were approved. If the club premises certificate, or relevant part, cannot be enclosed with the application, an explanation must be given. The club must then describe any additional steps it intends to take to promote the four licensing objectives as a result of the proposed variation.

Finally there is a checklist for the applicant to complete so that nothing is overlooked, together with a warning that it is an offence, liable on conviction to a fine up to level 5 on the standard scale, under s.158 to make a false statement in or in connection with the application.

Part 5

Part 5 makes provision for the applicant to sign the form. The form must be signed by a person who has authority to bind the club.

18.3.2 Obtaining an application form

For information on obtaining a form and making an application see **6.5.1** and **6.5.3**.

18.4 ADVERTISING

The application must be advertised in accordance with the Premises Licences Regulations, reg. 25 (s.84(4)) by displaying a notice at or on the premises and by publishing a notice in a local newspaper.

An applicant must advertise his application by displaying a notice containing prescribed information on the premises for a period of not less than 28 consecutive days starting on the day after the day on which the application was given to the relevant licensing authority.

The notice must be:

- of a size equal to or larger than A4;
- of a pale blue colour; and
- printed legibly in black ink or typed in black in a font of a size equal to or larger than 16 points.

The notice must be displayed prominently at or on the premises to which the application relates where it can be conveniently read from the exterior of the premises. Where the premises cover an area of more than 50 metres square, a further notice in the same form and subject to the same requirements must be displayed every 50 metres along the external perimeter of the premises abutting any highway.

An applicant must publish a notice containing prescribed information in a local newspaper or, if there is none, in a local newsletter, circular or similar document, circulating in the vicinity of the premises on at least one occasion during the 10 working days starting on the day after the day on which the application was given to the relevant licensing authority.

The notices to be displayed at or on the premises and to be published in a local newspaper must:

- briefly describe the proposed variation;
- state the name of the club;
- state the postal address of the club premises, if any, or if there is no postal address for the premises a description of those premises sufficient to enable the location and extent of the premises to be identified;
- state the postal address and, where applicable, the worldwide web address where the register of the relevant licensing authority is kept and where and when the record of the application may be inspected;
- state the date by which an interested party or a responsible authority may make representations to the relevant licensing authority;
- state that representations shall be made in writing; and
- state that it is an offence knowingly or recklessly to make a false statement in connection with an application and the maximum fine for which a person is liable on summary conviction for the offence.

A suggested form of notice is given in Box 18.1.

18.5 NOTICE TO RESPONSIBLE AUTHORITIES

An applicant must also give notice of his application to each responsible authority by giving each responsible authority a copy of his application together with its accompanying documents, if any. Notice is to be given on the same day as the day on which the application is given to the relevant

---

BOX 18.1   SUGGESTED FORM OF NOTICE OF AN APPLICATION TO VARY A CLUB PREMISES CERTIFICATE

Licensing Act 2003

Notice of application to vary a Club Premises Certificate

PREMISES: [insert address of premises]

Notice is hereby given that [insert the full name of the club] has applied to the [insert the full name of the licensing authority] on [insert the date of application to the licensing authority] to vary a club premises certificate under the Licensing Act 2003.

The proposed variation is: [set out details of the proposed variation].

Any person who wishes to make a representation in relation to this application must give notice in writing of his/her representation by [insert the date by which all relevant representations must be received by the licensing authority, i.e. 28 consecutive days starting on the day after the day on which the application is given to the licensing authority] stating the grounds for making said representation to [insert contact details for the licensing authority]. The public register where applications are available to be viewed by members of the public can be viewed at [insert details]. The Licensing Authority must receive representations by the date given above. The Licensing Authority will have regard to any such representation in considering the application. It is an offence, under section 158 of the Licensing Act 2003, to knowingly or recklessly make a false statement in or in connection with an application for a club premises certificate and the maximum fine on being convicted of such an offence is £5000.

---

licensing authority. A responsible authority may then make representations to the relevant licensing authority about the application.

18.6   DETERMINATION OF THE APPLICATION

18.6.1   Preliminary determination

When a licensing authority receives an application for a variation, it must initially determine whether the application has been made properly in accordance with the Act and with the Premises Licences Regulations. An incomplete application is invalid and will be returned to the applicant. Any failure to observe the notice requirements will also render the application invalid.

18.6.2   Unopposed applications

Where a licensing authority has received an application to vary a club premises certificate and is satisfied that the applicant has complied with all the procedural requirements, and no relevant representations have been received there is no need for a hearing and it must grant the application (s.85(2)). See **14.6.2** for the relevant provision in the Guidance.

18.6.3 Applications where representations have been made

Where relevant representations are made, the authority must hold a hearing to consider them, unless the authority, the applicant and each person who has made such representations agree that a hearing is unnecessary (s.85(3)(a)). A hearing must be held within 20 working days beginning with the day after the end of the period during which representations may be made (Hearings Regulations, reg. 5 and Sched. 1, para. 9). Notice of the hearing must be given to the club and persons who have made relevant representations no later than 10 working days before the day or the first day on which the hearing is to be held (Hearings Regulations, reg. 6(4) and Sched. 2, para. 9). The club must be sent the relevant representations with the notice of hearing (Hearings Regulations, reg. 7(2) and Sched. 3, para. 9).

The hearing should focus only on the steps needed to promote the particular licensing objective which has given rise to the representation. Following the hearing the licensing authority may, having regard to the representations, and if it considers it necessary for the promotion of the licensing objectives, modify the conditions of the certificate, or reject the whole or part of the application (s.85(4)). The conditions are treated as being modified if any of them is altered or omitted or any new condition is added. The club premises certificate may be varied in such a way so that it has effect subject to different conditions in respect of different parts of the premises or different licensable activities (s.86(7)). If the licensing authority does not consider that any steps are necessary, it can grant the variation in accordance with the application.

'Relevant representations' are representations which:

- are about the likely effect of the grant of the application on the promotion of the licensing objectives;
- are made by an interested party or a responsible authority within the period of 28 consecutive days starting on the day after the day on which the applicant gave the application to the licensing authority;
- have not been withdrawn; and
- in the case of representations made by an interested party (who is not also a responsible authority) are not, in the opinion of the relevant licensing authority, frivolous or vexatious.

When granting an unopposed application or making its decision where relevant representations have been made, a licensing authority must consider its duties in relation to the mandatory conditions relating to supply of alcohol for consumption off the premises and to exhibition of films (s.85(7)).

18.7   NOTIFICATION OF A DECISION

When an application is granted either in whole or in part, the licensing authority must forthwith (see **2.9**) give notice of this to:

- the applicant;
- any person who made relevant representations in respect of the application; and
- the chief officer of police for the police area (or each police area) in which the premises are situated.

Where relevant representations were made, the notice must set out the authority's reasons for its decision as to any steps to take to promote the licensing objectives. The notice must also specify the time when the variation in question takes effect. This will either be the time specified in the application or, if that time is before the applicant is given the notice, such later time as the relevant licensing authority specifies in the notice.

Where an application, or any part of an application, is rejected the relevant licensing authority must forthwith (see **2.9**) give a notice to that effect stating its reasons for rejecting the application to:

- the applicant;
- any person who made relevant representations; and
- the chief officer of police for the police area (or each police area) in which the premises are situated.

The notice must accompanied by information regarding the right of a party to appeal against the determination.

Where a relevant licensing authority determines that any representations are frivolous or vexatious, it must give the person who made them its reasons for that determination.

18.8   INSPECTION OF PREMISES

A constable or an authorised person may, at any reasonable time before the determination of an application for the variation of a club premises certificate, enter the premises to which the application relates to inspect them.

A constable or an authorised person who is exercising the power to enter the premises must, if so requested, produce evidence of his authority to exercise the power (s.96(2)). Before an authorised person or a constable can enter and inspect any premises, at least 48 hours' notice must be given to the club (s.96(3)). The entry and inspection must take place at a reasonable time on a day which is not more than 14 days after the application for the variation was made, and the date of the inspection must be in the notice (s.96(3)). Anyone who intentionally obstructs an authorised person exercising the power of entry commits an offence, and is liable on summary conviction to a fine not exceeding level 2 on the standard scale (s.96(5) and (6)).

The relevant licensing authority may, on the application of a responsible authority, extend by not more than seven days the time allowed for carrying out an entry and inspection. The relevant licensing authority may allow such an extension of time only if it appears that reasonable steps had been taken for an authorised person or a constable authorised by the applicant to inspect the premises in good time, but it was not possible for the inspection to take place within the time allowed.

CHAPTER 19

Review of a club premises certificate

19.1 INTRODUCTION

The Act provides a procedure whereby a club premises certificate can be reviewed at any time on the application of an interested party, such as a resident living in the vicinity of the club premises, a responsible authority, such as the police because of a matter arising at the premises in connection with any of the licensing objectives, or a member of the club. This procedure is necessary as otherwise there would be no other opportunity to deal with problems which may arise during the currency of the club premises certificate. A review must be based on one of the licensing objectives.

A review of a club premises certificate is very similar to a review of a premises licence and reference should be made to **Chapter 15**.

19.2 WHO CAN APPLY FOR A REVIEW?

At any time an interested party, a responsible authority or a member of the club may apply to the relevant licensing authority for a review of the club premises certificate (s.87(1)). However, an application for a review need not be the first step where problems arise and the Guidance, para. 5.103 recommends that:

> It would therefore be good practice for authorised persons and responsible authorities to give licence holders early warning of their concerns about problems identified at the premises concerned and of the need for improvement. It is expected that a failure to respond to such warnings would lead to a decision to request a review.

A licensing authority cannot initiate a review. However, where a local authority is both the relevant licensing authority and a responsible authority, it may, in its capacity as a responsible authority, apply for a review of a club premises certificate and, in its capacity as licensing authority, determine the application (s.89). For example, an environmental health officer may request a review on a matter which relates to the promotion of one or more of the licensing objectives.

19.3 WHEN CAN AN APPLICATION BE MADE?

An application for a review may be made at any time where a club premises certificate has effect (s.87(1)). It is clear that an application can be made at any time as the Guidance, para. 5.100 states:

> At any stage, following the grant of a premises licence, a responsible authority, such as the police or the fire authority, or an interested party, such as a resident living in the vicinity of the premises, may ask the licensing authority to review the licence because of a matter arising at the premises in connection with any of the four licensing objectives.

19.4   MAKING AN APPLICATION

An application for a review of a club premises certificate must be made to the relevant licensing authority (s.87(1)). There is no fee payable for a review.

A copy of the application must also be sent to the club and each of the responsible authorities. The application must also be advertised (see **19.6**).

19.5   THE APPLICATION FORM

An application for a review must be in the prescribed form which is set out in the Premises Licences Regulations, Sched. 8.

19.5.1   Completing the application form

For details of completing the form see **6.5.2**.

In the opening statement, the name of the applicant or applicants who are applying for the review should be inserted.

The application form is then divided into three parts.

Part 1

The applicant must set out the postal address of the club premises. If the club premises have no postal address, the location of the club premises should be described or the Ordnance Survey map reference should be given. The name of the club holding the club premises certificate and the number of the club premises certificate should then be given, if these are known.

Part 2

Part 2 deals with the details of the applicant and the reason for the review. The applicant must state whether he is an interested party, a responsible authority, or a member of the club. In the first case he must indicate how he claims to be an interested party. He must then give such details as his name and address, telephone number and confirmation, where relevant, that he is at least 18 years old.

The applicant must then state which of the licensing objectives the application relates to and the grounds for review and provide as much information as possible to support the application, such as details of problems which have occurred.

The form also asks whether the applicant has applied for a review in relation to the club premises before and, if so, the date of that application. If the applicant has made representations before in relation to the club premises he must set them out and indicate when they were made.

Part 2 also includes a checklist for the applicant so that nothing is overlooked, together with a warning that it is an offence, liable on conviction to a fine up to level 5 on the standard scale, under s.158 to make a false statement in or in connection with the application.

Part 3

Part 3 provides for the applicant to sign the form. The form can also be signed by the applicant's solicitor or other duly authorised agent, and someone signing on behalf of the applicant must state in what capacity they sign. Where there are joint applicants, both applicants or their respective agents must sign the application form.

19.5.2   Obtaining an application form

For how to obtain the form see **6.5.1**.

19.5.3   Making an application

For details on how to make the application see **6.5.3**.

19.5.4   Notice to other persons

The applicant must give a copy of the application form together with any accompanying documents to each responsible authority and to the club on the same day as it is given to the licensing authority. It must also be advertised (see **19.6**). An interested party or a responsible authority may then make a representation to the licensing authority within the period of 28 days starting on the day after the day on which the application for review was given to the licensing authority.

19.6 ADVERTISING THE APPLICATION

Once a licensing authority has received an application for review, it must advertise it by displaying prominently for a period of no less than 28 consecutive days starting on the day after the day on which the application was given to the licensing authority a notice which is:

- of a size equal to or larger than A4;
- of a pale blue colour; and
- printed legibly in black ink or typed in black in a font of a size equal to or larger than 16 points.

The notice must be displayed:

- at, on or near the site of the club premises to which the application relates where it can conveniently be read from the exterior of the premises by the public and in the case of a premises covering an area of more than 50 metres square, one further notice in the same form and subject to the same requirements shall be displayed every 50 metres along the external perimeter of the premises abutting any highway; and
- at the offices, or the main offices, of the licensing authority in a central and conspicuous place.

If the licensing authority has a website which it uses to advertise applications it receives, then a notice of the application for review must also be published on that website.

All the notices must state:

- the address of the premises about which an application for a review has been made;
- the dates between which interested parties and responsible authorities may make representations to the relevant licensing authority;
- the grounds of the application for review;
- the postal address and, where relevant, the worldwide web address where the register of the relevant licensing authority is kept and where and when the grounds for the review may be inspected; and
- that it is an offence knowingly or recklessly to make a false statement in connection with an application and the maximum fine for which a person is liable on summary conviction for the offence.

19.7 REJECTION OF THE APPLICATION

Once an application for review has been received by a licensing authority, it must initially consider whether the grounds for review stated in the application are relevant to the licensing objectives. Any ground for review specified in the application may, at any time, be rejected by the licensing authority if it is satisfied that the ground is not relevant to one or more of the licensing objectives, or, in the case of an application made by an interested party or a club member, that the ground is frivolous or vexatious, or is a repetition (s.87(4)).

A ground will not be relevant if it does not relate to one or more of the licensing objectives. Rejection of a ground because it is frivolous or vexatious will be similar to a rejection of a relevant representation by an interested party on an application for a premises licence.

A ground for review is a repetition under s.87(5) if:

- it is identical or substantially similar to:

  - a ground for review specified in an earlier application for review made in respect of the same club premises certificate which has been determined; or
  - representations considered by the relevant licensing authority before it originally granted the club premises certificate; and

- a reasonable interval has not elapsed since that earlier application for review or the grant of the club premises certificate. The Guidance, para. 5.105 recommends that more than one review originating from an interested party should not be permitted within a period of 12 months on similar grounds save in compelling circumstances or where it arises following a closure order.

Rejection on the ground of repetition is similar to that in relation to the review of premises licences.

If a licensing authority rejects a ground for review, it must notify the applicant in writing of its decision as soon as reasonably practicable and, if the ground was rejected because it was frivolous or vexatious, it must include a statement of its reasons for making that decision (s.87(6)).

If the applicant had raised more than one ground in his application and not all of them are rejected then the application is only treated as being rejected in respect of the ground which has been rejected and it will still be valid in relation to any ground which has not been rejected (s.87(7)). Even though one of the grounds stated in the application may have been rejected the obligation to give notice still applies. By way of example, if a licensing authority receives an application which sets out two grounds for review and it decides that one of the grounds is frivolous it must give notice of this to the applicant together with the reasons for its decision, and then proceed to determine the application on the basis of the remaining ground.

19.8 DETERMINATION OF THE APPLICATION FOR REVIEW

The position is the same as for a review of a premises licence and the paragraphs in the Guidance on such reviews apply equally here. Once the 28-day period for making representations has ended, the licensing authority must hold a hearing within 20 working days beginning with the day after the end of the 28-day period to consider the application and any relevant representations (Hearings Regulations, reg. 5 and Sched. 1, para. 10). Notice of the hearing must be given to the club, persons who have made relevant representations and the applicant for the review no later than 10 working days before the day or the first day on which the hearing is to be held (Hearings Regulations, reg. 6(4) and Sched. 2, para. 10). There is no provision for dispensing with the hearing if all the parties consider it unnecessary. The club must be given the relevant representations with the notice of hearing (Hearings Regulations, reg. 7(2) and Sched. 3, para. 10).

When determining the application, the licensing authority must have regard to the application and any relevant representations. It may decide that no action is required in order to promote the licensing objectives, or that informal action should be taken, for example by giving the club an informal warning or a recommendation to improve matters within a specified period of time.

If however the licensing authority considers that formal action is required, it may take such of the following steps, if any, which it considers necessary for the promotion of the licensing objectives:

- modify the conditions of the certificate (this will involve any of the conditions of the licence being altered or omitted or the addition of a new condition);
- exclude a qualifying club activity from the scope of the certificate;
- suspend the certificate for a period not exceeding three months; or
- withdraw the certificate (s.88(3)).

When making its determination, the licensing authority must have regard to the requirements in the Act to include mandatory conditions in the certificate.

If a licensing authority decides that none of these steps is necessary, then it need take no action.

Where a licensing authority takes one of the above steps, it may provide that the modification or exclusion is to have effect for a specified period only, not exceeding three months, as it may specify.

19.9 NOTIFICATION OF THE DECISION

Once an application for a review has been determined, the licensing authority must notify the following of its decision and its reasons:

- the club;
- the applicant;
- any person who made relevant representations; and
- the chief officer of police for the police area (or each police area) in which the premises are situated.

The decision will not, however, take effect until the end of the period for appealing against the decision, or if the decision is appealed against, until the appeal is disposed of. An appeal may be made by the club, the applicant or any person who made relevant representations within 21 days.

19.10 RELEVANT REPRESENTATIONS

For the purposes of a review, s.88(7) and (8) provides that representations are relevant if they:

- are relevant to one or more of the licensing objectives;
- are made by the club, a responsible authority or an interested party within the 28-day period prescribed for making representations;
- have not been withdrawn; and
- if they are made by an interested party, who is not also a responsible authority, are not, in the opinion of the relevant licensing authority, frivolous or vexatious.

While a club member is entitled to apply for a review, he does not appear to be able to make relevant representations, unless he can qualify as an interested party, for example because he lives in the vicinity of the club.

Where the licensing authority decides that a representation is frivolous or vexatious, it must notify the person who made it of its reasons for its decision.

19.11 INSPECTION OF PREMISES

A constable or an authorised person may, at any reasonable time before the determination of an application for a review of a club premises certificate, enter the premises to which the application relates to inspect them (s.96(1)).

A constable or an authorised person who is exercising the power to enter the premises must, if so requested, produce evidence of his authority to exercise the power (s.96(2)). Before an authorised person or a constable can enter and inspect any premises, at least 48 hours' notice must be given to the club (s.96(3)). The entry and inspection must take place at a reasonable time on a day which is not more than 14 days after the application for the review was made, and the date of the inspection must be in the notice (s.96(3)). Anyone who intentionally obstructs an authorised person exercising the power of entry commits an offence, and is liable on summary conviction to a fine not exceeding level 2 on the standard scale (s.96(5) and (6)).

The relevant licensing authority may, on the application of a responsible authority, extend by not more than seven days the time allowed for carrying out an entry and inspection. The relevant licensing authority may allow such an extension of time only if it appears that reasonable steps had been taken for an authorised person or a constable authorised by the applicant to inspect the premises in good time, but it was not possible for the inspection to take place within the time allowed.

CHAPTER 20

Permitted temporary activities

20.1 INTRODUCTION

Part 5 of the Act introduces a system for authorising temporary licensable activities. It allows licensable activities to be carried on by virtue of a temporary event notice on a temporary basis without the need for a premises licence or club premises certificate. No authorisation is required for these temporary events from the relevant licensing authority. All that is required is that an individual, the 'premises user', must give notice to the licensing authority and the police. In general, only the police may intervene to prevent such an event taking place or to agree a modification of the arrangements for such an event. The system is characterised by an exceptionally light touch bureaucracy. The Guidance at para. 8.2 states that:

> The licensing authority may only ever intervene of its own volition if the limits set out in the 2003 Act on the number of temporary event notices that may be given in various circumstances would be exceeded. Otherwise, the licensing authority is only required to issue a timely acknowledgement.

According to the Guidance, para. 8.4 such a light touch is possible because of the limitations directly imposed on the use of the system by the Act itself. These limitations apply to:

- the number of times a premises user may give a temporary event notice (50 times per year for a personal licence holder and 5 times per year for other people);
- the number of times a temporary event notice may be given in respect of any particular premises (12 times in a calendar year);
- the length of time a temporary event may last for these purposes (96 hours);
- the maximum aggregate duration of the periods covered by temporary event notices at any individual premises (15 days); and
- the scale of the event in terms of the maximum number of people attending at any one time (fewer than 500).

Situations where a temporary event notice might be used would include the running of a temporary bar at a wedding reception or at a fundraising event being held in an unlicensed venue, the provision of live music in premises which are not licensed for the provision of entertainment, or the provision of late night refreshment, e.g. the supply of hot food, at the end of a quiz night.

The Guidance, para. 8.9 acknowledges that:

Many premises users giving temporary event notices will not have commercial backgrounds or ready access to legal advice. They will include, for example, people acting on behalf of charities, community and voluntary groups, schools, churches and hospitals all of which may stage public events to raise funding at which licensable activities will take place. Licensing authorities should therefore ensure that local publicity about the system of permitted temporary activities is clear and understandable and should strive to keep the arrangements manageable and user-friendly for these groups.

A temporary event notice can be given by any individual, including holders of personal licences. Where it is given by a person who does not hold a personal licence the Guidance, paras. 8.19–8.21 provides:

8.19 The 2003 Act provides that any individual person aged 18 or over may give a temporary event notice whether or not they hold a personal licence. They will not therefore have met the tests and qualifications described in Part 6 of the Act. Where alcohol is not to be sold, this should not matter. However, many events will involve combinations of licensable activities. In the absence of a premises user holding a personal licence showing these tests and qualifications have been met, the Act limits the number of notices that may be given by any non-personal licence holder to 5 occasions per year. In every other respect, the Guidance and information set out in paragraphs 8.2 to 8.14 above applies.

8.20 . . . the police will be alive to notifications given by individuals in the area known to have a criminal background. They can also be expected to give particular attention to events staged primarily for children and will be able to intervene, for example, if they have exceptional concerns about any premises user with a known background in paedophilia.

8.21 It should be noted that temporary event notices may be given in respect of club premises covered by club premises certificates by non-personal licence holders. This means, for example, that a club which under its certificate is normally only permitted to supply alcohol to its members and their guests may during the period covered by a temporary event notice (subject to the limitation on numbers and occasions) under the authority of the notice and the responsibility of the individual giving the notice (the premises user) admit members of the public and sell alcohol to them as well as provide regulated entertainment. Only 12 such notices may be given in respect of the same club premises in any calendar year and the maximum aggregate duration of 15 days will also apply.

20.2 MEANING OF 'PERMITTED TEMPORARY ACTIVITY'

Section 98 provides that a licensable activity is a permitted temporary activity if:

- it is carried on in accordance with a temporary event notice which has been properly given;
- the statutory requirements as to acknowledgement of the notice and notification of police are met in relation to the notice;
- the notice has not been withdrawn; and
- a counter notice has not been given.

A potential problem with these requirements is that it appears that if a licensing authority does not acknowledge the temporary event notice, the licensable activity will not be a permitted temporary activity. A licensing authority can thus prevent a temporary event from going ahead by not acknowledging the notice. It is doubtful that this was Parliament's intention.

20.3 THE RELEVANT LICENSING AUTHORITY

In relation to temporary event notices, the 'relevant licensing authority' in relation to any premises is the licensing authority in whose area the premises are situated, or where the premises are situated in the areas of two or more licensing authorities, each of those authorities. This means that where premises are situated in two or more licensing areas, a temporary event notice must be given to each of the licensing authorities.

20.4 PERSONS ENTITLED TO GIVE A TEMPORARY EVENT NOTICE

A temporary event notice may only be given by an individual aged 18 or over who proposes to use premises for one or more licensable activities during a period not exceeding 96 hours (s.100(1)–(3)). Such a person is referred to in the Act as the 'premises user'.

20.5 FORM AND CONTENT OF A TEMPORARY EVENT NOTICE

Section 100(4)–(6) provides that a temporary event notice must be in the prescribed form and contain:

- a statement of the following matters:
  - the licensable activities which are proposed ('the relevant licensable activities');

- the period, not exceeding 96 hours, during which it is proposed to use the premises for those activities ('the event period');
- the times during the event period when the premises user proposes that those licensable activities shall take place;
- the maximum number of persons, being under 500, which the premises user proposes should, during those times, be allowed on the premises at the same time;
- where the relevant licensable activities include the supply of alcohol, whether supplies are proposed to be for consumption on the premises or off the premises, or both; and
- such other matters as may be prescribed.

- where the relevant licensable activities include the supply of alcohol, the notice must make it a condition of using the premises for such supplies that all such supplies are made by or under the authority of the premises user. The supply of alcohol means the sale by retail of alcohol, or the supply of alcohol by or on behalf of a club to, or to the order of, a member of the club (s.100(9)); and
- such other information as may be prescribed.

The prescribed form of temporary event notice is contained in the Licensing Act 2003 (Permitted Temporary Activities) (Notices) Regulations 2005, SI 2005/2918 ('Permitted Temporary Activities Regulations'). As most of the information that must be given in a temporary event notice is contained in the Act, 'the ... regulations concern the additional information that needs to be sought to ensure that the arrangements function efficiently and sensibly in the public interest' (Consultation on Draft Regulations to be Made under the Licensing Act 2003 Permitted Temporary Activities and Temporary Event Notices, para. 1.22).

The 'event period' is a period not exceeding 96 hours. This will allow licensable activities to take place on four consecutive days. However, there is no express requirement that they must take place on consecutive days. It would appear that licensable activities can take place on non-consecutive days provided those activities do not exceed 96 hours in total. For example, for an event lasting a week there might be licensable activities on Monday and Tuesday, none on Wednesday, and then licensable activities on Thursday and Friday. If the licensable activities do not exceed 96 hours the statutory requirements will be satisfied even though the licensable activities take place on non-consecutive days. Having said that it may well be that the provision will be interpreted to require the licensable activities to take place on consecutive days as this was the position with occasional permissions under the previous law (see *R.* v. *Bromley Licensing Justices ex p. Bromley Licensed Victuallers' Association* [1984] 1 All ER 794 where 'a period not exceeding twenty four hours' was taken to mean a continuous period of 24 hours).

231

The Secretary of State may by order alter the period of 96 hours and the maximum number of people attending at any one time during the event (499 persons) (s.100(8)).

20.5.1 Obtaining a form of temporary event notice

The Permitted Temporary Activities Regulations are silent on whether a relevant licensing authority must provide a potential applicant with a temporary event notice on request. The provisions to this effect in the Premises Regulations only apply to forms listed in the schedules to those regulations and not to other forms. It is assumed that in practice licensing authorities will make printed copies available and may also provide electronic versions on their websites which a potential applicant can download, print off and complete.

20.5.2 Completing the temporary event notice

For details of how to complete the notice see **6.5.2**.

The temporary event notice in the Permitted Temporary Activities Regulations is divided into 10 parts, as follows.

Part 1 – personal details

This section asks for details of the premises user, such as his full name, any previous names, his date of birth, current address (the licensing authority will use this address to correspond with the premises user unless he specifies an alternative correspondence address, such as his business address), telephone number, and fax number and e-mail address (both these are optional).

Part 2 – the premises

This section asks for details of the premises where the premises user intends to carry on the licensable activities. If the premises do not have an address, for example they are an open space, the Ordnance Survey references should be given. Where only part of the premises is to be used, a clear description of the area to be used must be given. Any licensable activities carried on outside this area will be unauthorised so it is important that the description cover all the area where the licensable activities are to be carried on.

The nature of the premises must be described, for example, a church or village hall, a restaurant, an open field, a beer tent or a public house. The nature of the event must also be described, for example, a wedding with a pay bar, the supply of beer at a fair, etc. These descriptions will help the police decide whether any crime prevention issues are likely to arise.

Part 3 – the licensable activities

The applicant must state which licensable activities he intends to carry on at the premises, the dates on which he intends to use the premises for these licensable activities, the times it is proposed to carry on licensable activities and the maximum number of people at any one time that it is intended to allow to be present at the premises. If the licensable activities will include the supply of alcohol, the applicant must state whether the supplies will be for consumption on or off the premises or both.

Part 4 – personal licence holders

If the applicant holds a personal licence, he must give details of it, for example, the name of the licensing authority which issued the personal licence, the licence number and its dates of issue and expiry.

Part 5 – previous temporary event notices

An applicant must indicate whether he has previously given a temporary event notice in respect of any premises for events falling in the same calendar year as the event for which he is now giving this temporary event notice and, if he has, he must state the number of temporary event notices. He must also indicate whether he has already given a temporary event notice for the same premises in which the event period ends 24 hours or less before, or begins 24 hours or less after the event period proposed in this temporary event notice.

Part 6 – associates and business colleagues

An applicant must indicate whether any associate or any person with whom he is in business carrying on licensable activities has given a temporary event notice for an event in the same calendar year as the event for which he is now giving a temporary event notice (see **20.11.4**), and if he has, he must state the number of temporary event notices the associate or business colleague has given. He must also indicate whether any associate or any person with whom he is in business carrying on licensable activities has already given a temporary event notice for the same premises in which the event period ends 24 hours or less before, or begins 24 hours or less after the event period proposed in this temporary event notice.

Part 7 – checklist

This part is made up of a checklist so that an applicant does not overlook anything.

Part 8 – condition

This section contains a declaration that it will be a condition of the temporary event notice that where the relevant licensable activities described in part 3 include the supply of alcohol that all such supplies are made by or under the authority of the premises user.

Part 9 – declaration

By signing this part the applicant is making a declaration that the information in the form is correct to the best of his knowledge and belief. If he signs and has not complied with the declaration, he may be making a false statement in relation to the temporary event notice which is an offence which, on conviction, is liable to a fine not exceeding level 5 on the standard scale.

Part 10 – acknowledgement

An applicant must leave this blank as it is for the licensing authority to use in order to acknowledge receipt of the temporary event notice.

20.5.3 Making an application

There is no provision for a temporary event notice to be given electronically. Two copies of the temporary event notice must be sent to the relevant licensing authority at least 10 working days before the licensable activities are to start. A copy must also be sent to the chief officer of police for the area in which the premises are situated.

20.5.4 Checklist for a temporary event notice

- Two copies of completed and signed temporary event notice sent to the relevant licensing authority;
- one copy of completed and signed temporary event notice sent to the chief officer of police; and
- fee of £21 enclosed with copies sent to relevant licensing authority.

20.6 NOTICE PERIOD

A temporary event notice must be given to the relevant licensing authority no later than 10 working days before the day on which the event period begins, and must be accompanied by the prescribed fee of £21 (s.100(7)). The notice must be given in duplicate. The notice must be given in accordance with s.184.

Section 193 defines 'working day' as any day other than a Saturday, a Sunday, Christmas Day, Good Friday or a day which is a bank holiday under the Banking and Financial Dealings Act 1971 in England and Wales. '10 working days' notice means 10 working days exclusive of the day on which the event is to start (Guidance, para. 8.12).

It is not apparent whether the 10-day notice period starts from the time the licensing authority receives the notice or from the time the notice is given. It is possible that this could be an issue in a case where the police object as there may not be sufficient time for the licensing authority to hold a hearing before the event is due to take place. While a licensing authority has no power to extend the 10-day notice period, a licensing authority may encourage a longer period of notice to be given, as the Guidance, para. 8.11 states:

> Although . . . ten working days is the minimum possible notice that may be given, licensing authorities should publicise locally their preferences in terms of forward notice and encourage notice givers to provide the earliest possible notice of events likely to take place. Licensing authorities should also consider publicising a preferred maximum time in advance of an event that applications should be made. For example, if an application is made too far in advance of an event, it may be difficult for the police to make a sensible assessment and could lead to objections that could be otherwise avoided.

The Guidance also provides at para 8.17:

> The possibility of police intervention is another reason why event organisers should be encouraged by local publicity not to rely on giving the minimum amount of notice and to contact local police licensing officers at the earliest possible opportunity about their proposals.

Where an individual wishes to hold more than one temporary event, he can give notice of them all at the same time if he wishes provided the first event is at least 10 working days away. The Guidance, para. 8.10 provides:

> On each occasion at least 10 working days notice must be given, but there is nothing to prevent simultaneous notification of multiple events at a single time so long as the first event is at least ten days away. For example, an individual personal licence holder wishing to exhibit and sell beer at a series of country shows may wish to give several notices simultaneously. However, this would only be possible where the events are to take place in the same licensing authority (and police area) and the premises to be used at the show would be occupied by no more than 499 people at any one time.

20.7 MINIMUM PERIOD BETWEEN EVENT PERIODS

There must be a minimum of 24 hours between events notified by a premises user in respect of the same premises. If this is not the case then the temporary event notice will be void. This is to prevent evasion of the 96-hour limit on such events and the need to obtain a full premises licence or club premises certificate for more major or permanent events (Guidance, para. 8.22).

Section 101 provides that a temporary event notice given by a premises user will be void if the event period specified in it does not:

- end at least 24 hours before the event period specified in any other temporary event notice given by the relevant premises user in respect of the same premises before or at the same time as the notice; or
- begin at least 24 hours after the event period specified in any other such notice.

A temporary event notice in respect of which a counter notice has been given or which has been withdrawn is disregarded when calculating the minimum period of 24 hours.

Section 101 attempts to prevent a premises user circumventing the 24-hour minimum period by having consecutive notices given by others on his behalf. It provides that a temporary event notice which is given by an individual who is an associate of the relevant premises user is treated as a notice given by the relevant premises user. While the definition of an 'associate' is very wide it does not include a friend of the premises user which therefore provides a premises user with a possibility for circumventing the minimum period. Section 101(3) provides that an individual is an associate of another person if he is:

- the spouse of that person:
- a child, parent, grandchild, grandparent, brother or sister of that person;
- an agent or employee of that person;
- the spouse of a child, parent, grandchild, grandparent, brother or sister of that person; or
- the spouse of an agent or employee of that person.

A person living with another as that person's husband or wife is to be treated as that person's spouse, and when the Civil Partnership Act 2004 is in force, a civil partner will be specifically included in the definition in s.101(3) with a spouse.

A temporary event notice given by an individual who is in business with the premises user will be treated as a temporary event notice given by the premises user if that business relates to one or more licensable activities, and both notices relate to one or more licensable activities to which the business relates, although not necessarily the same activity or activities. There is no definition in the Act of when an individual will be in business with a premises user.

Where two temporary event notices are given in respect of different parts of the same premises, they will be regarded as given in respect of the same premises.

20.8 ACKNOWLEDGEMENT OF A TEMPORARY EVENT NOTICE BY A LICENSING AUTHORITY

A licensing authority which receives a temporary event notice (in duplicate) must acknowledge receipt of the notice by sending or delivering one of the duplicate notices to the premises user (s.102). This must be done before the end of the first working day following the day on which it was received, or if the day on which it was received was not a working day, before the end of the second working day following that day. If the licensing authority does not acknowledge receipt then it may be that the premises user cannot stage the temporary event, as one of the conditions for a permitted temporary activity is that the acknowledgement requirements in s.102 are met. There is no sanction available for a premises user to take against a licensing authority which does not acknowledge receipt.

If a temporary event notice is not submitted in duplicate there is no requirement on a licensing authority to acknowledge receipt, which will mean that the premises user cannot stage the temporary event.

The licensing authority must acknowledgement receipt of the temporary event notice on the copy of the notice it returns to the premises user. The receipt must be in the prescribed form. The Permitted Temporary Activities Regulations provide that this acknowledgement is the signature of a person authorised to acknowledge receipt in part 10 of the temporary event notice or a copy of the notice.

A licensing authority does not need to acknowledge a notice if it has sent or delivered a counter notice to the premises user under s.107 stating that the prescribed number of events would be exceeded if the event went ahead.

Once the licensing authority acknowledges receipt of the temporary event notice, the premises user is authorised to hold his temporary event in accordance with the Act. The Guidance, para. 8.15 provides:

> In the case of an event proceeding under the authority of a temporary event notice, failure to adhere to the requirements of the 2003 Act, such as the limitation of no more than 499 being present at any one time, would mean that the event was unauthorised. In such circumstances, the premises user would be liable to prosecution.

20.9 WITHDRAWAL OF A TEMPORARY EVENT NOTICE

Section 103 allows a premises user to withdraw a temporary event notice by giving the relevant licensing authority a notice to that effect no later than 24 hours before the beginning of the event period specified in the temporary event notice. A notice once withdrawn will not count towards an individual's limit on the number of temporary event notices he can submit during a calendar year.

20.10 POLICE INTERVENTION

Notice of a temporary event must be given to the police who may then object on the basis of the crime prevention objective. It is not possible for anyone else, for example a local resident or a responsible authority to object. A temporary event may always be closed down by the police for up to 24 hours where there is, or is likely imminently to be, disorder on or in the vicinity of and related to the premises and their closure is necessary in the interests of public safety, or a public nuisance is being caused by noise coming from the premises and the closure of the premises is necessary to prevent that nuisance.

20.10.1 Notice to the police

A premises user must give a copy of his temporary event notice to the relevant chief officer of police no later than 10 working days before the day on which the event period specified in the notice begins (s.104(1)). For these purposes 'relevant chief officer of police' means:

- where the premises are situated in one police area, the chief officer of police for that area; or
- where the premises are situated in two or more police areas, the chief officer of police for each of those areas.

The notice must be given to the chief officer of police in accordance with s.184. Section 184(3) provides that it may be given by delivering it to him, or by leaving it at his proper address, or by sending it by post to him at that address.

20.10.2 Objection by the police

If a chief officer of police receives a copy of a temporary event notice and is satisfied that allowing the premises to be used in accordance with the notice would undermine the crime prevention objective, he must give an objection notice setting out the reasons for his decision. This notice must be given to the relevant licensing authority and the premises user no later than 48 hours after the chief officer of police has been given a copy of the temporary event notice.

The Guidance at para. 8.16 states that the most important purpose of the notification requirements is to give the police an opportunity to consider whether they should object to the event taking place in order to prevent crime and disorder. It goes on to state:

> Such cases might arise because of concerns about the scale, location or timing of the event. The general run of cases where alcohol is supplied away from licensed premises at a temporary bar under the control of a personal licence holder (e.g. at weddings or small social, community, charitable or sporting events) should not give rise to the use of these police powers. The 2003 Act provides that the police may issue an objection notice because they believe the event would undermine the

crime prevention objective set out in the Act. The police must issue any objection notice within 48 hours of being notified, but they can subsequently withdraw their objection notice. If the police do not intervene, they will still be able to rely on their powers of closure under Part 8 of the 2003 Act should disorder or noise nuisance subsequently arise. The issuing of such an objection notice requires the consideration of the objection by the licensing authority at a hearing.

The police cannot object if the chief officer of police has received a copy of a counter notice given by the licensing authority that the permitted limits for temporary event notices have been exceeded (see **20.11**).

20.10.3   Counter notice following a police objection

If the police give an objection notice, the relevant licensing authority must hold a hearing to consider the objection notice, unless the premises user, the chief officer of police who gave the objection notice and the authority agree that a hearing is unnecessary (s.105).

The hearing must be held within seven working days beginning with the day after the end of the period within which a chief officer of police may give an objection notice. The end of the period during which the police may give an objection notice is 48 hours after the premises user has given a copy of the temporary event notice to the police. Notice of the hearing must be given to the premises user and the chief officer of police no later than two working days before the day or the first day on which the hearing is to be held.

Following the hearing the licensing authority must, having regard to the objection notice, give the premises user a counter notice if it considers that this is necessary for the promotion of the crime prevention objective.

At the hearing the licensing authority can only consider the crime prevention objective and nothing else. The Guidance, para. 8.16 states:

> Consideration by the licensing authority is confined to the crime prevention objective. It may not, for example, uphold a police objection notice on grounds of public nuisance. At the hearing, the police and the premises user may be heard by the relevant licensing committee. A hearing would not be necessary if the objection notice is withdrawn by the police.

If the licensing authority gives a counter notice to the premises user, it must give with it a notice setting out its reasons for giving the counter notice. There is no provision in either the Act or the Permitted Temporary Activities Regulations about the form that a counter notice should take. Copies of both notices must also be given to the chief officer of police. The Licensing authority must give notice forthwith (see **2.9**) on making the decision and the notice must be accompanied by information setting out the right of a party to appeal against the decision. If the licensing authority decides not to give a counter notice, it must give the premises user and the chief officer of police notice of its decision. There is no requirement for it to give its reasons for not giving a counter notice.

A decision as to whether or not to give a counter notice must be made, and the appropriate notices given, at least 24 hours before the beginning of the event period specified in the temporary event notice (s.105(4)). The Act does not set out the effect of non-compliance with this provision but it seems clear that a failure to comply with it will mean that the premises user will not be able to proceed with his event.

Where the premises are situated in the area of more than one licensing authority, the authorities must act jointly and hold a joint hearing (s.105(5)). It is not clear whether each authority will need to give its own notices or whether notices can be given by one of them on behalf of them all.

The provisions as to counter notices do not apply if the objection notice has been withdrawn, or if the premises user has been given a counter notice by the licensing authority that the permitted limits for temporary event notices have been exceeded (see **20.11**).

20.10.4 Modification of a temporary event notice following a police objection

Where a chief officer of police has given an objection notice in respect of a temporary event notice, and the objection notice has not been withdrawn, he may, with the agreement of the premises user, modify the temporary event notice (s.106). He may do this at any time before a hearing to consider the objection notice is held or dispensed with, and provided the premises user has not been given a counter notice by the licensing authority that the permitted limits for temporary event notices have been exceeded (see **20.11**).

A modification is made by making changes to the copy of the temporary event notice which the licensing authority returned to the premises user. A copy of the modified temporary event notice must be sent or delivered by the chief officer of police to the relevant licensing authority before a hearing is held or dispensed with.

Where a temporary event notice is modified the objection notice is treated as having been withdrawn from the time the temporary event notice is modified, and from that time the modified temporary event notice has effect (s.106(3)).

Where the premises are situated in more than one police area, the chief officer of police may modify the temporary event notice only with the consent of the chief officer of police for the other police area or each of the other police areas in which the premises are situated (s.106(5)).

The procedure for modifying a temporary event notice may prove difficult in practice. The police have to make changes to the notice which the licensing authority returned to the premises user. This is a copy of the temporary event notice held by the licensing authority, and the Act is silent as to how changes will be made to this notice. It may well be that in practice the police will modify their copy of the temporary event notice and then send a copy of it to the premises user and the licensing authority.

20.11   LIMITS ON TEMPORARY EVENT NOTICES

20.11.1   Permitted limits – personal licence holders

An individual who holds a personal licence may give a maximum of 50 temporary event notices in a calendar year (s.107(2)). Where an individual gives temporary event notices to different licensing authorities it may be difficult, in the absence of a central register, to keep track of the number of temporary event notices he has given. Section 8 requires licensing authorities to keep a register containing, among other information, a record of temporary event notices received by it. The central licensing register project is currently working with licensing authorities to examine ways in which such a system might best be developed. Until such time as this is operational licensing authorities will be reliant on an applicant disclosing the number of temporary event notices he has given.

The Secretary of State may, by order, change the maximum number of temporary event notices which can be given in a calendar year.

20.11.2   Permitted limits – non personal licence holders

An individual who does not hold a personal licence may give a maximum of five temporary event notices in a calendar year (s.107(3)). As mentioned above until there is a central register, licensing authorities will be reliant on an applicant disclosing the number of temporary event notices he has given.

The Secretary of State may, by order, change the maximum number of temporary event notices which can be given in a calendar year.

20.11.3   Permitted limits – individual premises

No more than 12 temporary event notices can be given in respect of the same premises in a calendar year and these cannot cover a period of more than 15 days (s.107(4) and (5)).

As s.193 defines 'premises' as meaning 'any place', it could be argued that temporary event notices could be given in respect of part of a building or open space. However in calculating the permitted limit, s.107(13)(a) provides that 'a temporary event notice is in respect of the same premises . . . if it is in respect of the whole or any part of the relevant premises or premises which include the whole or any part of those premises'.

The Secretary of State may, by order, change the maximum number of temporary event notices which can be given in a calendar year and/or the maximum number of days which they can cover in a calendar year.

20.11.4 Calculating the permitted limits

For calculation of the permitted limits, the number of events are calculated by reference to a calendar year. If an event straddles two calendar years, it counts towards the limits for each of those years (s.107(6)).

No account is taken of any temporary event notice in respect of which a counter notice has been given by the licensing authority, either following an objection notice by the police or because the permitted limits for temporary event notices have been exceeded (s.107(9)).

In determining the number of temporary event notices given by an individual, a temporary event notice given by his associate or by someone who is in business with him is treated as a notice given by him (s.107(10)). For these purposes 'an associate' has the same meaning as in s.101 (see 20.7). Where the notice is given by someone who is in business with the individual, it will be treated as a notice given by him if the business relates to one or more licensable activities, and the temporary event notices relate to one or more licensable activities to which the business relates, but not necessarily the same activity or activities.

20.11.5 Giving a counter notice

Where a licensing authority receives a temporary event notice in respect of any premises, and is satisfied that one of the permitted limits will be exceeded if the event proceeds, it must give the premises user a counter notice (s.107(1)).

A counter notice must be in the prescribed form and be given to the premises user in the prescribed manner, which is set out in the Permitted Temporary Activities Regulations, Sched. 2. This is a straightforward form of counter notice in which the licensing authority states that it has received a temporary event notice and then indicates which one of the permitted limits would be exceeded if the activities were to take place. It must be given at least 24 hours before the beginning of the event period specified in the temporary event notice.

A copy of the counter notice must forthwith (see **2.9**) be sent by the licensing authority to the chief officer of police for the police area, or each of the police areas, in which the premises are situated.

A counter notice must be given by being:

- delivered to the relevant premises user in person;
- left at the 'appropriate address' which will be the postal address indicated in section 1(8) of the temporary event notice, or if there is no such address, the postal address indicated in section 1(6) of the notice;
- sent to the 'appropriate address' by ordinary post, i.e. ordinary pre-paid first-class or second-class post (with or without special arrangements for delivery); or
- sent by e-mail to an 'appropriate e-mail address' which will be an e-mail

address indicated in section 1(9) of the temporary event notice, or if sections 1(8) and (9) of the notice have not been completed, an e-mail address indicated in section 1(7) of the notice (Permitted Temporary Activities Regulations, reg. 6).

20.12 RIGHT OF ENTRY WHERE A TEMPORARY EVENT NOTICE HAS BEEN GIVEN

Section 108 gives a constable or an authorised officer the right, at any reasonable time, to enter the premises to which a temporary event notice relates in order to assess the likely effect of the notice on the promotion of the crime prevention objective. There is no right for the use of reasonable force when gaining entry. Nor is there any provision as to when entry can be made, so entry could take place either before or during the event to which the notice relates.

For these purposes, an 'authorised officer' is an officer of the licensing authority in whose area the premises are situated, or if the premises are situated in the area of more than one licensing authority, an officer of any of those authorities, authorised for the purposes of the Act (s.108(5)). An authorised officer who exercises the right of entry must, if so requested, produce evidence of his authority (s.108(2)).

Anyone who intentionally obstructs an authorised officer exercising his right of entry commits an offence. A person guilty of such an offence is liable on summary conviction to a fine not exceeding level 2 on the standard scale. Obstructing a constable exercising the right of entry will be an offence of obstructing a constable in the execution of his duties under the Police Act 1996, s.89(2). A person guilty of such an offence is liable on summary conviction to imprisonment for a term not exceeding one month (this will increase to 51 weeks when the Criminal Justice Act 2003 takes effect) or to a fine not exceeding level 3 on the standard scale, or to both.

20.13 DUTY TO KEEP AND PRODUCE A TEMPORARY EVENT NOTICE

Whenever premises are being used for one or more licensable activities which are or are purported to be permitted temporary activities, the premises user must under s.109 make sure either:

- that a copy of the temporary event notice is prominently displayed at the premises; or
- that the temporary event notice is kept at the premises in his custody, or in the custody of a person who is present and working at the premises and whom he has nominated for this purpose, and where the temporary event notice is in the custody of a nominated person, ensure that a notice

specifying that fact and the position held at the premises by that person is prominently displayed at the premises.

A premises user will commit an offence if he fails, without reasonable excuse, to comply with these requirements. A person guilty of such an offence is liable on summary conviction to a fine not exceeding level 2 on the standard scale.

Where the temporary event notice is not displayed as required and no notice is displayed specifying that the temporary event notice is in the custody of a nominated person and the position held at the premises by that person, a constable or an authorised officer may require the premises user to produce the temporary event notice for examination (s.109(5)). An authorised officer when exercising this power must, if so requested, produce evidence of his authority. A person commits an offence if he fails, without reasonable excuse, to produce a temporary event notice in accordance with this requirement. A person guilty of such an offence is liable on summary conviction to a fine not exceeding level 2 on the standard scale.

Where a notice is displayed specifying that the temporary event notice is in the custody of a nominated person and the position held at the premises by that person, a constable or an authorised officer may require the person specified in the notice to produce the temporary event notice for examination (s.109(6)). An authorised officer when exercising this power must, if so requested, produce evidence of his authority. A person commits an offence if he fails, without reasonable excuse, to produce a temporary event notice in accordance with this requirement. A person guilty of such an offence is liable on summary conviction to a fine not exceeding level 2 on the standard scale.

20.14   THEFT, LOSS, ETC. OF A TEMPORARY EVENT NOTICE

If a temporary event notice which has been acknowledged is lost, stolen, damaged or destroyed, the premises user may apply to the licensing authority which acknowledged the notice, or, if there is more than one such authority, any of them, for a copy of the notice (s.110). The licensing authority must then issue the premises user with a copy of the temporary event notice if it is satisfied that the notice has been lost, stolen, damaged or destroyed, and where it has been lost or stolen, the premises user has reported that loss or theft to the police. The copy must be a copy of the notice in the form it existed immediately before it was lost, stolen, damaged or destroyed, and must be certified by the licensing authority as a true copy. The Act then applies to the copy as it applies in relation to an original temporary event notice.

An application must be accompanied by the prescribed fee of £10.50. An application cannot be made more than one month after the end of the event period specified in the temporary event notice.

CHAPTER 21

Offences

21.1 INTRODUCTION

Part 7 of the Act contains the main offences in the Act. There are a number of other offences in the Act which cover failure to comply with procedural requirements, and these have been dealt with earlier in this text where appropriate.

The offences in Part 7 are divided into six categories as follows:

- unauthorised licensable activities;
- drunkenness and disorderly conduct;
- smuggled goods;
- children and alcohol;
- confiscation of alcohol;
- vehicles and trains; and
- false statements relating to licensing, etc.

There are also offences relating to licensing law in other statutes, dealing with the following:

- giving intoxicating liquor to children under 5;
- confiscation of alcohol; and
- alcohol consumption in designated public places.

21.2 UNAUTHORISED LICENSABLE ACTIVITIES

21.2.1 Unauthorised licensable activities

Section 136(1)(a) provides that it is an offence to carry on or attempt to carry on a licensable activity on or from any premises otherwise than under and in accordance with a premises licence, a club premises certificate or a temporary event notice. Section 136(1)(b) provides that it is an offence to knowingly allow a licensable activity to be carried on without such authorisation.

These offences are very wide in their scope. They will cover not only premises which have no authorisation for any licensable activities, but also premises that have authorisation but not for the particular licensable activity which is being carried on and premises which have authorisation for the licensable activity in question but where a breach of conditions has occurred. The Guidance, para. 14.6 provides:

> These offences therefore cover premises that are entirely unlicensed, for example, an unlicensed drinking den or unlicensed film exhibitions; and premises that are licensed for one activity, for example, premises licensed for the sale of alcohol but not for another, for example the provision of regulated entertainment. In addition, the offence refers to an activity carried on otherwise than in accordance with a premises licence, club premises certificate or temporary event notice meeting the conditions of section 98(2)–(4) of the 2003 Act. Accordingly, these offences relate to breaches of the terms and conditions included in such licences, certificates or notices including any relating to hours during which the licensable activities may take place.

The offence in s.136(1)(a) is committed by a person who carries on or attempts to carry on an unauthorised licensable activity. Persons carrying on a licensable activity will clearly include persons who have some role in the organisation or management of the licensable activity, for example, the premises licence holder, the club secretary or club committee or a premises user. Whether any other persons will be liable will depend on the interpretation of 'carries on'. There is a due diligence defence to this offence (see **21.2.4**).

The offence in s.136(1)(b) requires a person to 'knowingly' allow a licensable activity to be carried on without authorisation. This will require not only that they have a positive belief that the licensable activity is being carried on but also that they have a positive belief that there is no authorisation for it (see *Westminster City Council* v. *Croyalgrange Ltd* [1986] 1 WLR 674, a case relating to a sex establishment, where it was held that knowledge was needed not only as to the use of the premises but also as to the entertainment being carried on without a licence). A person will allow a licensable activity to be carried on where he has positively acted in such a way as to allow the activity to go ahead and also where he has failed to exercise control to prevent it going ahead where he has power to do so (*Barking and Dagenham London Borough Council* v. *Bass Taverns* [1993] COD 453).

Where the licensable activity in question is the provision of regulated entertainment, s.136(2) provides that a person does not commit an offence if his only involvement in the provision of the entertainment is that he:

* performs in a play;
* participates as a sportsman in an indoor sporting event;
* boxes or wrestles in a boxing or wrestling entertainment;
* performs live music;
* plays recorded music;

- performs dance; or
- does something coming within para. 2(1)(h) of Sched. 1 (entertainment similar to music, dance, etc.).

Thus the offences do not apply to performers or participants in regulated entertainment. However if the individual also organised or helped to organise the event, then subject to the defence of due diligence, he may commit an offence (the Guidance, para. 14.7).

A person guilty of an offence under s.136 is liable on summary conviction to imprisonment for a term not exceeding six months or to a fine not exceeding £20,000, or to both (s.136(4)).

21.2.2 Exposing alcohol for unauthorised sale

Section 137(1) provides that it is an offence to expose for sale by retail on any premises any alcohol in circumstances where the sale by retail of that alcohol on those premises would not be authorised by a premises licence, a club premises certificate or a temporary event notice. It is not necessary that there is a sale or attempted sale of the alcohol as all that is required is that the alcohol is exposed in such a way that any sale would be unauthorised. The offence can be committed by anyone who exposes the alcohol for sale.

An offence under this provision may also be committed where the sale by retail of alcohol is permitted, but there is a breach of the conditions of that authorisation, for example exposing alcohol for sale outside authorised hours will be an offence.

A person guilty of this offence is liable on summary conviction to imprisonment for a term not exceeding six months or to a fine not exceeding £20,000, or to both. In addition, a court which convicts a person of this offence may order that the alcohol in question and its containers are forfeited and either destroyed or dealt with in such other manner as the court may order.

There is a due diligence defence to this offence (see **21.2.4**).

21.2.3 Keeping alcohol on premises for unauthorised sale

Section 138(1) provides that a person commits an offence if he has in his possession or under his control alcohol which he intends to sell by retail or supply by or on behalf of a club to, or to the order of, a member of the club in circumstances where that activity would be an unauthorised licensable activity, i.e. it is not authorised by a premises licence, a club premises certificate or a temporary event notice. The offence is committed where a person has possession or control of the alcohol. There is no requirement that he must own it or have any other proprietary right in it.

247

A person guilty of this offence is liable on summary conviction to a fine not exceeding level 2 on the standard scale. In addition, a court which convicts a person of this offence may order that the alcohol in question, and its containers, be forfeited and either destroyed or dealt with in such other manner as the court may order.

There is a due diligence defence to this offence (see **21.2.4**).

21.2.4 Defence of due diligence

Section 139 provides a due diligence defence for a person who has been charged with:

- an offence of carrying on an unauthorised licensable activity (s.136(1)(a));
- exposing alcohol for unauthorised sale (s.137); or
- keeping alcohol on premises for unauthorised sale (s.138).

It will be a defence for a person charged with these offences if:

- his act was due to a mistake, or to reliance on information given to him, or to an act or omission by another person, or to some other cause beyond his control; and
- he took all reasonable precautions and exercised all due diligence to avoid committing the offence.

Both elements of the defence must be satisfied for the defence to be effective. Whether the defence is established will be a question of fact in each case. The burden of satisfying the court falls on the person raising this defence. An example of where it might apply is given by the Guidance, para. 14.9 as follows:

> For example, in the case of a manager of premises assured inaccurately by the premises licence holder (his employer) that the premises were licensed for the provision of regulated entertainment such as live music, he may have a defence that he had relied on false information given to him and had taken all reasonable precautions and exercised all due diligence to avoid committing the offence.

21.3 DRUNKENNESS AND DISORDERLY CONDUCT

21.3.1 Allowing disorderly conduct on licensed premises

Section 140 makes it an offence to knowingly allow disorderly conduct on licensed premises, premises which have a club premises certificate or premises which may be used for a permitted temporary activity.

This offence may be committed by:

- any person who works at the premises, whether paid or unpaid, in a capacity which authorises him to prevent the conduct;

- in the case of licensed premises, the holder of the premises licence, and the designated premises supervisor;
- in the case of premises which have a club premises certificate, any member or officer of the club who at the time the conduct takes place is present on the premises in a capacity which enables him to prevent it; and
- in the case of premises used for a permitted temporary activity, the premises user in relation to the temporary event notice in question.

According to the Guidance, para. 14.15:

> This is an extremely important offence and is central to the management of premises where alcohol is sold for consumption on those premises, though it applies equally to premises where other licensable activities are taking place. Its existence is central to the safety of law-abiding customers on the premises. . . . The licensing authority should draw the attention of any person, business or club granted a licence, club premises certificate or giving a temporary event notice to this offence and of the licensing authority's readiness to prosecute any person who fails in his duty in this respect. It is important to note the words 'knowingly to allow' disorderly conduct on relevant premises. The outbreak of disorder may not of itself give rise to this offence. It is the failure to address the problem either through direct action or calling the police that is likely to give rise to an offence.

There is no definition in the Act of what will amount to 'disorderly conduct'. However it is suggested that it will include such matters as allowing drunkenness or violent behaviour on licensed premises, allowing licensed premises to be used by prostitutes or as a brothel, or permitting illegal gaming on licensed premises.

The offence requires a person to have knowledge of the disorderly conduct. Apart from in relation to premises where a club premises certificate has effect, there is no requirement that the appropriate person must be on the premises at the time the conduct takes place. In this situation it may be argued that there is no liability as that person has no personal knowledge of the conduct (see *Vane* v. *Yiannopoullos* [1965] AC 486) unless he has completely delegated his authority to someone else who is present.

A person guilty of this offence is liable on summary conviction to a fine not exceeding level 3 on the standard scale.

21.3.2   Sale of alcohol to a person who is drunk

Section 141 provides that it is an offence for a person on licensed premises, premises which have a club premises certificate or premises which may be used for a permitted temporary activity, to knowingly sell or attempt to sell alcohol to a person who is drunk, or to knowingly allow alcohol to be sold to such a person.

The offence may be committed by:

- any person who works at the premises, whether paid or unpaid, in a capacity which authorises him to sell the alcohol concerned;
- in the case of licensed premises, the holder of the premises licence and the designated premises supervisor;
- in the case of premises which have a club premises certificate, any member or officer of the club who at the time of the sale or attempted sale takes place is present on the premises in a capacity which enables him to prevent it; and
- in the case of premises used for a permitted temporary activity, the premises user in relation to the temporary event notice in question.

The offence also covers a supply of alcohol by or on behalf of a club to or to the order of a member of the club (s.141(3)).

There must be a sale of alcohol to a person who is drunk or an attempt to sell alcohol to such a person. Thus, the offence would not be committed where there was a bona fide gift of alcohol to someone who was drunk (*Petherick* v. *Sargent* (1862) 26 JP 135).

The offence requires a person to have knowledge of both the sale and that the person is drunk. Apart from in relation to premises where a club premises certificate has effect, there is no requirement that the appropriate person must be on the premises at the time the sale takes place (see **21.3.1** as to delegation).

The Act is silent as to when a person is 'drunk'. It is suggested that 'drunk' should be given its ordinary meaning. In *Neale* v. *RJME (a Minor)* (1985) 80 Cr App R 20 the case involved an offence of drunken disorderly behaviour in a public place. Robert Goff LJ when considering the meaning of 'drunk' said at p.23:

> The primary meaning set out in the Shorter Oxford Dictionary (1933) is as follows: 'That has drunk intoxicating liquor to an extent which affects steady self-control.' ... In my judgment, that is indeed the natural and ordinary meaning of the word 'drunk' in ordinary common speech in 1984.

A person guilty of the offence is liable on summary conviction to a fine not exceeding level 3 on the standard scale.

The Guidance, para. 14.17 recommends rigorous enforcement of this offence as follows:

> Licensing authorities and the police should note that anti-social behaviour once customers are beyond the direct control of licensees and managers of licensed premises will sometimes (some drunkenness will arise through consumption at private parties) be a result of sales made earlier on licensed premises when an individual was drunk. It is therefore important that these offences are prosecuted effectively to ensure that there is a strong deterrent in respect of such sales. The control of excessive consumption and drunkenness on relevant premises should reduce the risk of anti-social behaviour occurring elsewhere after customers have left the premises.

21.3.3 Obtaining alcohol for a person who is drunk

Section 142 provides that it is an offence for a person, on licensed premises, premises which have a club premises certificate or premises which may be used for a permitted temporary activity, to knowingly obtain or attempt to obtain alcohol for consumption on those premises by a person who is drunk.

A person guilty of this offence is liable on summary conviction to a fine not exceeding level 3 on the standard scale.

21.3.4 Failure to leave licensed premises

A person who is drunk or disorderly commits an offence under s.143 if, without reasonable excuse, he fails to leave licensed premises, premises which have a club premises certificate or premises which may be used for a permitted temporary activity when requested to do so by a police constable or by a person specified below, or he enters or attempts to enter such premises after a police constable or a person specified below has requested him not to enter them.

The persons specified for these purposes are:

- any person who works at the premises, whether paid or unpaid, in a capacity which authorises him to make such a request;
- in the case of licensed premises, the holder of the premises licence and the designated premises supervisor;
- in the case of premises which have a club premises certificate, any member or officer of the club who is present on the premises in a capacity which gives him authority to make such a request; and
- in the case of premises used for a permitted temporary activity, the premises user in relation to the temporary event notice in question.

A person guilty of this offence is liable on summary conviction to a fine not exceeding level 1 on the standard scale. There is defence of reasonable excuse available to a person charged with this offence. This would assist a person who was unable to leave because he was ill, disabled or injured.

If requested to do so by one of the persons specified above, a police constable must help to expel from relevant premises a person who is drunk or disorderly, or help to prevent such a person from entering relevant premises (s.143(4)).

21.4 SMUGGLED GOODS

A person will commit an offence under s.144 if he knowingly keeps or allows to be kept, on any licensed premises, premises which have a club premises certificate or premises which may be used for a permitted temporary activity, any goods which have been imported without payment of duty or which have otherwise been unlawfully imported. A court which convicts a person of this offence may order that the goods in question, and any container for them, are to be forfeited and either destroyed or dealt with in such other manner as the court may order.

The persons who can commit this offence are:

- any person who works at the premises, whether paid or unpaid, in a capacity which gives him the authority to prevent those goods from being kept on the premises;
- in the case of licensed premises, the holder of the premises licence and the designated premises supervisor;
- in the case of premises which have a club premises certificate, any member or officer of the club who is present on the premises at the time when the goods are kept on the premises, in a capacity which gives him authority to prevent them being so kept; and
- in the case of premises used for a permitted temporary activity, the premises user in relation to the temporary event notice in question.

In relation to this offence, the Guidance, para. 14.22 provides that the reasoning behind this offence is that:

> The sale of contraband cigarettes and alcohol is a matter of considerable concern to the Government. In addition, some of the goods sold have not been manufactured by responsible manufacturers but are fake products smuggled from other countries, for example Eastern European countries and China on behalf of organised criminal gangs, and could therefore contain dangerous ingredients.

The scope of the offence extends beyond items imported without payment of duty. It also covers any goods which have been unlawfully imported, such as obscene materials and drugs.

A person guilty of this offence is liable on summary conviction to a fine not exceeding level 3 on the standard scale. The Guidance, para. 14.23 provides that licensing authorities should liaise closely with HM Revenue and Customs in respect of the investigation and prosecution of this offence.

21.5 OFFENCES ON VEHICLES AND TRAINS

21.5.1 Prohibition on sale of alcohol on moving vehicles

It is an offence under s.156 for a person to sell by retail alcohol on or from a vehicle at a time when the vehicle is not permanently or temporarily parked.

There is no ban on the consumption of alcohol on moving vehicles, as the Guidance, para. 14.24 states: 'It should be noted that this does not amount to a ban on the consumption of alcohol on coach trips: only the sale by retail of alcohol is prohibited on moving vehicles.' A vehicle is defined in s.193 as 'a vehicle intended or adapted for use on roads'. This will include coaches and minibuses, as well as caravans and trailers.

A person guilty of this offence is liable on summary conviction to imprisonment for a term not exceeding three months or to a fine not exceeding £20,000, or to both.

It is a defence under s.156(3) in relation to this offence if the defendant can prove that:

- his act was due to a mistake, or to reliance on information given to him, or to an act or omission by another person, or to some other cause beyond his control; and
- he took all reasonable precautions and exercised all due diligence to avoid committing the offence.

An example of where this defence could be used would be where a person mistakenly believed that the drink he was serving was non-alcoholic.

21.5.2   Power to prohibit sale of alcohol on trains

A magistrates' court acting for a local justice area may make an order under s.157 prohibiting the sale of alcohol, during such period as it may decide, on any railway vehicle at such station or stations as may be specified, being stations in that area, or travelling between such stations as may be specified, at least one of which is in the court's area.

An order can only be made on the application of a senior police officer, i.e. a police officer of, or above, the rank of inspector. Before granting an order the court must be satisfied that it is necessary to prevent disorder.

Once an order is made, the senior police officer who applied for the order, or if the chief officer of police of the force in question has designated another senior police officer for the purpose, that other officer, must, forthwith, serve a copy of the order on the train operators affected by the order. Any person who then knowingly sells or attempts to sell alcohol in contravention of the order, or who allows the sale of alcohol in contravention of the order will commit an offence.

A person guilty of an offence under s.157 is liable on summary conviction to imprisonment for a term not exceeding three months or to a fine not exceeding £20,000, or to both.

A 'railway vehicle' has the meaning given by the Railways Act 1993, s.83, that is, it includes anything which, whether or not it is constructed or adapted to carry any person or load, is constructed or adapted to run on flanged wheels over or along track, and 'station' has the meaning given by the Railways Act 1993, s.83, that is any land or other property which consists of premises used as or for the purposes of or otherwise in connection with a railway passenger station or railway passenger terminal, including any approaches, forecourt, cycle store or car park, whether or not the land or other property is, or the premises are, also used for other purposes. 'Train operator' means a person authorised by a licence under the Railways Act 1993, s.8 to operate railway assets within the meaning of s.6 of that Act.

21.6   FALSE STATEMENTS

Section 158 provides that a person commits an offence if he knowingly or recklessly makes a false statement in or in connection with:

- an application for the grant, variation, transfer or review of a premises licence or club premises certificate;
- an application for a provisional statement;
- a temporary event notice, an interim authority notice or any other notice under the Act;
- an application for the grant or renewal of a personal licence; or
- a notice by freeholder of his right to be notified of changes to the licensing register.

A person is treated as making a false statement if he produces, furnishes, signs or otherwise makes use of a document that contains a false statement.

A person must act knowingly or recklessly. A person will act recklessly if he is aware of the risk of the statement being false and it is, in the circumstances known to him, unreasonable to take that risk (see *R.* v. *G* [2003] UKHL 50; [2004] 1 AC 1034 where it was held that this is a subjective test).

A person guilty of making a false statement will be liable on summary conviction to a fine not exceeding level 5 on the standard scale.

21.7   PROSECUTIONS

Section 186 provides that proceedings for an offence under the Act may be brought by a licensing authority, by the Director of Public Prosecutions, or in the case of sales of alcohol to children (offences under s.146 or s.147, see **Chapter 22**), by a local weights and measures authority.

All offences under the Act are summary only offences. Prosecutions for such offences must normally be brought within six months of the commission of the offence. However in relation to any offence under the Act, the provision in the Magistrates' Courts Act 1980, s.127(1) that an information must be laid within that six-month period is amended so that an information must be laid within 12 months of an offence (s.186(3)).

In respect of proceedings by a licensing authority, the Guidance, para. 12.3 provides that:

licensing authorities, when considering instituting proceedings for offences under the 2003 Act, are expected to be concerned primarily with offences involving the sale and consumption of alcohol on premises licensed under a premises licence or where it is authorised by the giving of a temporary event notice or where the supply of alcohol is authorised by a club premises certificate.

21.8   OFFENCES BY BODIES CORPORATE, PARTNERSHIPS AND UNINCORPORATED ASSOCIATIONS

21.8.1   Bodies corporate

If an offence committed by a body corporate, for example a limited company, is shown to have been committed with the consent or connivance of an officer of that body corporate, or to be attributable to any neglect on his part, then the officer as well as the body corporate is guilty of the offence and is liable to prosecution and punishment (s.187(1)).

An 'officer' in relation to a body corporate, means:

- a director, member of the committee of management, chief executive, manager, secretary or other similar officer of the body, or a person purporting to act in any such capacity; or
- an individual who is a controller of the body.

Where the affairs of a body corporate are managed by its members, for example where it is a members' club, the acts and defaults of a member in connection with his functions of management will have the same effect as if he were a director of the body, and so he may be prosecuted and punished (s.187(2)).

21.8.2   Partnerships

If an offence committed by a partnership is shown to have been committed with the consent or connivance of a partner, or to be attributable to any neglect on his part, the partner as well as the partnership will be guilty of the offence and be liable to be prosecuted and punished accordingly (s.187(4)). 'Partner' includes a person purporting to act as a partner.

21.8.3   Unincorporated associations

Where an offence is committed by an unincorporated association, other than a partnership, and it is shown that it was committed with the consent or connivance of an officer of the association or a member of its governing body, or is attributable to any neglect on the part of such an officer or member, then that officer or member as well as the association is guilty of the offence and liable to be prosecuted and punished accordingly (s.187(6)).

21.8.4 Overseas bodies

The Secretary of State may make regulations providing for the application of any of the above provisions, with such modifications as the Secretary of State considers appropriate, to a body corporate or unincorporated association formed or recognised under the law of a territory outside the United Kingdom (s.187(7)).

21.8.5 Jurisdiction and procedure

Any fine imposed on an unincorporated association on its conviction for an offence is to be paid out of the funds of the association (s.188(1)).

Proceedings for an offence alleged to have been committed by an unincorporated association must be brought in the name of the association, and not in that of any of its members (s.188(2)). Rules of court relating to the service of documents have effect as if the association were a body corporate (s.188(3)).

In proceedings for an offence brought against an unincorporated association, the Criminal Justice Act 1925, s.33 and the Magistrates' Courts Act 1980, Sched. 3, which lay down the procedure for prosecuting a corporation, apply as they do in relation to a body corporate (s.188(4)).

Proceedings for an offence may be taken against a body corporate or unincorporated association at any place at which it has a place of business and against an individual at any place where he is for the time being (s.188(5)).

21.9 EXCLUSION ORDERS

The Licensed Premises (Exclusion of Certain Persons) Act 1980 provides that where a court convicts a person of an offence which was committed on licensed premises (i.e. premises with a premises licence authorising the supply of alcohol for consumption on the premises) and it is satisfied that in committing that offence he resorted to violence or offered or threatened to resort to violence, the court may make an exclusion order which prohibits him from entering those premises or any other specified premises, without the express consent of the licensee of the premises or his servant or agent. In addition the Violent Crime Reduction Bill proposes that where a person is convicted by or before a court in England and Wales of an offence committed on licensed premises the court must consider making an exclusion order in respect of the convicted person, and if it decides not to make an order, it must state that fact in open court and give reasons.

An exclusion order may only be made either in addition to any sentence which is imposed in respect of the offence of which the person is convicted, or in addition to an order discharging him absolutely or conditionally.

The duration of an exclusion order must be specified in it but it must be for at least three months and not more than two years.

A person who enters any premises in breach of an exclusion order is guilty of an offence and is liable on summary conviction to a fine not exceeding level 3 on the standard scale or to imprisonment for a term not exceeding one month (this will be increased to 51 weeks when the Criminal Justice Act 2003 comes into force) or both. The court which convicts a person of this offence must also consider whether or not the exclusion order should continue in force, and may, if it thinks fit, by order terminate the exclusion order or vary it by deleting the name of any specified premises.

The licensee of licensed premises or his servant or agent may expel from those premises any person who has entered or whom he reasonably suspects of having entered the premises in breach of an exclusion order; and a constable shall on the demand of the licensee or his servant or agent help to expel from licensed premises any person whom the constable reasonably suspects of having entered in breach of an exclusion order.

Where a court makes an exclusion order or an order terminating or varying an exclusion order, the proper officer of the court shall send a copy of the order to the licensee of the premises to which the order relates. In relation to a magistrates' court, the proper officer is the designated officer for the court, and in relation to the Crown Court the proper officer is the appropriate officer.

CHAPTER 22

Offences involving children

22.1 INTRODUCTION

A range of offences relating to children and alcohol are contained in sections 145 to 155. The broad effect of the offences relating to children are that:

1. Young persons who are aged over 16, but under 18, can go into licensed premises at the licence holder's discretion but cannot consume or buy alcohol there, except if they are accompanied by an adult at a table meal and an adult is purchasing beer, wine or cider for consumption with the table meal.

2. A child under 16 can go into licensed premises at the licence holder's discretion, but if the premises are licensed primarily or exclusively for the supply of alcohol for consumption on the premises, in other words the premises are a pub or a bar, then the child must be accompanied by an adult.

3. A child under 16 can enter licensed premises where the premises are licensed, but not primarily or exclusively for the supply of alcohol for consumption on the premises, for example a restaurant, and he only needs to be accompanied by an adult if there is a supply of alcohol taking place and it is between 12 midnight and 5 am.

4. The prohibitions on children's access to licensed premises only apply while such premises are open for the purpose of being used for the supply of alcohol for consumption there.

There are also powers to confiscate alcohol from persons under the age of 18 in the Confiscation of Alcohol (Young Persons) Act 1997.

22.2 UNACCOMPANIED CHILDREN PROHIBITED FROM CERTAIN PREMISES

22.2.1 Premises used exclusively or primarily for supplies of alcohol for consumption on the premises

Section 145 provides that it is an offence for a person, knowing that premises are those to which this offence applies, to allow an unaccompanied child under the age of 16 to be on those premises at a time when they are open for the purposes of being used for the supply of alcohol for consumption there. A child is unaccompanied if he is not in the company of an individual aged 18 or over.

The premises to which this offence applies are licensed premises, premises which have a club premises certificate or premises which may be used for a permitted temporary activity which:

- are exclusively or primarily used for the supply of alcohol for consumption on the premises; or
- are open for the purposes of being used for the supply of alcohol for consumption on the premises by virtue of a temporary event notice and, at the time the temporary event notice has effect, they are exclusively or primarily used for such supplies.

The 'supply of alcohol' means the sale by retail of alcohol, or the supply of alcohol by or on behalf of a club to, or to the order of, a member of the club.

It will be a question of fact as to whether premises are exclusively or primarily used for the supply of alcohol for consumption on the premises, and reference to the use of the premises as a whole should be made. The Guidance, para. 3.34 provides:

> It is not intended that the definition 'exclusively or primarily' in relation to the consumption of alcohol should be applied in a particular way by reference to turnover, floor space or any similar measure. The expression should be given its ordinary and natural meaning in the context of the particular circumstances. It will normally be quite clear that the business being operated at the premises is predominantly the sale and consumption of alcohol. Mixed businesses may be harder to pigeonhole and it would be sensible for both operators and enforcement agencies to consult where necessary about their respective interpretations of the activities taking place on the premises before any moves are taken which might lead to prosecution.

This means that where the exclusive or primary use is the supply of alcohol for consumption on the premises, unaccompanied children under 16 will not be allowed to be on the premises at any time. But this does not mean that unaccompanied children between the ages of 16 and 18 will have access to licensed premises. The Guidance, para. 3.35 provides:

The fact that the new offence may effectively bar children under 16 unaccompanied by an adult from premises where the consumption of alcohol is the exclusive or primary activity does not mean that the 2003 Act automatically permits unaccompanied children under the age of 18 to have free access to other premises or to the same premises even if they are accompanied or to premises where the consumption of alcohol is not involved. Subject only to the provisions of the 2003 Act and any licence or certificate conditions, admission will always be at the discretion of those managing the premises. The 2003 Act includes on the one hand, no presumption of giving children access or on the other hand, no presumption of preventing their access to licensed premises. Each application and the circumstances obtaining at each premises must be considered on its own merits.

No offence is committed if the unaccompanied child is just passing through the premises solely for the purpose of passing to or from some other place to or from which there is no other convenient means of access or egress (s.145(5)). As this is not a defence, it is suggested that the burden of proof would be on the prosecution.

A person guilty of this offence is liable on summary conviction to a fine not exceeding level 3 on the standard scale.

22.2.2 Premises open for the supply of alcohol for consumption on the premises

Section 145 also provides that it is an offence for a person to allow an unaccompanied child under the age of 16 to be on licensed premises, premises which have a club premises certificate or premises which may be used for a permitted temporary activity at a time between the hours of midnight and 5 am when the premises are open for the purposes of being used for the supply of alcohol for consumption there. A child is unaccompanied if he is not in the company of an individual aged 18 or over.

The 'supply of alcohol' means the sale by retail of alcohol, or the supply of alcohol by or on behalf of a club to, or to the order of, a member of the club.

Thus, where there is no exclusive or primary use it will only be an offence to allow unaccompanied children to be on the premises between midnight and 5.00 am. The Guidance, para. 3.33 provides: 'Accordingly, between 5 am and midnight the offence would not necessarily apply to many restaurants, hotels, cinemas and even many pubs where the main business activity is the consumption of both food and drink.' No offence is committed if the unaccompanied child is just passing through the premises solely for the purpose of passing to or from some other place to or from which there is no other convenient means of access or egress (s.145(5)). As this is not a defence, it is suggested that the burden of proof would be on the prosecution.

A person guilty of this offence is liable on summary conviction to a fine not exceeding level 3 on the standard scale.

22.2.3   Persons who can commit these offences

The offences in s.145 can only be committed by:

- any person who works at the premises in a capacity, whether paid or unpaid, which authorises him to request the unaccompanied child to leave the premises;
- in the case of licensed premises, the holder of a premises licence in respect of the premises and the designated premises supervisor under the licence;
- in the case of premises in respect of which a club premises certificate has effect, any member or officer of the club who is present on the premises in a capacity which enables him to make such a request; and
- in the case of premises which may be used for a permitted temporary activity, the premises user.

22.2.4   Defences

A person charged with one of these offences by reason of his own conduct has a defence under s.145(6) if:

- he believed that the unaccompanied child was aged 16 or over or that an individual accompanying him was aged 18 or over; and
- either he had taken all reasonable steps to establish the individual's age, or nobody could reasonably have suspected from the individual's appearance that he was aged under 16 or, as the case may be, under 18.

A person will be treated as having taken all reasonable steps to establish an individual's age if he asked the individual for evidence of his age, and the evidence would have convinced a reasonable person (s.145(7)).

Where a person is charged with one of these offences by reason of the act or default of some other person, it is a defence that he exercised all due diligence to avoid committing it (s.145(8)).

22.3   SALE OF ALCOHOL TO CHILDREN

There are three offences relating to the sale of alcohol to children. The principal offence is in s.146(1) which provides that it is an offence for a person to sell alcohol to an individual aged under 18.

In addition, a club commits an offence under s.146(2) if alcohol is supplied by it or on its behalf to, or to the order of, a member of the club who is aged under 18, or to the order of a member of the club, to an individual who is aged under 18.

Finally, s.146(3) provides that a person commits an offence if he supplies alcohol on behalf of a club to, or to the order of, a member of the club who is aged under 18, or to the order of a member of the club, to an individual who is aged under 18.

These offences may be committed by a corporate body (unlike under the Licensing Act 1964; see *Haringey LBC* v. *Marks & Spencer Plc*; *Liverpool City Council Trading Standards Office* v. *Somerfield Stores Ltd* [2004] EWHC 1141; [2005] 1 WLR 1742). The Interpretation Act 1978 provides that, unless the contrary intention appears, a person includes a corporate body. There is nothing in the Act to indicate such a contrary intention. In addition, the Act specifically provides for a corporate body to be capable of committing offences under the Act. The Guidance also states at para. 12.3: 'It should be noted that a body corporate, partnership or unincorporated association (see section 187 of the 2003 Act) may be the subject of proceedings for an offence under section 146.'

The offence under s.146(1) can be committed anywhere and is not limited to sales on licensed premises. It is thought that most prosecutions will arise out of sales on licensed premises. The Guidance, para. 12.3 states:

> licensing authorities, when considering instituting proceedings for offences under the 2003 Act, are expected to be concerned primarily with offences involving the sale and consumption of alcohol on premises licensed under a premises licence or where it is authorised by the giving of a temporary event notice or where the supply of alcohol is authorised by a club premises certificate.

Liability for all three offences is strict and only arises where there is a sale or supply. Section 146(4) provides for a defence of 'reasonable belief'. A person charged with one of these offences by reason of his own conduct has a defence if he believed that the individual was aged 18 or over, and either he had taken all reasonable steps to establish the individual's age, or nobody could reasonably have suspected from the individual's appearance that he was aged under 18.

This defence applies where the person has been charged 'by reason of his own conduct'. This implies that the person must have made the sale or supply personally for the defence to apply.

The second limb of this defence, that nobody could reasonably have suspected from the individual's appearance that he was aged under 18, will cover the situation where the purchaser who was under 18 looked exceptionally old for his age.

Where a purchaser does not look 'exceptionally old', a person will have to take 'all reasonable steps' to establish his age. Section 146(5) provides that a person is treated as having taken all reasonable steps to establish an individual's age if he asked the individual for evidence of his age, and the evidence would have convinced a reasonable person. Such evidence could be provided by a proof of age card. However if it is proved by the prosecution that the evidence of age was such that no reasonable person would have been convinced by it because for example the proof of age was either an obvious forgery or clearly belonged to another person, the defence will fail.

There are several proof of age schemes in existence, for example the Portman Group proof of age card (**www.portman-group.org.uk**), CitizenCard (**www.citizencard.net**) and VALIDATEUK (**www.validateuk.co.uk**). The PASS (Proof of Age Standards Scheme) accreditation system has been established by the British Retail Consortium to approve and accredit the various proof of age schemes that exist. It is an umbrella system, audited by the Trading Standards Institute, under which reliable proof of age card schemes carry the same hologram logo in order that retailers can readily distinguish such cards from forgeries or cards issued under unreliable schemes. The Government in the Guidance, para. 12.8 recommends that licensing authorities should promote the PASS arrangements.

Where a person is charged with one of these offences by reason of the act or default of some other person, it is a defence that he exercised all due diligence to avoid committing it (s.146(6)).

A person guilty of one of these offences is liable on summary conviction to a fine not exceeding level 5 on the standard scale (s.146(7)).

Every local weights and measures authority in England and Wales, i.e. a trading standards department, is under a duty to enforce within its area these provisions, so far as they apply to sales of alcohol made on or from premises to which the public have access (s.154). The 'test purchasing' of alcohol is allowed (see **22.6**), and so a weights and measures inspector may make, or authorise any person to make on his behalf, such purchases of goods as appear expedient for the purpose of determining whether these provisions are being complied with. 'Test purchasing' was first introduced into the Licensing Act 1964 by the Criminal Justice and Police Act 2001. The Government's intention behind the test purchasing measure was to increase the chance of detection of non-compliance and therefore increase the deterrent effect of the law on retailers. The Guidance recommends in paras. 12.4 and 12.5 that:

> Licensing authorities are expected to maintain close contact with the police, young offenders' teams and trading standards officers about the extent of unlawful sales and consumption of alcohol by minors and to be involved in the development of any strategies to control or prevent these unlawful activities and to pursue prose-cutions. For example, where as a matter of policy, warnings are given to retailers prior to any decision to prosecute in respect of an offence, it is important that each of the enforcement arms should be aware of the warnings each of them has given.
>
> The Government primarily sees the development of these offences as having a deterrent effect on sales of alcohol to children by raising the risk of detection and by making the consequences of non-compliance significant. The Government is not proposing that a regime of constant test purchasing exercises is pursued in all areas for all licensed premises. The need for and extent of test purchasing opera-tions in any area is a matter for the police and trading standards officers to judge on the basis of their local knowledge and available resources, which will establish how far such operations are necessary in each licensing authority area.

22.4   ALLOWING THE SALE OF ALCOHOL TO CHILDREN

Section 147 provides that a person who works, whether paid or unpaid, at licensed premises, premises which have a club premises certificate or premises which may be used for a permitted temporary activity, in a capacity which authorises him to prevent the sale, will commit an offence if he knowingly allows the sale of alcohol on those premises to an individual aged under 18.

A person who works on the premises in a capacity, whether paid or unpaid, which authorises him to prevent the supply, and any member or officer of the club who at the time of the supply is present on the relevant premises in a capacity which enables him to prevent it commits an offence if he knowingly allows alcohol to be supplied on those premises by or on behalf of a club to or to the order of a member of the club who is aged under 18, or to the order of a member of the club, to an individual who is aged under 18.

There is no statutory defence and a person guilty of an offence is liable on summary conviction to a fine not exceeding level 5 on the standard scale.

These offences may be committed by a corporate body and the Guidance at para. 12.10 states: 'It should be noted that a body corporate, partnership or unincorporated association (see section 187 of the 2003 Act) may be the subject of proceedings for an offence under section 147.'

Every local weights and measures authority in England and Wales is under a duty to enforce within its area these provisions, so far as they apply to sales of alcohol made on or from premises to which the public have access. A weights and measures inspector may make, or authorise any person to make on his behalf, such purchases of goods as appear expedient for the purpose of determining whether these provisions are being complied with.

22.5   SALE OF LIQUEUR CONFECTIONERY TO CHILDREN UNDER 16

An offence is committed under s.148 by a person who sells liqueur confectionery to an individual aged under 16, or by a person who supplies such confectionery on behalf of a club to or to the order of a member of the club who is aged under 16, or to the order of a member of the club, to an individual who is aged under 16.

A club commits an offence if liqueur confectionery is supplied by it or on its behalf to or to the order of a member of the club who is aged under 16, or to the order of a member of the club, to an individual who is aged under 16.

'Liqueur confectionery' is confectionery which:

- contains alcohol in a proportion not greater than 0.2 litres of alcohol, of a strength not exceeding 57 per cent, per kilogram of the confectionery; and

- either consists of separate pieces weighing not more than 42 g or is designed to be broken into such pieces for the purpose of consumption.

Liability for these offences is strict though defences of 'reasonable belief' and 'due diligence' are provided.

A person charged with one of these offences by reason of his own conduct has a defence if he believed that the individual was aged 16 or over, and either he had taken all reasonable steps to establish the individual's age or nobody could reasonably have suspected from the individual's appearance that he was aged under 16 (s.148(3)). A person is treated as having taken all reasonable steps to establish an individual's age if he asked the individual for evidence of his age and the evidence would have convinced a reasonable person.

Where a person is charged with one of these offences by reason of the act or default of some other person, for example an employee, it is a defence that he exercised all due diligence to avoid committing it.

While children aged 16 and 17 can buy alcohol in the form of liqueur chocolates they cannot buy or be sold any other foodstuffs which contain alcohol of a strength exceeding 0.5 per cent alcohol by volume (Guidance, para. 12.12).

A person guilty of one of these offences is liable on summary conviction to a fine not exceeding level 2 on the standard scale.

22.6 PURCHASE OF ALCOHOL BY OR ON BEHALF OF CHILDREN

22.6.1 Purchase of alcohol by a child

Section 149(1) provides that it is an offence for an individual under 18 to buy or attempt to buy alcohol or, where he is a member of a club, to have alcohol supplied to him or to his order by or on behalf of the club, as a result of his act or default, or to attempt to have alcohol supplied to him or to his order by or on behalf of the club. A child guilty of such an offence is liable on summary conviction to a fine not exceeding level 3 on the standard scale.

Test purchases to find out whether under-age sales are taking place are allowed. No offence is committed where the individual buys or attempts to buy the alcohol at the request of a constable, or a weights and measures inspector appointed under the Weights and Measures Act 1985, s.72(1), who is acting in the course of his duty (s.149(2)). The Guidance, para. 12.13 provides: 'It is expected that enforcement officers will have regard to the LACORS/TSI Code of Best Practice on test purchasing operations which includes advice on the protection of children engaged in such operations.'

A person guilty of this offence is liable on summary conviction to a fine not exceeding level 3 on the standard scale.

22.6.2   Purchase of alcohol for a child

As well as being an offence for children to buy alcohol, it is also an offence for a person to buy or attempt to buy alcohol on behalf of an individual aged under 18, or where he is a member of a club, on behalf of an individual aged under 18 to make arrangements whereby alcohol is supplied to him or to his order by or on behalf of the club, or to attempt to make such arrangements (s.149(3)).

The Guidance, para. 12.14 provides that such an offence will be committed: 'if a child gives money to an adult to buy alcohol in an off-licence for consumption by the child. The offence also applies where a member of a club has alcohol supplied to a child or attempts to do so.' A person charged with this offence has a defence if he had no reason to suspect that the individual was aged under 18 (s.149(6)).

A person guilty of this offence is liable on summary conviction to a fine not exceeding level 5 on the standard scale.

22.6.3   Purchase of alcohol for consumption by a child

Section 149(4) provides that it is an offence for a person to buy or attempt to buy alcohol for consumption on relevant premises by an individual aged under 18, or where he is a member of a club by some act or default of his, alcohol is supplied to him, or to his order, by or on behalf of the club for consumption on relevant premises by an individual aged under 18, or he attempts to have alcohol so supplied for such consumption.

Under s.149(5) an offence is not committed where:

- the person buying or being supplied the alcohol, or attempting to do so, is aged 18 or over;
- the individual consuming the alcohol is aged 16 or 17;
- the alcohol is beer, wine or cider;
- its purchase or supply is for consumption at a table meal on relevant premises; and
- the individual is accompanied at the meal by an individual aged 18 or over.

It is not necessary that the person who purchases the alcohol accompanies the 16- or 17-year-old at the meal. All that is required is that someone aged 18 or over accompanies the 16- or 17-year-old at the meal.

A 'table meal' is defined in s.159 as a meal eaten by a person seated at a table, or at a counter or other structure which serves the purpose of a table and is not used for the service of refreshments for consumption by persons not seated at a table or structure serving the purpose of a table. The Guidance, para. 12.15 states that it would not be sufficient for a person to claim that bar snacks amounted to a table meal. It is clear that something more than a snack will therefore be required. In *Solomon* v. *Green* (1955) 119 JP 289 it was held that sandwiches and sausages on sticks constituted a meal though it was said that this was a borderline decision. In *Timmins* v. *Millman* (1965) 109 Sol Jo 31 the court decided that a substantial sandwich accompanied by beetroot and pickles, eaten at a table, might be a table meal.

A person charged with this offence has a defence if he had no reason to suspect that the individual was aged under 18.

A person guilty of this offence is liable on summary conviction to a fine not exceeding level 5 on the standard scale.

22.7   CONSUMPTION OF ALCOHOL BY CHILDREN

Section 150(1) provides that an individual aged under 18 commits an offence if he knowingly consumes alcohol on licensed premises, premises which have a club premises certificate or premises which may be used for a permitted temporary activity.

This offence does not involve strict liability and requires there to be knowing consumption of alcohol for the offence to be proved.

No offence will be committed if a child inadvertently consumes alcohol. The Guidance, para. 12.16 provides: 'The offence is not committed if the child inadvertently consumes the alcohol, for example, if his drink is spiked.'

Nor will an offence be committed if the individual is aged 16 or 17, the alcohol is beer, wine or cider, its consumption is at a table meal on licensed premises, premises which have a club premises certificate or premises which may be used for a permitted temporary activity, and the individual is accompanied at the meal by an individual aged 18 or over.

A child guilty of such an offence is liable on summary conviction to a fine not exceeding level 3 on the standard scale.

22.7.1   Allowing the consumption of alcohol by children

Section 150(2) provides that a person who works at licensed premises, premises which have a club premises certificate or premises which may be used for a permitted temporary activity in a capacity, whether paid or unpaid, which authorises him to prevent the consumption, and where the alcohol was supplied by a club to or to the order of a member of the club, any member or officer of the club who is present at the premises at the time of the consumption in a capacity which enables him to prevent it, commits an offence if he knowingly allows the consumption of alcohol on those premises by an individual aged under 18.

No offence will be committed if the individual is aged 16 or 17, the alcohol is beer, wine or cider, its consumption is at a table meal on licensed premises,

premises which have a club premises certificate or premises which may be used for a permitted temporary activity, and the individual is accompanied at the meal by an individual aged 18 or over.

This offence does not involve strict liability and it requires there to be knowing consumption of alcohol for the offence to be proved.

A person guilty of this offence is liable on summary conviction to a fine not exceeding level 5 on the standard scale.

22.8   DELIVERING ALCOHOL TO CHILDREN

Section 151(1) provides that a person who works on licensed premises, premises which have a club premises certificate or premises which may be used for a permitted temporary activity, in any capacity, whether paid or unpaid, commits an offence if he knowingly delivers to an individual aged under 18 alcohol sold on the premises, or alcohol supplied on the premises by or on behalf of a club to or to the order of a member of the club. The offence will cover, for example, circumstances where a child takes delivery of a consignment of alcohol ordered by an adult by telephone, in a case where the exceptions mentioned below do not apply (Guidance, para. 12.17).

A person who works on the premises in a capacity, whether paid or unpaid, which authorises him to prevent the delivery of the alcohol commits an offence under s.151(2) if he knowingly allows anybody else to deliver to an individual aged under 18 alcohol sold on licensed premises, premises which have a club premises certificate or premises which may be used for a permitted temporary activity. This offence would cover, for example, a person who authorised a delivery of the sort mentioned above in the knowledge that the recipient would be a child (Guidance, para. 12.17).

In addition, s.151(4) provides that a person who works on the premises in a capacity, whether paid or unpaid, which authorises him to prevent the supply, for example the club steward, and any member or officer of the club who at the time of the supply in question is present on the premises in a capacity which enables him to prevent the supply, commits an offence if he knowingly allows anybody else to deliver to an individual aged under 18 alcohol supplied on licensed premises, premises which have a club premises certificate or premises which may be used for a permitted temporary activity by or on behalf of a club to or to the order of a member of the club.

There are a number of exceptions in s.151(6). None of these offences will be committed where:

- the alcohol is delivered at a place where the buyer or, as the case may be, person supplied lives or works, for example, where a child answers the door and signs for the delivery of his father's order at his house;
- the individual aged under 18 works on licensed premises, premises which have a club premises certificate or premises which may be used for a

permitted temporary activity in a capacity, whether paid or unpaid, which involves the delivery of alcohol, for example, where a 16-year-old office worker is sent to collect a delivery for his employer; or

- the alcohol is sold or supplied for consumption on licensed premises, premises which have a club premises certificate or premises which may be used for a permitted temporary activity.

A person guilty of one of these offences is liable on summary conviction to a fine not exceeding level 5 on the standard scale.

22.9   SENDING A CHILD TO OBTAIN ALCOHOL

Section 152(1) provides that it is an offence for a person to knowingly send an individual aged under 18 into licensed premises, premises which have a club premises certificate or premises which may be used for a permitted temporary activity in order to obtain alcohol sold or to be sold on for consumption off the premises, or alcohol supplied or to be supplied by or on behalf of a club to or to the order of a member of the club for such consumption.

The Guidance, para. 12.18 states:

> This offence would cover, for example, circumstances where a parent sends their child to an off-licence to collect some alcohol which had been bought over the telephone. The offence is committed regardless of whether the child is sent to the actual premises from where the alcohol is sold or supplied, or whether he is sent to other premises to which the alcohol has been sent.

It is immaterial whether the individual aged under 18 is sent to obtain the alcohol from the licensed premises, premises which have a club premises certificate or premises which may be used for a permitted temporary activity or from other premises from which it is delivered in pursuance of the sale or supply (s.152(2)).

An offence is not committed:

- where the individual aged under 18 works on the relevant premises in a capacity, whether paid or unpaid, which involves the delivery of alcohol; or
- where the individual aged under 18 is sent by a constable, or a weights and measures inspector, i.e. a trading standards officer, who is acting in the course of his duty to carry out a 'test purchase'. The Government expects that enforcement officers will have regard to the Local Authorities Coordinators of Regulatory Services/Trading Standards Institute Code of Best Practice on test purchasing operations which includes advice on the

protection of children engaged in such operations (Guidance, para. 12.18).

A person guilty of this offence is liable on summary conviction to a fine not exceeding level 5 on the standard scale.

22.10 PROHIBITION OF UNSUPERVISED SALES BY CHILDREN

Section 153 provides that it is an offence for a 'responsible person' on any licensed premises, premises which have a club premises certificate or premises which may be used for a permitted temporary activity knowingly to allow an individual aged under 18 to make on the premises any sale of alcohol, or any supply of alcohol by or on behalf of a club to or to the order of a member of the club, unless the sale or supply has been specifically approved by that or another responsible person. An offence is therefore not committed where the sale or supply is specifically approved, and there is no minimum age for the individual making the sale or supply.

For these purposes, a 'responsible person' is:

- in relation to licensed premises the holder of the premises licence, the designated premises supervisor, or any individual aged 18 or over who is authorised by them;
- in relation to premises in respect of which there is in force a club premises certificate, any member or officer of the club present on the premises in a capacity which enables him to prevent the supply in question; and
- in relation to premises which may be used for a permitted temporary activity the premises user, or any individual aged 18 or over who is authorised by him.

An offence will not be committed where the alcohol is sold or supplied for consumption with a table meal, it is sold or supplied in premises which are being used for the service of table meals, or in a part of any premises which is being so used, and the premises are, or the part is, not used for the sale or supply of alcohol otherwise than to persons having table meals there and for consumption by such a person ancillary to his meal. This means that someone under 18 who works as a waiter in a restaurant can serve alcohol in the restaurant, or in a public house in a part set aside for table meals.

A person guilty of this offence is liable on summary conviction to a fine not exceeding level 1 on the standard scale.

22.11 GIVING INTOXICATING LIQUOR TO CHILDREN UNDER 5

It is an offence under the Children and Young Persons Act 1933, s.5 for a person to give, or cause to be given, to any child under the age of 5 any alcohol except upon the order of a duly qualified medical practitioner, or in case of sickness, apprehended sickness or other urgent cause.

A person guilty of this offence is liable, on summary conviction, to a fine not exceeding level 1 on the standard scale.

The meaning of alcohol for the purposes of this provision is the same as that in the Licensing Act 2003 except that denatured alcohol, methyl alcohol, naphtha and alcohol contained in liqueur confectionery are to be disregarded.

22.12 CONFISCATION OF ALCOHOL

Section 1 of the Confiscation of Alcohol (Young Persons) Act 1997 which gives the police the power to confiscate alcohol from young persons has been amended by the Licensing Act 2003 to allow alcohol in sealed containers to be confiscated.

It provides that where a constable reasonably suspects that a person in a relevant place is in possession of alcohol and that either:

- he is under 18;
- he intends that any of the alcohol should be consumed by a person who is under 18 in that or any other relevant place; or
- a person under 18 who is, or has recently been, with him has recently consumed alcohol in that or any other relevant place,

the constable may require him to surrender anything in his possession which is, or which the constable reasonably believes to be, alcohol or a container for such alcohol, and to give him his name and address. The constable must inform the person of his suspicion and that failing without reasonable excuse to comply with his requirement to surrender is an offence. A constable may not however require a person to surrender any sealed container unless he reasonably believes that the person is, or has been, consuming, or intends to consume, alcohol in any relevant place.

A 'relevant place' for these purposes means:

- any public place, other than licensed premises; or
- any place, other than a public place, to which the person has unlawfully gained access;

and for this purpose a place is a public place if at the material time the public or any section of the public has access to it, on payment or otherwise, as of right or by virtue of express or implied permission.

271

Anything which is surrendered to a police officer may be disposed of in any manner he considers appropriate.

Anyone who fails without reasonable excuse to comply with a requirement to surrender alcohol to a police officer will commit an offence and is liable on summary conviction to a fine not exceeding level 2 on the standard scale, and a constable may arrest without warrant a person who fails to comply with a requirement imposed on him.

22.12.1   Alcohol consumption in designated public places

If a constable reasonably believes that a person is, or has been, consuming alcohol in a designated public place or intends to consume alcohol in such a place, he may require that person:

- not to consume in that place anything which is, or which the constable reasonably believes to be, alcohol; and
- to surrender anything in his possession which is, or which the constable reasonably believes to be, alcohol or a container for such alcohol.

A constable may dispose of anything which has been surrendered to him in such manner as he considers appropriate.

A constable who imposes a requirement must inform the person concerned that failing without reasonable excuse to comply with the requirement is an offence, and a person who fails without reasonable excuse to comply with a requirement commits an offence and is liable on summary conviction to a fine not exceeding level 2 on the standard scale.

A 'designated public place' is a public place which has been identified in an order as such by a local authority. Such an order may be made by a local authority if it is satisfied that nuisance or annoyance to members of the public or a section of the public, or disorder has been associated with the consumption of alcohol in that place. The order may identify a place either specifically or by description or revoke or amend orders previously made.

The procedure to be followed in connection with the making of these orders is laid down in the Local Authorities (Alcohol Consumption in Designated Public Places) Regulations 2001, SI 2001/2831. Before making an order, a local authority must consult the chief officer of police for the police area in which the public place proposed to be identified in the order is situated, the parish or community council in whose area the public place is situated, the chief officer of police, the local authority and the parish or community council for any area near to the public place which they consider may be affected by the designation, and the licensee of any licensed premises in that place or which they consider may be affected by the designation. It must also take reasonable steps to consult the owners or occupiers of any land proposed to be identified, and publish a notice in a newspaper circulating in the local authority's area which identifies specifically or by description the place proposed to be identified, sets out the effect of an order being made in relation to that place, and invites representations as to whether or not an order should be made, and an order cannot be made until at least 28 days after the publication of this notice. Before making an order, the local authority must consider any representations as to whether or not a particular public place should be identified in an order whether made as a result of its consultation, in response to an advertised notice, or otherwise. After making an order and before it takes effect, a local authority must publish a notice in a newspaper circulating in its area which identifies the place which has been identified in the order, sets out the effect of the order in relation to that place and indicates the date on which the order will take effect. Before an order takes effect, a local authority must post in the place identified such signs as it considers sufficient to draw the attention of members of the public in that place to the effect of the order. A copy of the order must be sent to the Secretary of State.

A place cannot be a designated public place or a part of such a place if it is:

- premises in respect of which a premises licence or club premises certificate has effect;
- a place within the curtilage of such premises;
- premises which may for the time being be used by virtue of a temporary event notice for the supply of alcohol or which could have been so used within the last 20 minutes; or
- a place where facilities or activities relating to the sale or consumption of alcohol are for the time being permitted by virtue of a permission granted under the Highways Act 1980, s.115E (highway related uses).

Any bylaw which prohibits, by the creation of an offence, the consumption in a particular public place of alcohol (including any liquor of a similar nature which falls within the bylaw), or makes any incidental, supplementary or consequential provision (whether relating to the seizure or control of containers or otherwise) shall not apply to any designated public place.

CHAPTER 23

Closure of premises

23.1 INTRODUCTION

Part 8 of the Act has extended the pre-existing powers of the police to seek a court order to close licensed premises in a geographical area that is experiencing or likely to experience disorder, and to close down instantly individual licensed premises that are disorderly, likely to become disorderly or are causing nuisance as a result of noise from the premises. These powers are now available in relation to premises which have been licensed for the provision of regulated entertainment and late night refreshment and to premises in respect of which a temporary event notice has effect.

The Secretary of State has issued guidance to police officers about the operation of those powers, and this can be found in Chapter 11 of the Guidance. This guidance has no binding effect on police officers but is provided to support and assist them in interpreting and implementing Part 8 of the Act in the interests of public safety, the prevention of disorder and the reduction of antisocial behaviour.

The Government sees the use of the powers of closure as an important deterrent against disorder and public nuisance through noise. The Guidance at para. 11.8 provides:

> The Government intends that the extended police powers contained in sections 161–170 of the 2003 Act should place licence holders, those giving temporary event notices and designated premises supervisors, who will usually have day to day management control of the premises, under pressure to maintain order and minimise anti-social behaviour on licensed premises, and thereby to deter disorder and nuisance behaviour often caused by excessive consumption of alcohol. The powers are intended to make these individuals more alive to their responsibilities to the wider community. As such, the potential as well as the actual use by the police of these powers should itself be beneficial in terms of preventing disorder on and noise nuisance from the relevant premises. The powers therefore have significant deterrent value.

The Anti-social Behaviour Act 2003 also contains provision for the temporary closure of premises with a premises licence or a temporary event notice where a public nuisance is being caused because of noise coming from the premises, or where there is production, supply or use of class A drugs on the premises.

23.2 ORDERS TO CLOSE PREMISES IN AN AREA EXPERIENCING DISORDER

Section 160 provides that where there is or is expected to be disorder in any local justice area, a magistrates' court acting in the area may make an order requiring all premises which have a premises licence or are subject to a temporary event notice and are situated at or near the place of the disorder or expected disorder, to be closed for a period not exceeding 24 hours. An application for an order must be made by a police officer of the rank of superintendent or above. The period of closure must be specified in the order.

An order can only be made if the magistrates' court is satisfied that it is necessary to make an order to prevent disorder. The proceedings are civil ones and, while the Act and Guidance are silent, it is suggested that the standard of proof will be on the balance of probabilities. This power is intended to be used in emergencies where there is disorder, or where there is expected to be disorder. An example of when such an order may be used would be where there is going be a local 'derby' football match and the police anticipate some public disorder. Evidence which might be used could include the fact that disorder has taken place when the event last took place, and that there is intelligence to suggest that disorder may re-occur.

In relation to these orders, the Guidance provides in paras 11.10 to 11.12:

11.10 Such orders should . . . normally be sought where public order problems are anticipated, as a result of intelligence or publicly available information, which may very often be fuelled by the ready availability of alcohol. Examples of future events which might justify action by the police . . . could include football fixtures with a history of public order problems; and political demonstrations which are thought likely to be hi-jacked by extreme or violent groups. Accordingly, if a football match is taking place on a Saturday, and intelligence is received on the preceding Thursday, which indicates that fans may cause disorder, a senior police officer should not rely on the powers in sections 161–170 of the 2003 Act (instant closure without court involvement) on that Thursday specifying closure of premises near the football ground during the following Saturday. This is because the orders under sections 161–170 must be made and served at the time the senior police officer forms his or her reasonable belief that the disorder is happening or is imminent, or that the noise nuisance is being caused, and such orders will come into force as soon as they are served. However, where it is possible to anticipate disorder in this way, the courts should be involved and make the decision on the application of a police officer of the rank of superintendent or above as to whether widespread closure is justified.

11.11 When seeking an order under section 160 of the 2003 Act, the burden of proof will fall on the police to satisfy the court that their intelligence or evidence is sufficient to demonstrate that such action is necessary. Police officers should recognise that such action may do serious damage to the businesses affected (and in circumstances where those businesses are being conducted properly) and disrupt the activities of consumers and other law-abiding citizens. It is therefore essential that orders are sought only where necessary to prevent disorder.

11.12 Where serious disorder is anticipated, many holders of premises licences and premises users who have given temporary event notices will want to co-operate with the police, not least for the protection of their premises and customers. So far as possible, and where time is available, police officers should initially seek voluntary agreement to closure in an area for a particular period of time. The courts should therefore only be involved where other alternatives are not available.

Once a closure order has been made, s.160(4) and (5) provide that the following persons will commit an offence if they knowingly keep open any premises to which the order relates, or allow any such premises to be kept open, during the period of the order:

- any manager of the premises (this means a person who works at the premises in a capacity whether paid or unpaid which authorises him to close them);
- in the case of licensed premises, the holder of a premises licence in respect of the premises, and the designated premises supervisor under the licence;
- in the case of premises in respect of which a temporary event notice has effect, the premises user in relation to that notice.

In order to be guilty of an offence a person must have knowledge of the facts both that the premises are open and that they are subject to a closure order.

A person guilty of such an offence is liable on summary conviction to a fine not exceeding level 3 on the standard scale (s.160(6)).

Section 171 provides that premises are 'open' if a person who is not a premises licence holder in respect of the premises, any designated premises supervisor under such a licence, the premises user in relation to any temporary event notice which has effect in respect of the premises, a manager of the premises, a person who usually lives at the premises, or a member of the family of an appropriate person or a person who usually lives at the premises enters the premises and buys or is otherwise supplied with food, drink or anything usually sold on the premises, or while he is on the premises, they are used for the provision of regulated entertainment.

In deciding whether the premises are open the following are to be disregarded:

- where no premises licence has effect in respect of the premises, any use of the premises for activities (other than licensable activities) which do not take place during an event period specified in a temporary event notice having effect in respect of the premises;
- any use of the premises for a qualifying club activity under and in accordance with a club premises certificate; and

- any exempt supply of hot food and drink by clubs, hotels, etc. (see **5.4**) in circumstances where a person will neither be admitted to the premises nor be supplied with hot food and drink on or from the premises, except by virtue of being a member of a recognised club or a guest of such a member.

A constable may use such force as may be necessary for the purpose of closing premises which have been ordered to be closed (s.160(7)).

23.3 CLOSURE OF IDENTIFIED PREMISES

23.3.1 Closure orders for identified premises

Section 161 provides that a senior police officer of or above the rank of inspector may make a closure order for a period not exceeding 24 hours in relation to any premises which have a premises licence or a temporary event notice, if he reasonably believes that:

- there is, or there is likely imminently to be, disorder on, or in the vicinity of and related to, the premises and their closure is necessary in the interests of public safety; or
- a public nuisance is being caused by noise coming from the premises and the closure of the premises is necessary to prevent that nuisance.

These orders may only be made where it is necessary in the interests of public safety or to prevent the nuisance caused by noise coming from the premises, and should not be used where it has been possible to anticipate the disorder arising, for example, in connection with intelligence about likely future disorder at a football fixture or in connection with a demonstration. The appropriate course then is to seek a closure order from the magistrates' court.

23.3.2 Closure because of disorder

Before making a closure order because of disorder, a police officer will need reasonable belief that:

- disorder is actually taking place on the premises or in the vicinity or is likely to be imminent;
- the disorder or imminent disorder relates to the premises; and
- it is necessary to close the premises in the interests of public safety.

There is no definition in the Act of what amounts to 'in the vicinity' of licensed premises and so this will be a matter of fact for a court to determine. There must be a causal connection between any disorder or likely disorder and the licensed premises themselves. The senior police officer

277

cannot close the premises unless 'closure is necessary in the interests of public safety' and so closure of the premises must directly affect the danger to the public safety being caused by the disorder, or likely disorder, taking place or expected imminently to take place on or in the vicinity of and related to the premises.

Another question arises as to when any future disorder is likely to take place in order to justify a closure order being made. The disorder should be likely to be imminent, and there also has to be a causal connection between the likely disorder and the particular licensed premises involved, which makes closure of those particular premises under this provision necessary in the interests of public safety. This means that the expected incident must be happening or be imminent in which case, closure of the licensed premises should actively diminish the probability that disorder will take place in the immediate future (Guidance, para. 11.27).

23.3.3   Closure because of noise

Before making a closure order because of noise, a police officer will need reasonable belief that:

- a public nuisance is being caused;
- such nuisance is being caused by noise;
- a public nuisance by noise is coming from the premises; and
- closure of the premises is necessary to prevent the nuisance caused by the noise.

The Guidance, para. 11.28 provides:

The 2003 Act does not define the term 'public nuisance'. Parliament has decided not to constrain the interpretation of the term by providing a more restrictive definition. Whether or not there is 'public nuisance' will depend upon the circumstances of the particular case. Ultimately any questions of interpretation will be decided by the courts. However this means that senior police officers are required to judge reasonably whether the noise is causing a nuisance. Such judgements will inevitably have a subjective quality and officers will need to bring their experience to bear in making them. However, it is important to note that the 'noise' in question must be emitted from the licensed premises. Noise nuisance arising solely from people in the street outside licensed premises would not be sufficient to justify the use of these powers. In addition, the power should only be used where the senior police officer reasonably believes that a nuisance is being caused to the public. Accordingly, the senior police officer should normally have cause to believe that particular individuals in the vicinity are being annoyed by the noise from the licensed premises. Liaison with local government enforcement officers with existing powers for controlling noise nuisance would therefore be beneficial. It will ultimately be for senior police officers to decide, in the circumstances of any case, whether it is appropriate for them to deploy these powers, which are likely ultimately to lead to the review of the premises licence for the premises affected with the possibility of a licensing authority determining that it is necessary for the promotion of the licensing objectives to take steps in relation to that licence, which may include its revocation.

23.3.4   The decision to make a closure order

A police officer will usually decide to make a closure order based on the activities taking place. The Guidance, para. 11.21 provides:

> Where the police attend an incident, following complaints about disorder or noise nuisance to local residents, or attend at the request of the licensee, and a senior police officer of inspector rank or above reasonably believes that closure is necessary under the terms of the 2003 Act, police officers should advise the licence holder, designated premises supervisor, premises user or manager of the premises immediately. Wherever possible, police officers should then give the licence holder, manager, designated premises supervisor or premises user an opportunity to close the premises voluntarily, on police advice, until the following day. A closure order will normally only have to be made if police advice is disputed or rejected and it becomes necessary to take action to impose closure. When giving advice to close voluntarily, police officers should make clear that they are not engaging in a negotiation. The view of the senior police officer will be final until a court decides otherwise.

However, when making his decision as to whether or not to make a closure order in respect of any premises, a police officer must under s.161(3) have regard, in particular, to the conduct of the following people in relation to the disorder or nuisance:

- any person who holds a premises licence in respect of the premises;
- any designated premises supervisor under such a licence;
- the premises user in relation to any temporary event notice which has effect in respect of the premises; or
- a manager of the premises (this means a person who works at the premises in a capacity whether paid or unpaid which authorises him to close them).

The Guidance, para. 11.14 provides:

> This means that if the licence holder or manager or designated premises supervisor or premises user has acted incompetently, inadequately or has actually provoked or caused the problems, the officer may take that into account when deciding whether to make a closure order. On the other side of the coin, if the licensee, manager or designated premises supervisor or premises user has called the police in promptly and acted sensibly in his or her attempts to prevent disorder or noise nuisance, that good conduct should also be taken into account.

Before making a closure the Guidance, para. 11.17 provides:

> The police should, whenever possible, seek the voluntary co-operation of licensees, premises users, designated premises supervisors and managers in resolving

incidents of disorder, potential disorder and noise nuisance rather than move directly to a decision to use a closure order.

The senior police officer may make his decision on the basis on information which has been supplied to him by other police officers. However, he remains accountable for his decision. The Guidance suggests that it would be good practice for a senior police officer to attempt to attend the premises wherever possible in order to make a full and personal assessment, though it is recognised that it will be difficult for officers, particularly in rural force areas, to always attend the premises. Where it is not possible for the senior officer to attend, it will be important that the information supplied to him is comprehensive and contemporaneously recorded, so that he can be clear about the reasons upon which his decision was based when he is subsequently required to present them to the magistrates' court.

23.3.5　Giving a closure order

There is no prescribed form of closure order. However, s.161(4) provides that a closure order must:

• specify the premises to which it relates;
• specify the period for which the premises are to be closed;
• specify the grounds on which it is made; and
• state details of the statutory powers to extend and cancel the order, referral to the magistrates' court and review.

A specimen closure order is contained in the Guidance, annex L.

A closure order will take effect at the time a constable gives notice of it to an appropriate person who is connected with any of the activities to which the disorder or nuisance relates (s.161(5)). It is not necessary for the senior police officer who made the order to be present when it is served.

Notice of a closure order must always be given in writing, and be handed by a police constable to the holder of the premises licence, designated premises supervisor, premises user or the manager of the premises. If a licensee, premises user, designated premises supervisor or manager of the premises refuses to accept the written notice of a closure order, the constable should note this so that it can be reported to the magistrates' court. The written notice should then be left in plain sight of the relevant person on whom it is being served. He should also be advised orally that the notice contains details of his rights and duties under the Act.

An offence is committed by a person who, without reasonable excuse, permits relevant premises to be open in contravention of a closure order or any extension of it (s.161(6)). A person guilty of this offence is liable on summary conviction to imprisonment for a term not exceeding three months or to a fine not exceeding £20,000, or to both (s.161(7)).

23.3.6　Length of a closure order

Subject to very limited exceptions, a closure order cannot exceed 24 hours. However, the Guidance at para. 11.34 stresses that this does not mean that the duration should always automatically be set for 24 hours. The premises should only be closed for the period which the police estimate it will take to end the threat to public safety, or the nuisance to the public. In practice, therefore, closure orders could last between 30 minutes and 24 hours depending on the circumstances of each case. An extension to that closure period can be made only if the senior police officer reasonably believes that the court would not have determined its consideration by the end of that period and certain conditions are met.

The Guidance, para. 11.35 gives the following by way of example:

> If, for example, a closure is made at 9pm on a Monday evening because of disorder caused by gangs fighting in a public house, closure might only be appropriate for up to the time when the premises licence requires the premises to close, perhaps midnight. This could be because the senior police officer reasonably believes that there is a threat of gang members (those not arrested) returning to the premises before closing time but after the police have left. However, if the threat is not expected to have subsided by closing time, it may be appropriate to impose a closure for a period extending into the following day.

23.3.7　Extension of a closure order

Once a closure order has taken effect, the senior police officer must as soon as reasonably practicable apply to the magistrates' court so that it can consider the order. However if, before the end of a period of closure under a closure order or any extension of a closure order, the responsible senior police officer reasonably believes that a magistrates' court acting in the local justice area in which the premises are situated will not have determined whether to exercise its powers in respect of the closure order, and any extension of it, by the end of the closure period, and the conditions for an extension are satisfied, he may extend the closure period for a further period of up to 24 hours beginning with the end of the previous closure period (s.162).

It is not clear whether the maximum period of closure without the magistrates being involved would be 48 hours, or whether it could be longer. Section 162 provides that the senior police office may 'extend the closure period' and that the 'closure period' is the period when the premises 'are to be closed under a closure order or any extension of it'. This would seem to indicate that there could be more than one extension period.

For these purposes 'responsible senior police officer' means either the police officer of, or above, the rank of inspector who made the order, or any other police officer of, or above, the rank of inspector who has been

281

designated for the purpose by the chief officer of police for the police area in which the premises are situated.

The conditions which must be satisfied for an extension are that:

- in the case of an order made because there is, or is likely imminently to be, disorder on, or in the vicinity of and related to, the premises and their closure is necessary in the interests of public safety, closure is necessary in the interests of public safety because of disorder or likely disorder on, or in the vicinity of and related to, the premises; or
- in the case of an order made because a public nuisance is being caused by noise coming from the premises and the closure of the premises is necessary to prevent that nuisance, closure is necessary to ensure that no public nuisance is, or is likely to be, caused by noise coming from the premises.

An extension comes into force when a constable gives notice of it to an appropriate person connected with any of the activities to which the disorder or nuisance relates or is expected to relate. But the extension will not come into force unless the notice is given before the end of the initial closure period.

23.3.8 Cancellation of a closure order

Section 163 allows the responsible senior police officer to cancel a closure order and any extension of it at any time after the order has been made, but before a magistrates' court acting in the local justice area in which the premises are situated has determined whether to exercise its powers in respect of the order and any extension.

The responsible senior police officer must cancel a closure order and any extension of it if he does not reasonably believe that:

- in the case of an order made because there is, or is likely imminently to be, disorder on, or in the vicinity of and related to, the premises and their closure is necessary in the interests of public safety, closure is necessary in the interests of public safety because of disorder or likely disorder on, or in the vicinity of and related to, the premises; or
- in the case of an order made because a public nuisance is being caused by noise coming from the premises and the closure of the premises is necessary to prevent that nuisance, closure is necessary to ensure that no public nuisance is, or is likely to be, caused by noise coming from the premises.

Where a closure order and any extension are cancelled, the responsible senior police officer must give notice of the cancellation to an appropriate person, i.e. the licence holder, manager, designated premises supervisor or premises user, connected with any of the activities related to the disorder, or anticipated disorder or nuisance in respect of which the closure order was made.

23.3.9 Application to a magistrates' court and its powers

The responsible senior police officer must, as soon as is reasonably practicable after a closure order comes into force, apply to a magistrates' court acting in the local justice area in which the premises are situated so that it can consider the order and any extension of it (s.164). The application must be made by way of complaint.

The responsible senior officer must also notify the relevant licensing authority:

- that a closure order has come into force;
- of the contents of the order and of any extension of it; and
- of the application to the magistrates' court.

Section 165 provides that the magistrates' court must as soon as reasonably practicable after receiving an application for it to consider the order and any extension:

- hold a hearing to consider whether it is appropriate to exercise any of the court's powers in relation to the closure order or any extension of it; and
- determine whether to exercise any of those powers.

The powers conferred on a magistrates' court must be exercised in the place required by the Magistrates' Courts Act 1980 for the hearing of a complaint and may be exercised by a single justice. All evidence at the hearing must be given on oath.

The powers of a magistrates' court when considering an order and any extension are that it may:

- revoke the closure order and any extension of it;
- order the premises to remain, or to be, closed until such time as the relevant licensing authority has reviewed the premises licence (see **23.3.11**);
- order the premises to remain or to be closed until that time subject to such exceptions as may be specified in the order, for example the premises might be allowed to open during the daytime but not in the evening; or
- order the premises to remain or to be closed until that time unless such conditions as may be specified in the order are satisfied, for example the premises might only open when the designated premises supervisor is physically present.

In determining whether the premises will be, or will remain, closed the magistrates' court must, in particular, consider whether:

- in the case of an order made because there is, or is likely imminently to be, disorder on, or in the vicinity of and related to, the premises and their closure is necessary in the interests of public safety, closure is necessary in the interests of public safety because of disorder or likely disorder on the premises, or in the vicinity of and related to, the premises; and

- in the case of an order made because a public nuisance is being caused by noise coming from the premises and the closure of the premises is necessary to prevent that nuisance, closure is necessary to ensure that no public nuisance is, or is likely to be, caused by noise coming from the premises.

The magistrates' court does not seem to be limited to considering only these two matters. It could also consider factors such as the impact of the closure on the premises licence holder and on the local community.

In the case of licensed premises, the magistrates' court must notify the relevant licensing authority if it decides to exercise any of its powers.

The magistrates' court cannot exercise any of its powers if, before it discharges its functions, the premises cease to be premises in respect of which a premises licence or a temporary event notice is in effect. Any order which the court may make will also cease to have effect if the premises cease to be premises in respect of which a premises licence or a temporary event notice is in effect.

An offence is committed by anyone who, without reasonable excuse, permits premises in respect of which a premises licence or a temporary event notice is in effect to be open in contravention of a closure order made or remaining in force following a magistrates' court hearing. A person guilty of such an offence is liable on summary conviction to imprisonment for a term not exceeding three months or to a fine not exceeding £20,000, or to both.

23.3.10 Appeals from the magistrates' court

Any person who is aggrieved by a decision of a magistrates' court in respect of a closure order may appeal to the Crown Court (s.166). A notice of appeal must be given to the designated officer for the magistrates' court within 21 days beginning with the day the decision being appealed against was made.

23.3.11 Review of a premises licence following a closure order

The relevant licensing authority must review a premises licence when a closure order has come into force in relation to the premises in respect of which the premises licence has effect, and it has received a notice of the magistrates' court's decision, in relation to the order and any extension of it (s.167).

Regulation 37 of the Premises Licences Regulations provides that the licensing authority must within one working day starting on the day after the day on which it received the notice of the magistrates' court's decision, give the holder of the premises licence and each responsible authority written notice of:
- the review;

- the dates between which interested parties and responsible authorities may make representations relating to the review to the relevant licensing authority;
- the closure order and any extension of it; and
- any order made in relation to the closure order by the magistrates' court.

The relevant licensing authority must also advertise the review by displaying prominently a notice which is:

- of a size equal to or larger than A4;
- of a pale blue colour; and
- printed legibly in black ink or typed in black in a font of a size equal to or larger than 16 points.

The notice must be displayed:

- at, on or near the site of the premises to which the review relates where it can conveniently be read from the exterior of the premises by the public and in the case of a premises covering an area of more than 50 metres square, one further notice in the same form and subject to the same requirements shall be displayed every 50 metres along the external perimeter of the premises abutting any highway; and
- at the offices, or the main offices, of the licensing authority in a central and conspicuous place;

Where the relevant licensing authority maintains a website for advertising applications given to it, a notice must also be published on that website.

The notice must be displayed for a period of no less than seven consecutive days starting on the day after the day on which the relevant licensing authority received the notice of the magistrates' court's decision.

The notice must include the following information:

- the address of the premises about which an application for a review has been made;
- the dates between which interested parties and responsible authorities may make representations to the relevant licensing authority;
- the grounds of the application for review;
- the postal address and, where relevant, the worldwide web address where the register of the relevant licensing authority is kept and where and when the grounds for the review may be inspected; and
- that it is an offence knowingly or recklessly to make a false statement in connection with an application and the maximum fine for which a person is liable on summary conviction for the offence.

An interested party or a responsible authority may make representations at any time up to and including seven days starting on the day after the day on which the relevant licensing authority received the notice of the magistrates' court's decision.

Where the relevant licensing authority determines that any representations are frivolous or vexatious, it must notify the person who made them of the reasons for that determination. 'Relevant representations' are representations which:

- are relevant to one or more of the licensing objectives;
- are made by the holder of the premises licence, a responsible authority or an interested party within the prescribed seven-day period;
- have not been withdrawn; and
- if they are made by an interested party, who is not also a responsible authority, are not, in the opinion of the relevant licensing authority, frivolous or vexatious.

The relevant licensing authority must then hold a hearing to consider the closure order and any extension of it, any order made by the magistrates' court, and any relevant representations. The hearing must be held within 10 working days beginning with the day after the day the licensing authority received notice from the magistrates' court (Hearings Regulations, reg. 5 and Sched. 1, para. 15). Notice of the hearing must be given to the premises licence holder and anyone who has made relevant representations no later than five working days before the day or the first day on which the hearing is to be held (Hearings Regulations, reg. 6(3)(a) and Sched. 2, para. 15). The premises licence holder must be given the relevant representations with the notice of hearing (Hearings Regulations, reg. 7(2) and Sched. 3, para. 14).

Following the hearing, the relevant licensing authority must, after it has considered the closure order and any extension of it, any order made by the magistrates' court, and any relevant representations, take such of the following steps, if any, as it considers necessary for the promotion of the licensing objectives:

- to modify the conditions of the premises licence;
- to exclude a licensable activity from the scope of the licence;
- to remove the designated premises supervisor from the licence;
- to suspend the licence for a period not exceeding three months; or
- to revoke the licence.

For this purpose the conditions of a premises licence are modified if any of them is altered or omitted or any new condition is added.

The requirement to take any necessary steps for the promotion of the licensing objectives is subject to the requirements to include mandatory conditions in premises licences (see **7.12**).

Where the authority modifies the conditions of the premises licence or excludes a licensable activity from the scope of the licence, it may provide that the modification or exclusion is only to have effect for a specified period of up to three months.

Once a licensing authority has determined a review of a closure order it must notify the determination and its reasons for making it to:

- the holder of the premises licence;
- any person who made relevant representations; and
- the chief officer of police for the police area, or each police area in which the premises are situated.

23.3.12   When does a review determination take effect?

A decision in relation to a review of a closure order will usually not have effect until 'the relevant time', which will be either the end of the period given for appealing against the decision, or if the decision is appealed against, the time the appeal is disposed of (s.168). However this will not be the case where the relevant licensing authority has decided to take one or more of the steps it can take to modify the conditions on the licence, exclude a licensable activity from the licence, remove the designated premises supervisor or suspend the licence, and the premises to which the licence relates have been closed, by virtue of an order of the magistrates' court until the licensing authority's decision was made. In these circumstances the decision takes effect when it is notified to the holder of the premises licence, though this is subject to the right of relevant licensing authority, on such terms as it thinks fit, to suspend the operation of its decision, in whole or in part, until the relevant time or to suspend it pending appeal.

The premises must remain closed, but the premises licence will continue in force, until the relevant time where the relevant licensing authority has decided on a review to revoke the premises licence, and the premises to which the licence relates have been closed, by virtue of an order of the magistrates' court, until that decision was made. The magistrates can in such a situation modify the closure order pending appeal.

23.3.13   Opening premises in contravention of a closure following a review

A person commits an offence if, without reasonable excuse, he allows premises to be open during the relevant time in contravention of an order by a relevant licensing authority to revoke the premises licence. A person guilty of this offence is liable on summary conviction to imprisonment for a term not exceeding three months or to a fine not exceeding £20,000, or to both.

A constable may use such force as may be necessary for the purposes of closing premises in compliance with a closure order.

There is no requirement in the Act for the licence holder or the police to clear the premises of customers following the service of a closure order, and the presence of customers in the premises does not give rise to an offence. A customer does not commit an offence if he is not asked to leave and remains on the premises. A person who is drunk or disorderly who refuses to leave after being asked commits an offence (see **21.3.4**).

23.4 POLICE IMMUNITY FROM LIABILITY FOR DAMAGES

Section 170 provides immunity for the police from liability for damages. A constable is not liable for damages in respect of any act or omission of his in the performance or purported performance of his functions in relation to a closure order or any extension of it. Nor is a chief officer of police liable for damages in respect of any act or omission of a constable under his direction or control in the performance or purported performance of a function of the constable's in relation to a closure order or any extension of it. For these purposes the damages are damages awarded in proceedings for judicial review, the tort of negligence or misfeasance in public office. This does not affect any other exemption from liability for damages, whether at common law or otherwise.

These exemptions do not apply if the act or omission is shown to have been in bad faith, or so as to prevent an award of damages in respect of an act or omission on the grounds that the act or omission was unlawful as a result of the Human Rights Act 1998, s.6(1) which provides that it is unlawful for a public authority to act in a way which is incompatible with a Convention right.

These are controversial provisions given that the initial closure may be made by way of a subjective decision by a police inspector.

23.5 CLOSURE UNDER THE ANTI-SOCIAL BEHAVIOUR ACT 2003

The Anti-social Behaviour Act 2003 contains provision for:

- the temporary closure of premises with a premises licence or a temporary event notice by the chief executive officer of a local authority if he reasonably believes that a public nuisance is being caused by noise coming from the premises, and the closure of the premises is necessary to prevent that nuisance. This provision came into force on 31 March 2004;
- the closure of premises with a premises licence or a temporary event notice where they have been used for the production, supply or use of class A drugs. This enables the police to quickly close premises where there is a class A drug problem. This power came into force on 20 January 2004.

CHAPTER 24

Hearings

24.1 INTRODUCTION

The procedure to be followed in respect of all hearings required to be held by a licensing authority under the Act is set out in the Hearings Regulations. Local authorities have also been issued with guidance on hearings by the Local Authorities Coordinators of Regulatory Services.

A hearing might arise following a relevant representation being made in respect of the following applications:

- the grant, transfer, review or variation of a premises licence;
- the grant of a provisional statement;
- the grant, review or variation of a club premises certificate; and
- the grant or renewal of a personal licence.

A hearing could also arise from:

- the cancellation of an interim authority notice following a police objection;
- an objection notice following a police objection to a temporary event notice; and
- convictions coming to light following the grant or renewal of a personal licence.

Where it is not possible to resolve, in the first instance, a relevant representation the licensing authority should:

- arrange a public hearing within the prescribed timescales for the type of application as laid down by the Hearings Regulations;
- notify all the relevant parties of the forthcoming hearing within the prescribed timescales as laid down by the Hearings Regulations;
- provide the applicant with copies of the relevant representations that have been made by interested parties and responsible authorities;
- supply appropriate information at each hearing; and
- supply appropriate information to all parties to a hearing.

24.2 WHEN MUST A HEARING BE HELD?

When required a licensing authority must arrange for a hearing to be held within the period prescribed by the Hearings Regulations. There is no requirement that the hearing must be completed within this period, it merely has to have started before the period ends. Where a hearing will take longer than a day, it must be arranged so that it takes place on consecutive working days, so it could be held on the last day of the prescribed period and continue on the following day or days as required.

24.3 NOTICE OF HEARING

A licensing authority must give notice of a hearing to those persons who have been prescribed by the Hearings Regulations as being required to receive a notice of the date on which and the time and place at which the hearing is to be held.

The general rule is that notice of the hearing must be given by the licensing authority no later than 10 working days before the day or the first day on which the hearing is to be held. There are the following exceptions to this:

1. Where the hearing is in respect of the cancellation of an interim authority notice following a police objection (s.48(3)(a)), or a counter notice which has been given following a police objection to a temporary event notice (s.105(2)(a)), notice of the hearing must be given by the licensing authority no later than two working days before the day or the first day on which the hearing is to be held.
2. Where the hearing is in respect the review of a premises licence following a closure order (s.167(5)(a)) notice of the hearing must be given by the licensing authority no later than five working days before the day or the first day on which the hearing is to be held.

In all cases the notice of the hearing must be accompanied by information which explains:

- that a party has the right to attend the hearing and to be assisted or represented at the hearing by any person who may or may not be legally qualified;
- that a party is entitled to make representations at the hearing, to question any other party, if allowed to, and to address the licensing authority;
- the consequences if a party does not attend or is not represented at the hearing;
- the procedure to be followed at the hearing; and
- any particular points on which the licensing authority considers that it will want clarification at the hearing from a party.

In respect of certain hearings the notice must also be accompanied by relevant documents, e.g. relevant representations.

24.4   ACTION FOLLOWING RECEIPT OF A NOTICE OF A HEARING

Following the receipt of a notice that there is to be a hearing, a recipient must himself give notice to the licensing authority stating whether he intends to attend or be represented at the hearing, whether he intends to call any witnesses, or whether he considers a hearing to be unnecessary.

In most cases, this notice must be given no later than five working days before the day on which the hearing is to be held. The exceptions to this are as follows:

- in the case of a hearing in respect of the cancellation of an interim authority notice following a police objection, or a counter notice following a police objection to a temporary event notice, the notice must be given no later than one working day before the day or the first day on which the hearing is to be held; and
- in the case of a hearing in respect of a review of a premises licence following a closure order the notice must be given no later than two working days before the day or the first day on which the hearing is to be held.

If a party wishes anyone else to appear at the hearing, other than the person he intends to represent him, for example a witness, the notice must include a request for permission for that person to appear at the hearing together with details of that person's name and a brief description of the point on which that person may be able to assist the licensing authority in relation to the application, representations or notice of the party making the request.

24.5   DISPENSING WITH A HEARING

A licensing authority may dispense with a hearing if all the relevant parties, i.e. the applicant, any interested parties and responsible authorities, agree that it would not be necessary to hold a hearing. Each person must give notice to the licensing authority that he does not think there should be a hearing. The licensing authority, if it then agrees that a hearing is not necessary, must forthwith (see **2.9**) give notice to the parties that the hearing is not to take place.

24.6 WITHDRAWAL OF A REPRESENTATION

A party which has made a representation may withdraw it by giving notice to the licensing authority either no later than 24 hours before the day of the hearing, or orally at the hearing.

24.7 POWER TO EXTEND TIME

A licensing authority may extend a time limit for holding a hearing or for giving notice if it considers it to be necessary in the public interest. If a time limit is extended the licensing authority must forthwith give notice to the parties setting out the period of extension and the reasons why it has decided to extend the time limit.

A licensing authority may also adjourn a hearing to a specified date, or arrange for a hearing to be held on specified additional dates, if it considers that this is necessary for its consideration of any representations or notice made by a party. Where a hearing is adjourned to a specified date the licensing authority must forthwith notify the parties of the date, time and place to which the hearing has been adjourned. Where a hearing is to be held on a specified additional date the licensing authority must forthwith notify the parties of the additional date on which and time and place at which the hearing is to be held.

A licensing authority may not exercise its powers to extend time, adjourn a hearing to a specified date, or arrange for a hearing to be held on a specified additional date in such a way that the effect will be that it would fail to reach a determination on the review of a premises licence following a closure order within the specified period for reaching a determination, which is 28 days after the day on which the licensing authority receives notice of the magistrates' court's determination.

24.8 THE HEARING

The hearing must take place in public; however the licensing authority may exclude the public (which includes a party to the hearing and any person assisting or representing a party) for all or a part of the hearing if it considers that the public interest in doing so outweighs the public interest in the hearing, or that part of it, taking place in public.

Each licensing authority has established a licensing committee of 15 members. The prime purpose of the committee is to exercise all the licensing authority's functions under the Act and review strategy and licensing policy and make appropriate recommendations to the licensing authority. Licensing applications will usually be dealt with in two ways:

- by a licensing subcommittee of three members of the licensing committee; and
- by licensing officers within the delegations of the licensing committee as set out in the licensing authority's licensing policy.

A licensing officer should not make any recommendations to a licensing subcommittee in terms of the outcome of the committee hearing.

Anyone who has been given notice of the hearing may attend the hearing and may be assisted or represented by someone who may be legally qualified or not.

A party is entitled at the hearing:

- in response to a point in respect of which the licensing authority has given notice before the hearing to a party that it will want clarification, to give further information in support of their application, representations or notice (as applicable);
- if given permission by the licensing authority, to question any other party; and
- to address the licensing authority.

Members of the licensing authority may ask any question of any party or other person appearing at the hearing.

In considering any representations or notice made by a party the licensing authority may take into account documentary or other information produced by a party in support of their application, representations or notice (as applicable) either before the hearing or, with the consent of all the other parties, at the hearing.

The licensing authority must disregard any information given by a party or any person to whom permission to appear at the hearing is given by the licensing authority which is not relevant to their application, representations or notice (as applicable) or in the case of another person, the application, representations or notice of the party requesting their appearance, and the promotion of the licensing objectives or, in relation to a hearing to consider a notice given by a chief officer of police, the crime prevention objective.

24.9   PROCEDURE AT THE HEARING

It is up to each individual licensing authority to decide the procedure to be followed at the hearings it holds; however the Hearings Regulations specifically provide that:

1. At the beginning of a hearing, the licensing authority must explain to the parties the procedure which it proposes to follow at the hearing. It must also at this stage consider any requests for permission for another person

to appear at the hearing, and such permission must not be unreasonably withheld.

2. The hearing must take the form of a discussion led by the licensing authority and cross-examination is only allowed if the licensing authority considers that it is required for it to consider the representations, application or notice as the case may require.

3. The licensing authority must allow each of the parties an equal maximum period of time in which to exercise their rights of clarification, questioning and address (see above).

4. The licensing authority may require any person attending the hearing who in its opinion is behaving in a disruptive manner to leave the hearing and may refuse to permit that person to return, or permit him to return only on such conditions as the authority may specify, but such a person may, before the end of the hearing, make a written submission to the licensing authority of any information which he would have been entitled to give orally had he not been required to leave.

Enquiries should always be made with the licensing authority to obtain details of the procedures which will be adopted at a hearing. Each licensing authority should have such a procedure so that licensing applications are dealt with in accordance with the law, that probity is observed at all times, and that there is effective public participation in the process.

24.10 FAILURE OF PARTIES TO ATTEND THE HEARING

If a party has told the licensing authority that he does not intend to attend or be represented at a hearing, the hearing may proceed in his absence. If a party does not inform the licensing authority that he is not going to attend, and he subsequently fails to attend or be represented at a hearing, the licensing authority may either where it considers it to be necessary in the public interest adjourn the hearing to a specified date, or hold the hearing in the party's absence, in which case the licensing authority must consider at the hearing the application, representations or notice made by the party who has failed to attend. If the licensing authority adjourns the hearing to a specified date it must forthwith notify the parties of the date, time and place to which the hearing has been adjourned.

24.11 DETERMINATION OF THE APPLICATION

A licensing authority must make its decision within five working days beginning with the day or the last day on which the hearing was held. The exceptions to this are for hearings dealing with a counter notice following an objection by the police to a temporary event notice and a review of a premises licence following a closure order when the licensing authority must makes its determination at the conclusion of the hearing.

If all the parties agree that the hearing may be dispensed with, the licensing authority must make its determination within 10 working days beginning with the day on which the licensing authority gave notice to the parties that it agreed that a hearing is unnecessary and can be dispensed with.

Once a licensing authority has made a determination it must notify the parties. If the Act does not make provision for the period in which this notification must be given, the licensing authority must give it forthwith on making its determination. The notice must be accompanied by information setting out the right of a party to appeal. Where the Act provides for the chief officer of police to be notified of a determination and he was not a party to the hearing, the licensing authority must notify him of its determination forthwith on making it.

24.12 RECORD OF A HEARING

A licensing authority must make a record of a hearing in a permanent and intelligible form. This must be kept for six years from the date of the determination, or where an appeal has been made, the disposal of the appeal.

24.13 IRREGULARITIES

An irregularity due to a failure to comply with the Hearings Regulations before a licensing authority has made a determination will not of itself render the proceedings void. If the licensing authority considers that any person may have been prejudiced by an irregularity, it must take such steps as it thinks fit to cure the irregularity before it makes its determination. A licensing authority may correct clerical errors in documentation recording a determination or errors arising in such documentation because of an accidental slip or omission.

24.14 NOTICES

Any notices which are required to be given under the Hearings Regulations must be in writing. Notwithstanding this, the requirement shall be satisfied where:

- the text of the notice:

- is transmitted by electronic means;
- is capable of being accessed by the recipient;
- is legible in all material respects; and
- is capable of being reproduced in written form and used for subsequent reference;

- the person to whom the notice is to be given has agreed in advance that such a notice may be given to them by electronic means; and
- forthwith on sending the text of the notice by electronic means, the notice is given to the recipient in writing.

Where the text of the notice is transmitted by electronic means, the notice is given at the time it is transmitted.

24.15 THE IMPACT OF THE HUMAN RIGHTS ACT 1998

The Human Rights Act 1998 requires that a public body ensures that everything it does is compatible with Convention rights and makes it unlawful for a public authority to act incompatibly with those rights. Article 6 of the European Convention on Human Rights is the right to a fair trial, and the key elements of this include:

- the right to a fair hearing;
- the right to a public hearing;
- the right to a hearing before an independent and impartial tribunal; and
- the right to a hearing within a reasonable time.

A licensing authority is part of a public authority and therefore subject to the requirements of the Human Rights Act 1998. However it does not automatically follow that art. 6 will apply. When hearing an application, the proceedings of a licensing committee, being a non-judicial body as opposed to a judicial body, need not meet the full requirements of art. 6 where there is a right of appeal from the licensing committee to a court that does meet the full art. 6 standards and can consider all aspects of the case, even though that does not include a full re-hearing of the facts.

So, while it is good practice to make a hearing before the licensing committee as art. 6 compliant as possible, it will not be a breach of the Human Rights Act 1998 if it is not. In any event the hearing of all applications will be subject to the principles of natural justice and the requirement for decisions to be 'Wednesbury reasonable' (*Associated Provincial Picture Houses Ltd* v. *Wednesbury Corporation* [1948] 1 KB 223).

CHAPTER 25

Appeals

25.1 INTRODUCTION

Section 181 and Schedule 5 provide for appeals against decisions of a licensing authority. The procedures in relation to appeals are set out in Sched. 5. An appeal is made to a magistrates' court. There is no requirement that this must be the magistrates' court for the area in which the premises are situated (Courts Act 2003 (Consequential Provisions) Order 2005, SI 2005/886).

Any party involved in the decision may appeal. Thus an appeal may be brought by an applicant, a licence holder, a responsible authority or an interested party.

An appeal is brought by the appellant giving a notice of appeal to the designated officer for the magistrates' court within a period of 21 days beginning with the day on which the appellant was notified by the licensing authority of the decision to be appealed against. There is no requirement that notice of an appeal be given to any other person, for example a person who made a relevant representation, and nor does there seem to be any requirement for the court to notify such persons of the appeal. It is therefore unclear how they will know that an appeal has been made.

The licensing authority will always be a respondent to the appeal. Where a favourable decision has been made for an applicant licence holder, club or premises user against the representations of a responsible authority or an interested party or the objections of the chief officer of police, the holder of the premises licence, the holder of the personal licence, the holder of the club premises certificate, the person who gave an interim authority notice or the premises user will also be a respondent to the appeal and the person who made the relevant representation or the chief officer of police will be the appellant.

When dealing with an appeal against a decision of a licensing authority, s.181(2) provides that a magistrates' court may:

- dismiss the appeal;
- substitute for the decision appealed against any other decision which could have been made by the licensing authority; or

- remit the case to the licensing authority to dispose of it in accordance with the direction of the court.

The usual procedure will be for the magistrates' court to hold an initial hearing to decide whether it will hear the appeal itself or remit it back to the licensing authority. Where the court decides to hear the matter it will normally then adjourn to a separate contested hearing date. A pre-trial review may be conducted either at the initial hearing or on a separate date before the contested hearing in order to establish the length of time which the case will take.

There is nothing in the Act about the format the appeal hearing will take. The Guidance, para 10.7 provides that the court 'may review the merits of the decision on the facts and consider points of law or address both'. This would seem to suggest that the hearing would not proceed by way of a re-hearing but rather by way of a review of the decision of the licensing authority.

The magistrates may also make such order as to costs as they think fit (s.181(2)). In doing so it is unlikely that costs will be ordered against the police where they have acted in good faith or reasonably in objecting to an application or making a closure order (*R. v. Totnes Licensing Justices ex p. Chief Constable of Devon and Cornwall* (1992) 156 JP 587; *R. v. Merthyr Tydfil Crown Court ex p. Chief Constable of Dyfed Powys* (1998) 95(46) LSG 35).

25.2   PROCEDURE FOR AN APPEAL

The procedure for an appeal against the decision of a local authority is governed by the Magistrates' Courts Rules 1981, SI 1981/552, rule 34. This provides that 'Where under any enactment an appeal lies to a magistrates' court against the decision or order of a local authority or other authority, or other body or person, the appeal shall be by way of complaint for an order.'

Rule 14 governs the order of speeches and the calling of evidence as follows:

1. On the hearing of a complaint, except where the court determines under the Magistrates' Courts Act 1980, s.53(3) to make the order with the consent of the defendant without hearing evidence, the complainant shall call his evidence, and before doing so may address the court.
2. At the conclusion of the evidence for the complainant the defendant may address the court, whether or not he afterwards calls evidence.
3. At the conclusion of the evidence, if any, for the defence, the complainant may call evidence to rebut that evidence.
4. At the conclusion of the evidence for the defence and the evidence, if any, in rebuttal, the defendant may address the court if he has not already done so.

5. Either party may, with the leave of the court, address the court a second time, but where the court grants leave to one party it shall not refuse leave to the other.
6. Where the defendant obtains leave to address the court for a second time his second address shall be made before the second address, if any, of the complainant.

In practice, it may be more rational for the licensing authority to present its evidence first.

Evidence will be admitted on the same basis as at the original hearing before the licensing authority. The court will not be bound by the rules of evidence and so will be able to take into account everything which the licensing authority heard, including hearsay evidence (*Kavanagh* v. *Chief Constable of Devon and Cornwall* [1974] QB 624; *Westminster City Council* v. *Zestfair Ltd* (1989) 153 JP 613). The court can also take into account any local knowledge which the justices might have (*R.* v. *Howard ex p. Farnham Licensing Justices* [1902] 2 KB 363). In addition, the court can hear new evidence, for example, evidence which relates to events that have taken place since the licensing authority's decision.

25.3 LICENSING POLICY STATEMENTS AND THE SECRETARY OF STATE'S GUIDANCE

There is nothing in the Act requiring a magistrates' court to have regard to the relevant licensing authority's statement of licensing policy and the Guidance when reaching its decision. In relation to whether a magistrates' court dealing with an appeal must have regard to the relevant licensing authority's statement of licensing policy and the Guidance, the Guidance, para. 10.8 provides:

> In hearing an appeal against any decision made by a licensing authority, the magistrates' court concerned will have regard to that licensing authority's statement of licensing policy and this Guidance. However, the court would be entitled to depart from either the statement of licensing policy or this Guidance if it considered it is justified to do so because of the individual circumstances of any case. In other words, while the appellate court will normally consider the matter as if it was 'standing in the shoes' of the licensing authority, it would be entitled to find that the licensing authority should have departed from its own policy or the Guidance because the particular circumstances would have justified such a decision by the licensing authority. In addition, the appellate court is entitled to disregard any part of a licensing policy statement or this Guidance that it holds to be ultra vires the 2003 Act and therefore unlawful. The normal course for challenging a statement of licensing policy or this Guidance should be by way of judicial review, but where it is submitted to an appellate court that a statement of policy is itself ultra vires the 2003 Act and this has a direct bearing on the case before it, it would be inappropriate for the court, on accepting such a submission,

to compound the original error by relying on that part of the statement of licensing policy affected.

25.4 PREMISES LICENCES

An appeal may be made:

- where an application for a premises licence is rejected;
- where there is a grant, variation, transfer or review of a premises licence;
- where an interim authority notice seeking reinstatement of a licence following lapse is given; or
- where a provisional statement is issued.

25.4.1 Appeal against the rejection of an application relating to a premises licence

An applicant may appeal against a decision of a licensing authority to:

- reject an application for a premises licence;
- reject, in whole or in part, an application to vary a premises licence;
- reject an application to vary a premises licence to specify an individual as the premises supervisor; or
- reject an application to transfer a premises licence.

25.4.2 Appeal against a decision to grant a premises licence or to impose conditions

Where a licensing authority grants a premises licence, the licence holder may appeal against any decision to impose conditions on the licence, to exclude a licensable activity, or to refuse to specify a person as the designated premises supervisor.

A person who made relevant representations in relation to the application, i.e. a responsible authority or an interested party, may also appeal if he desires to contend:

- that the licence ought not to have been granted; or
- that, on granting the licence, the licensing authority ought to have imposed different or additional conditions, excluded a licensable activity, or refused to specify a person as the designated premises supervisor.

Where a licence has been granted, there is nothing in the Act to prevent the licence holder from operating the premises in accordance with the licence pending the determination of the appeal.

25.4.3 Variation of a premises licence

Where an application to vary a premises licence is granted, in whole or in part, the applicant may appeal against any decision to modify the conditions of the licence. There is a separate provision relating to variations by changing the designated premises supervisor.

A person who made relevant representations may also appeal against the decision if he desires to contend:

- that any variation made ought not to have been made; or
- that, when varying the licence, the licensing authority ought not to have modified the conditions of the licence, or ought to have modified them in a different way.

25.4.4 Variation of a premises licence to specify an individual as premises supervisor

The chief officer of police who gave a notice that was not withdrawn that granting an application to vary a premises licence to change the designated premises supervisor would undermine the crime prevention objective may appeal against the decision to vary the licence.

25.4.5 Transfer of a premises licence

The chief officer of police who gave a notice that was not withdrawn that granting an application to transfer a licence would undermine the crime prevention objective may appeal against the decision to transfer the premises licence.

25.4.6 Review of a premises licence

Where a licensing authority has made a decision in relation to an application for a review of a premises licence, an appeal may be made against that decision by:

- the applicant for the review;
- the holder of the premises licence; or
- any other person who made relevant representations in relation to the application.

The Violent Crime Reduction Bill proposes that the police should have the power to require a review of a premises licence, and that an appeal may be made against a decision following such a review by:

- the chief officer of police for the police area (or each police area) in which the premises are situated;

301

- the holder of the premises licence; or
- any other person who made relevant representations in relation to the application.

25.4.7 Interim authority notice

A chief officer of police who has given a notice that granting an application for an interim authority notice would undermine the crime prevention objective, and the notice has not been withdrawn, can appeal.

Where a relevant licensing authority has decided to cancel an interim authority notice, the person who gave the interim authority notice may appeal against the decision. Where the relevant licensing authority has decided not to cancel an interim authority notice, the chief officer of police may appeal against that decision.

Where an appeal is brought, the court to which it is brought may, on such terms as it thinks fit, order the reinstatement of the interim authority notice pending the disposal of the appeal, or the expiry of the interim authority period, whichever occurs first.

Where the court makes an order for reinstatement, the premises licence is reinstated from the time the order is made.

Where a licence is reinstated after it has been suspended because of the death, incapacity or insolvency of the licence holder, the reinstatement will cease to have effect on the date when the appeal which gave rise to the reinstatement is abandoned or dismissed.

25.4.8 Issue of provisional statement

An appeal against the issue of a provisional statement may be made by the applicant, or any person who made relevant representations in relation to the application.

25.4.9 General provision about appeals in relation to applications regarding premises licences

Any of the appeals outlined above must be made to a magistrates' court. Such an appeal is brought by the appellant giving notice of appeal to the designated officer for the magistrates' court within the period of 21 days beginning with the day on which the appellant was notified by the licensing authority of the decision which is being appealed against.

The decision of the licensing authority will have effect during the 21-day period for appeals. If an appeal is made, the decision will also have effect until the appeal is disposed of. Where the appeal is against a review of a premises licence, the licensing authority's decision will not have effect until the end of the appeal period or the disposal of the appeal (s.52(11)).

In respect of the following appeals, the holder of the premises licence is to be the respondent in addition to the licensing authority:

- an appeal by a person who made relevant representations in relation to an application for the grant of a premises licence;
- an appeal by a person who made relevant representations in relation to the issue of a provisional statement;
- an appeal by a person who made relevant representations in relation to an application for the variation of a premises licence;
- an appeal by a chief officer of police in relation to an application to vary the designated premises supervisor;
- an appeal by a chief officer of police in relation to the transfer of a premises licence; and
- an appeal by an applicant for the review of a premises licence or any person who made relevant representations in respect of such an application.

On an appeal by a chief officer of police against a decision not to cancel an interim authority notice, the person who gave the interim authority notice is to be the respondent in addition to the licensing authority.

25.5 CLUB PREMISES CERTIFICATES

An appeal may be made:

- where an application for a club premises certificate is rejected; or
- where there is a grant, variation, review or withdrawal of a club premises certificate.

25.5.1 Rejection of an application to grant or vary a club premises certificate

Where a licensing authority rejects an application for a club premises certificate, or rejects, in whole or in part, an application to vary a club premises certificate, the club that made the application may appeal against the decision.

25.5.2 Decision to grant a club premises certificate or to impose conditions

Where a licensing authority grants a club premises certificate, the club which made the application may appeal against a decision to impose conditions on the certificate, or to exclude a qualifying club activity.

A person who made relevant representations may also appeal against the decision if he desires to contend:

- that the certificate ought not to have been granted; or
- that, on granting the certificate, the licensing authority ought to have imposed different or additional conditions, or excluded a qualifying club activity.

25.5.3 Variation of a club premises certificate

A club which has applied for a variation of its club premises certificate may appeal against any decision to modify the conditions of the certificate.

A person who made relevant representations may also appeal against the decision if he desires to contend:

- that any variation made ought not to have been made; or
- that, when varying the club premises certificate, the licensing authority ought not to have modified the conditions of the certificate, or ought to have modified them in a different way.

25.5.4 Review of a club premises certificate

Where an application for a review of a club premises certificate is decided by a licensing authority, an appeal may be made against that decision by:

- the applicant for the review;
- the club that holds or held the club premises certificate; or
- any other person who made relevant representations in relation to the application.

25.5.5 Withdrawal of a club premises certificate

Where a relevant licensing authority has given notice withdrawing a club premises certificate, the club which holds or held the certificate may appeal against the decision to withdraw it.

25.5.6 General provision about appeals in relation to applications regarding a club premises certificate

Any of the appeals outlined above must be made to a magistrates' court. Such an appeal is brought by the appellant giving notice of appeal to the designated officer for the magistrates' court within the period of 21 days beginning with the day on which the appellant was notified by the licensing authority of the decision which is being appealed against.

The decision of the licensing authority will have effect during the 21-day period for appeals. If an appeal is made, the decision will also have effect until the appeal is disposed of. Where the appeal is against a review of a club premises certificate, the licensing authority's decision will not have effect until the end of the appeal period or the disposal of the appeal (s.88(11)).

In respect of the following appeals, the club which holds or held the certificate is to be the respondent in addition to the licensing authority:

- an appeal by a person who made relevant representations in relation to the grant of a club premises certificate, or the imposition of conditions;
- an appeal by a person who made relevant representations in relation to an application for the variation of a club premises certificate;
- an appeal by an applicant for the review of a club premises certificate or any person who made relevant representations in respect of such an application.

25.6 TEMPORARY EVENT NOTICES

When a temporary event notice is given, and a chief officer of police gives an objection notice:

- the premises user may appeal against a decision by the relevant licensing authority to give a counter notice; and
- the chief officer of police may appeal against a decision by the relevant licensing authority not to give a counter notice.

An appeal must be made to a magistrates' court. Such an appeal is brought by the appellant giving notice of appeal to the designated officer for the magistrates' court within the period of 21 days beginning with the day on which the appellant was notified by the licensing authority of the decision which is being appealed against. However, an appeal cannot be made later than five working days before the day on which the event period specified in the temporary event notice begins. The premises user must be the respondent to the appeal together with the relevant licensing authority, where the appellant is the chief officer of police.

25.7 PERSONAL LICENCES

An appeal may be made:

- where an application for either the grant or renewal of a personal licence is rejected;
- where there is a grant or renewal of a personal licence following police objection;
- where a personal licence is revoked following police objection on convictions coming to light after a grant or renewal; or
- where there is a decision not to revoke a personal licence following police objection on convictions coming to light after a grant or renewal.

25.7.1   Rejection of a grant or renewal

An applicant may appeal against a decision by the relevant licensing authority to reject an application for the grant of a personal licence or to reject an application for the renewal of a personal licence.

Where an appeal is made against a refusal to renew a personal licence, the licensing authority or the magistrates' court has the power to order that the personal licence remain in force if it would cease to have effect before the appeal or, if it has already ceased to have effect, to reinstate it.

25.7.2   Grant or renewal following police objection

Where a licensing authority grants an application for a personal licence or an application to renew a personal licence, the chief officer of police who gave an objection notice may appeal against that decision.

25.7.3   Revocation following police objection on convictions coming to light after a grant or renewal

A personal licence holder can appeal against a decision to revoke the personal licence.

25.7.4   Decision not to revoke following police objection on convictions coming to light after a grant or renewal

Where convictions come to light after the grant or renewal of a personal licence, the chief officer of police for the licensing authority's area who gave a notice that continuation of the licence would undermine the crime prevention objective, and does not later withdraw it, may appeal against a decision of the licensing authority not to revoke the licence.

25.7.5   General provision about appeals in relation to applications regarding personal licences

Any of the above appeals must be made to a magistrates' court. Such an appeal is brought by the appellant giving notice of appeal to the designated officer for the magistrates' court within the period of 21 days beginning with the day on which the appellant was notified by the licensing authority of the decision which is being appealed against. The personal licence holder must be the respondent to the appeal together with the relevant licensing authority, where the appellant is the chief officer of police.

Where objections have been raised by the chief officer of police, the personal licence holder must be the respondent to the appeal together with the relevant licensing authority.

Where the holder of a personal licence appeals against a decision not to renew his licence, the relevant licensing authority, or the magistrates' court to which the appeal has been made, may, on such conditions as it thinks fit:

* order that the licence is to continue in force until the relevant time, if it would otherwise cease to have effect before that time;
* where the licence has already ceased to have effect, order its reinstatement until the relevant time;

and for these purposes 'the relevant time' means either the time the appeal is dismissed or abandoned, or, where the appeal is allowed, the time the licence is renewed.

25.8 CLOSURE ORDERS

If on a review of a premises licence following a closure order the relevant licensing authority decides:

* to modify the conditions of the premises licence;
* to exclude a licensable activity from the scope of the licence;
* to remove a designated premises supervisor from the licence;
* to suspend the licence for not more than three months;
* to revoke the licence; or
* not to do anything;

an appeal may be made against that decision by the holder of the premises licence, or anyone else who made relevant representations in relation to the review.

Where an appeal is made against a decision to:

* modify the conditions of the premises licence;
* exclude a licensable activity from the scope of the licence;
* remove a designated premises supervisor from the licence; or
* suspend the licence for not more than three months;

the magistrates' court may, if the premises were closed when the decision was taken:

* suspend, on such terms as it thinks fit, the operation of the decision in whole or part, if the relevant licensing authority did not make an order suspending the operation of the decision in whole or part; or

- if the relevant licensing authority has made such an order, cancel it or substitute for it any order suspending the operation of the decision in whole or part which could have been made by the relevant licensing authority.

Where an appeal is made in respect of premises in respect of which the relevant licensing authority has decided to revoke the premises licence and the premises have been closed until that decision was made, the magistrates' court may, on such conditions as it thinks fit, order that the requirement that the premises must remain closed pending the appeal is not to apply to the premises.

An appeal must be made to a magistrates' court. Such an appeal is brought by the appellant giving notice of appeal to the designated officer for the magistrates' court within the period of 21 days beginning with the day on which the appellant was notified by the licensing authority of the decision which is being appealed against.

The holder of the premises licence must be the respondent to the appeal together with the relevant licensing authority where an appeal is brought by a person other than the holder of the premises licence.

25.9 IMPLEMENTING THE DETERMINATION OF THE MAGISTRATES' COURTS

Once a magistrates' court has reached a decision on an appeal, the relevant licensing authority should not delay its implementation. The Guidance at para. 10.10 provides that:

> Any attempt to delay such implementation will only bring the appeal system into disrepute. Standing orders should therefore be in place that on receipt of the decision, necessary action should be taken forthwith unless ordered by the magistrates' court or a higher court to suspend such action (for example, as a result of an ongoing judicial review). Except in the case of closure orders, the 2003 Act does not provide for a further appeal against the decision of the magistrates' courts and normal rules of challenging decisions of magistrates' courts will apply.

25.10 APPEALS TO THE HIGH COURT

25.10.1 By case stated

Section 111(1) of the Magistrates' Court Act 1980 provides that any person who is a party to any proceedings before a magistrates' court or is aggrieved by the court's order or determination may question the proceedings on the ground that the proceedings were wrong in law or were in excess of jurisdiction by applying to the magistrates to state a case for the opinion of the High Court on the question of law or jurisdiction involved. This right does not apply in respect of a decision against which there is a right of appeal to the High Court or which by virtue of the Licensing Act 2003 is final.

So an applicant for a licence, a licence holder, licensing authorities and persons who have made relevant representations will have a right of appeal by way of case stated. The magistrates must have finished dealing with the case before a case can be stated (*Streames* v. *Copping* [1985] QB 920).

An application for a case stated must be made within 21 days after the day on which the decision of the magistrates' court was made (Magistrates' Court Act 1980, s.111(2)). If the magistrates decide that an application is frivolous, they may refuse to state a case (Magistrates' Court Act 1980, s.111(5)). In such a case, if the applicant requires, the court must give him a certificate stating that the application has been refused. Where the magistrates refuse to state a case, the High Court may, on the application of the person who applied for the case to be stated, make a mandatory order requiring the justices to state a case (Magistrates' Court Act 1980, s.111(6)).

The requirements for making an application for a case stated are set out in the Magistrates' Courts Rules 1981, SI 1981/552, rules 76, 77 and 78. An application must be made in writing and signed by or on behalf of the applicant and shall identify the question or questions of law or jurisdiction on which the opinion of the High Court is sought. An application must be sent to the designated officer for the magistrates' court whose decision is questioned. Where one of the questions on which the opinion of the High Court is sought is whether there was evidence on which the magistrates' court could come to its decision, the particular finding of fact made by the magistrates' court which it is claimed cannot be supported by the evidence before the magistrates' court shall be specified in such application.

Within 21 days after the receipt of an application the designated officer must, unless the magistrates refuse to state a case, send a draft case to the applicant or his solicitor and a copy to the respondent or his solicitor. Within 21 days after receipt of the draft case, each party may make representations. These must be in writing and signed by or on behalf of the party making them and sent to the designated officer. Within 21 days after the latest day on which representations may be made, the magistrates can make such adjustments, if any, to the draft case as they think fit, after considering any such representations, and shall state and sign the case. Forthwith after the case has been stated and signed the designated officer must send it to the applicant or his solicitor.

Rule 81 provides that a case stated must state the facts found by the court and the question or questions of law or jurisdiction on which the opinion of the High Court is sought. Where one of the questions on which the opinion of the High Court is sought is whether there was evidence on which the magistrates' court could come to its decision, the particular finding of fact which it is claimed cannot be supported by the evidence before the magistrates' court shall be specified in the case. Unless one of the questions on which the opinion of the High Court is sought is whether there was evidence on which the magistrates' court could come to its decision, the case shall not contain a statement of evidence.

The powers of the High Court are set out in the Supreme Court Act, s.28A(3). The High Court must determine the question arising on the case and reverse, affirm or amend the determination in respect of which the case has been stated, or remit the matter to the magistrates' court, with the opinion of the High Court. It may make such other order in relation to the matter, including as to costs, as it thinks fit. The decision of the High Court is final.

25.10.2 Judicial review

An application may be made to judicially review the magistrates' decision. The Supreme Court Act, s.31 provides that an application can be made, with the leave of the High Court, for judicial review of a magistrates' court decision. Leave will only be granted where the High Court considers that the applicant has sufficient interest in the matter to which the application relates. If leave is granted, the High Court may grant a mandatory, prohibiting or quashing order, or it may award a declaration or damages. A mandatory order will compel the magistrates' court to carry out its functions properly. A quashing order will be appropriate to quash a decision where there has been some unlawfulness in the process used to reach the decision, whilst a prohibiting order can be used to prevent some unlawful action in the future.

The High Court may refuse to grant relief if it considers that the more appropriate remedy would have been an appeal by way of case stated.

An appeal in judicial review proceedings can be made to the Court of Appeal with leave of the Court of Appeal. A further appeal lies to the House of Lords with leave of either the Court of Appeal or the House of Lords.

APPENDIX A

Operating tool-kit – risk assessment

1 THE PREVENTION OF CRIME AND DISORDER

1.1 Management of the premises

1.1.1 Is there an effective door control policy in place to prevent overcrowding and to ensure that potential troublemakers are excluded? If yes, give details.

1.1.2 How do you monitor the number of people on the premises at any one time?

1.1.3 How many security staff do you employ?

1.1.4 Are all door staff registered with the Security Industry Authority scheme and have they all obtained the appropriate qualifications?

1.1.5 Do you hold regular security reviews and, if you do, what happens as a result of these?

1.1.6 How did you assess the number of door supervisors on the premises needed to cope with the numbers of customers?

1.1.7 Do you have a search policy and, if you do, give details.

1.1.8 Do you carry out risk assessments prior to holding specific events? If so, what issues do you consider?

1.1.9 Do you have an incident log of crime and disorder occurrences? If so, is this used, maintained and available for inspection as part of a risk assessment and intelligence gathering process?

1.1.10 Do you employ procedures to deal with customers under the influence alcohol and/or illegal drugs? If so, what are they?

1.1.11 Do you have procedures to deal with violence and antisocial behaviour in the premises? If so, what are they?

1.1.12 Are you involved in any relevant community radio schemes?

1.1.13 What procedures do you have to deal with handbag theft when it occurs as this can be prevalent in busy pubs and clubs?

1.1.14 How do you discourage customers from removing glass, bottles or cans from the premises?

1.1.15 Do you use only safety/toughened glass in your premises to reduce the potential injury from any assaults?

1.1.16 Is up-to-date information made available to customers detailing late night public transport to enable them to travel home safely?

1.1.17 Do you ensure that only telephone numbers for registered taxi firms are displayed?

1.1.18 Do you provide local police with details of events involving outside promoters (i.e. give one month's notice)?

1.1.19 Do you have contractual agreements with outside promoters and if so are police contacted before agreements are signed?

1.2 Implementing appropriate policies for the management of patron behaviour

1.2.1 Do you use practices outlined in the British Beer and Pub Association Drugs and Pubs: A Guide for Licensees (**www.beerandpub.com**)?

1.2.2 Do you have policies to search customers for drugs and/or weapons? If so, what are they?

1.2.3 How do you discourage the use or dealing of illicit substances in or around the premises?

1.2.4 Do you display materials that include the Frank National Drugs Help-line number (0800 776600)?

1.2.5 Do you actively promote drugs awareness among staff? If so, how do you do this?

1.2.6 What procedures do you have with regard to the retention or disposal of any controlled drugs found on the premises and any persons found in possession of them?

1.2.7 What measures do you take to ensure the safety of your customers in relation to drunkenness on the premises?

1.3 Drinks promotions

1.3.1 Are you a member of your local pub watch scheme, if there is one?

1.3.2 Do you use only responsible drinks promotions practices, for example, those outlined in the British Beer and Pub Association Point of Sale Promotions: A Good Practice Guide for Pub Owners and Licensees?

1.3.3 Do you actively promote sensible drinking policies, giving careful consideration to the use of happy hours and drink promotions that may encourage binge drinking?

1.3.4 Do you encourage promotions for non-alcoholic drinks?

1.3.5 Do you promote safe drink and drive practices?

1.4 Responsible management of the local environment around the premises

1.4.1 What procedures do you use to deal with violence and antisocial behaviour outside the premises?

1.4.2 Do you have a queuing policy to encourage good behaviour outside the premises? If so, give details.

1.4.3 Do you have procedures to promptly remove or repair hazardous or damaged objects, materials or property from the premises and the immediate area? If so, give details.

1.4.4 Are regular routine checks of premises and the immediate areas carried out, including the prompt removal of glass, antisocial deposits and graffiti? If so, give details.

1.4.5   Do you have procedures to remove graffiti and antisocial deposits from in and around the premises? If so, give details.

1.5   Entry and exit points

1.5.1   How many entry/exit points do the premises have?

1.5.2   Have the points of entry been reduced to a minimum?

1.5.3   Is there a separate point of entry for staff?

1.5.4   How are entry/exit points monitored?

1.5.5   Are emergency exit points alarmed so that staff are immediately notified of any unauthorised opening or tampering?

1.5.6   Are the doors signed as such?

1.6   Interior design

1.6.1   Is the burglar alarm linked to a system that will automatically contact the police if it is activated?

1.6.2   Are personal attack buttons incorporated in the burglar alarm system for use by staff in appropriate areas such as behind the bar or in the cash office?

1.6.3   Are all staff trained in their correct usage so that police are called to attend urgently when necessary?

1.6.4   Is the bar counter raised and widened for the better protection of staff?

1.6.5   Is the floor on the staff side raised to enable staff to monitor areas beyond the bar and to provide an added appearance of authority?

1.6.6   Are tills positioned so that staff face customers and are they protected from 'till snatch' by transparent screens or an under counter location?

1.6.7   Do staff have direct access to a place of safety behind the bar/counter area to retreat to if threatened with violence?

1.6.8   Are there reasonable means in place for the safe handling of cash both within and to and from the premises?

1.6.9   Have alcoves and blind spots been removed from the layout of the premises to improve natural surveillance? If not, has this lack of natural surveillance been compensated with CCTV coverage or other measures?

1.6.10   Have any wide-open areas been broken up into manageable, visible areas?

1.6.11   Is a cloakroom available to store coats and bags and is it clearly advertised?

1.6.12   Is the cloakroom queue managed at busy times and if so how?

1.6.13   Is furniture equipped with the facility for customers to secure their property?

1.7   Sanitary facilities

1.7.1   Are the entrances to the toilets visible from the bar?

1.7.2   Are toilet entrances located away from the main entrance/exit point?

1.7.3   Are toilet entrances located away from other at risk areas such as accommodation or kitchen entrances?

1.7.4   Are any cupboards or drawers located within the toilets kept locked?

1.7.5   Are the cisterns boxed in and secure to deter drug concealment?

1.7.6   Have all possible flat surfaces in the toilets been removed as otherwise these could facilitate drug use?

1.7.7   Do the cubicle doors have gaps at the top and bottom?

1.7.8   Is key access to the cubicles available to staff?

1.7.9   Are the toilets managed at peak times and kept in good order at other times?

1.7.10 Are there sufficient toilets to meet peak demand?

1.8   Closed circuit television

1.8.1   Have the premises been assessed to see whether CCTV is necessary?

1.8.2   Are the premises equipped with CCTV?

1.8.3   Do high-resolution cameras monitor all entry and exit points?

1.8.4   Does the CCTV monitor the cash office door?

1.8.5   Is the CCTV system registered with the Information Commissioner, if required?

1.8.6   Is there a written operational requirement for the CCTV system?

1.8.7   Is the recording equipment stored in a secure area with access restricted to authorised staff only?

1.8.8   Does the CCTV system record clear images which can be used as valid evidence in a court of law?

1.8.9   Describe your tape management system in detail (including storage of tapes).

2   PUBLIC SAFETY

2.1   Capacity

2.1.1   What is the maximum capacity of the premises?

2.1.2   If appropriate, what is the maximum capacity for separate areas within the premises?

2.1.3   How was this capacity arrived at?

2.2   Disabled persons

2.2.1   What facilities are available for the access and egress for disabled persons?

2.2.2   How does the evacuation procedure for the premises allow for the evacuation of disabled persons?

2.3   Emergency access

2.3.1   Does your site allow for access by emergency vehicles?

2.4   Fire escapes

2.4.1   Has a fire risk assessment of the premises been carried out?

2.4.2   If so, what are the results of this risk assessment?

2.4.3   Do the premises have sufficient exits and are these exits readily available at all times?

2.4.4   Do all the exit routes lead to a place of safety?

2.4.5   If the premises include an auditorium, has the layout of the seating been designed to facilitate easy means of escape from fire?

2.4.6   Are all staircases which form part of an escape route suitable?

2.5   Fire safety

2.5.1   Is the licensed area of the premises or the premises themselves separated by fire resisting construction from any adjoining building or any unlicensed part of a building?

2.5.2   Do all finishes, furniture and soft furnishings comply with the relevant standards?

2.5.3   Is the ventilation system and duct work fire rated and provided with dampers to provide fire separation of at least 30 minutes between the licensed part of the premises and unlicensed areas, and between the premises and escape routes?

2.5.4   If the premises have a stage, is there a safety curtain?

2.5.5   Do the premises have a sprinkler system, controls and arrangements for smoke ventilation, foam inlets, wet/dry risers, refuges for persons with impaired mobility, evacuation/fire fighting lifts, fire fighting staircases, gas cut off valves and other emergency cut offs, fire fighters switches, or main electrical intakes and if so, are these indicated with signs?

2.6   Fire and emergency warning systems

2.6.1   Do the premises have an automatic fire detection and a warning system?

2.6.2   Are there fire extinguishers, fire blankets, hose reels, or sprinklers in the premises?

2.6.3   Do the premises have a secondary supply of electricity?

2.7   Structure

2.7.1   Is the building structurally safe and can it support any extra loads imposed by the proposed use?

2.7.2   Are all changes in level and balconies within the premises protected by barriers or guard rails?

2.7.3   Are all barriers and guard rails of sufficient structural strength?

2.8   Building services

2.8.1   Is the electrical system mechanically and electrically safe?

2.8.2   When was the electrical system last assessed?

2.8.3   Are all electrical sockets for use by performers provided with RCD protection?

2.8.4   Are the premises provided with adequate levels of illumination?

2.8.5   Is there an emergency lighting system?

2.8.6   Do the premises have a mechanical ventilation system?

2.8.7   Do the premises have a heating system and is this arranged so as not to cause a safety or fire hazard?

2.8.8   Do the premises have a permanent water supply and adequate drainage?

2.9   Hygiene

2.9.1   Is free drinking water provided for customers?

2.10   Communication systems

2.10.1   What systems are in place within the premises to provide adequate facilities for communication with staff and the public?

2.10.2   What safety signs and notices are there within the premises?

2.11   Special installations and lifts

2.11.1   What special installations are there within the premises, e.g. lifts, stair lifts, escalators, moveable seating?

2.11.2   Are there any specific risks associated with such special installations?

2.11.3   What special effects are used such as real flame, lasers, pyrotechnics, smoke, fog, foam or firearms? Has a risk assessment been carried out with regard to these?

2.12   Commissioning and inspection test certificates

2.12.1   Do you have current up to date certificates for the following if appropriate:

- the electrical installation;
- emergency lighting batteries;
- fire alarm warning system;
- fire-fighting equipment;
- gas installation and gas appliances;
- boilers or clarifiers;
- passenger lifts and escalators;
- emergency telephones;
- public address systems and refuge alarms;
- safety curtains;
- mechanical installation and suspended or lifting equipment.

Please state which are on the premises.

2.13   Staff training

2.13.1   Have all staff been trained in public safety issues such as evacuation procedures, first aid, dealing with conflict, spotting persons under the influence of alcohol or drugs, etc.?

2.13.2   If so, what training have they recieved and is this documented?

2.14   Drink and drugs

2.14.1   What procedures are in place when dealing with persons who are believed to be suffering adversely from the effect of either drink or drugs?

3 PREVENTION OF PUBLIC NUISANCE

3.1 Noise

3.1.1 Are the premises located in close proximity to residential accommodation? If they are, what and where?

3.1.2 Are the premises attached to any residential premises?

3.1.3 Is it intended to hold live music events at the premises (acoustic or amplified)?

3.1.4 Has an acoustic report being carried out with regard to the premises?

3.1.5 If so, what recommended works have been carried out?

3.1.6 If amplified music is provided, do the premises have a sound-limiting device?

3.1.7 If so, is it located in a lockable cupboard to which only the licensee has access?

3.1.8 Are all socket outlets used to supply the music connected to the sound-limiting device?

3.1.9 Is there a policy of keeping all doors and windows closed while amplified music is being played within the premises?

3.1.10 Do the external doors have acoustic lobbies?

3.1.11 Do the door supervisors ensure that doors are not left open when amplified music is being played?

3.1.12 Is the ventilation/air conditioning system adequate for the number of customers?

3.1.13 Are there air-handling units external to the premises?

3.1.14 If so, are they sound insulated to avoid late night nuisance?

3.1.15 Are the air-handling units serviced on a regular basis?

3.2 People arriving, departing and in the vicinity of the premises

3.2.1 How is it ensured that customers queuing outside the premises do so in a quiet and orderly manner?

3.2.2 Are customers encouraged to leave the premises quietly?

3.2.3 Is information provided on local public transport provision?

3.2.4 What measures are taken to lessen the impact of noise and nuisance generated from cars and taxis attending the premises?

3.2.5 Do the premises have a beer garden or patio area?

3.2.6 Do the premises have tables and chairs outside?

3.2.7 If so, how is noise from the external areas controlled and is there a restricted hours of use policy?

3.3 Deliveries and collections

3.3.1 What measures are taken to control any possible noise nuisance arising from deliveries or collections?

3.4 Odours

3.4.1 If food is provided at the premises, what is done to avoid cooking odours becoming a nuisance?

3.4.2 How is waste stored and how often is it collected?

3.5 Litter and fly posting

3.5.1 What measures are employed to discourage customers from creating litter on the streets in the vicinity of the premises, e.g. food wrappings or promotional material?

3.5.2 What is done to ensure that there is no fly posting associated with the premises?

3.6 Light

3.6.1 Do the premises have external lighting?

3.6.2 If so, what is done to ensure that excess light is not causing a nuisance to neighbours?

4 PROTECTION OF CHILDREN FROM HARM

4.1 Prevention of alcohol sales to under 18s

4.1.1 How is it intended to prevent under-age drinking in the premises?

4.1.2 Are all the staff trained in the 'under-age' policy?

4.2 Restricting access for children to licensed premises

4.2.1 Is access to be restricted for under 18s?

4.2.2 If so how, why and when?

4.3 Other measures to prevent harm to children

4.3.1 What is the procedure for dealing with the safety of lost and found children?

4.3.2 Is it expected that unaccompanied children will be present in the premises and if so, what ratios of staff to children are there expected to be?

4.3.3 Is it anticipated that children will be performing at the premises? If so, what facilities are there for them?

4.4 Children, cinemas and television

4.4.1 If films, television programmes or videos are to be shown in the premises, how is it proposed to prevent children being exposed to strong language, violence and sexual content?

4.4.2 If the premises are a cinema, how is it proposed to control entry in accordance with the BBFC classification system and to prevent films being viewed by under-age children?

Licensing Act 2003 representation form

Your name	
Postal and e-mail address	
Contact telephone number	

Indicate your interest in the application. Please tick one:	☐ a person living in the vicinity of the premises ☐ a body representing persons who live in that vicinity ☐ a person involved in a business in the vicinity of the premises ☐ a body representing persons involved in a business in the vicinity of the premises

Name of the premises you are making a representation about	
Address of the premises you are making a representation about	

Which of the four licensing objectives does your representation relate to?	Please detail the evidence supporting your representation. Or the reason for your representation. Please use separate sheets if necessary
To prevent crime and disorder	
Public safety	
To prevent public nuisance	
To protect children from harm	

Signed: Date:

Draft pool of model conditions relating to the prevention of crime and disorder

1. The Licensee, that is the person in whose name the premises licence is issued, shall ensure that at all times when the premises are open for any licensable activity, there are sufficient competent staff on duty at the premises for the purpose of fulfilling the terms and conditions of the Licence and for preventing crime and disorder.

   (Note. Staffing requirements may vary dependent upon the size and nature of the premises and the licensable activities taking place and specified in the 'operating schedule'.)

2. 2.1 There shall be provided at the premises radio communication equipment to be operated in conjunction and in liaison with the local Police service.

   2.2 Any radio communication system provided under the provisions of condition 2.1. shall:

   (a) Be capable of sending and receiving messages to and from the local Police and other Licensees, designated premises supervisors, door supervisors, managers and club operators incorporated into any joint and mutually beneficial scheme operating in the area.

   (b) Be maintained in good working order at all times when the premises are being used for a licensable activity.

   (c) Be activated, made available to, and monitored by the designated premises supervisor or a responsible member of staff at all times when the premises are being used for a licensable activity.

   2.3 The Licensee, designated premises supervisor or other person having responsibility for monitoring radio communication system provided under the provisions of condition 2.1 shall comply with any instructions or directions received through the system from the Police.

   2.4 The Licensee, designated premises supervisor or other responsible person shall use the radio communication system provided under the provisions of condition 2.1 to notify and report any incident of crime and disorder to the police as soon as practically possible, in accordance with agreed protocols.

3. 3.1 The Licensee and designated premises supervisor shall ensure that:

   (either)

   • At all times that the premises are open for any licensable activity,

320

(or)

- Between . . . . and . . . . . on . . . . . (days) when the premises are open for a licensable activity,

there are employed at the premises:

(either)

- An appropriate number

(or)

- 'X' number

of door supervisors (as defined in the Private Security Industry Act 2001).

3.2   Door supervisors should be stationed in such numbers and in such positions as are detailed on the attached schedule and approved plan of the premises.

3.3   The Licensee shall ensure that where physical searching of patrons is to be undertaken, there is a sufficient number of appropriately trained staff to carry out such searches regardless of whether patrons are male or female.

> *(Note. This means that licensees would have to ensure that the door supervisors have been properly trained either to search members of their own sex and the opposite sex, or if searching is only to be carried out by door supervisors of the same sex as the patrons that there are sufficient door supervisors of both sexes on duty.)*

3.4   Door supervisors shall be provided with 'two-way' radios or similar systems capable of ensuring continuous communication between each other at all times that the premises are open for a licensable activity.

3.5   Door supervisors shall wear clothing of the same style, type and colour, which may be appropriate to the nature of the venue, but which will ensure they are clearly distinguishable and identifiable as door supervisors having regard to the events and activities taking place at the licensed premises.

3.6   The Licensee shall ensure that on each day that door supervisors are engaged for duty at the premises, their details (names and licence numbers) are recorded in an appropriate book kept at the premises. In conjunction with this record book, the Licensee shall also keep an incident book. This record book and incident book must be available for inspection by the Police or Authorised Officer at all times when the premises are open.

4.   4.1   Glass bottles containing beverages of any kind shall not be left in the possession of any patrons after service and following the discharge of the contents into an appropriate drinking vessel (see exception) . . .

Exception:

Glass bottles containing wine may be sold for consumption with a meal taken at a table, by customers who are seated in an area set aside exclusively for patrons taking table meals.

4.2 No persons carrying open or sealed glass bottles shall be admitted to the premises at any time that the premises are open for any licensable activity.

5. 5.1 One pint and half pint capacity drinking glassware, and highball (tumbler) drinking glassware, in which drinks are served, shall be of strengthened glass material (tempered glassware), so that in the event of breakage the glass will fragment with no sharp edges being left. Alternatively, drinks may be served in non-glassware drinking vessels (e.g. plastic, polystyrene, waxed paper).

(Note: Weights and measures legislation requires the use of 'stamped glasses' where 'meter-measuring equipment' is not in use.)

5.2 No glass drinking vessels or glass bottles shall be permitted *(in the areas described in the attached schedule and delineated on the approved plan.)*

5.3 No alcoholic drinks may be consumed in, or brought into, the (areas described in the attached schedule) (following areas) and delineated on the approved plan.

5.4 No patrons shall be allowed to leave the premises whilst in the possession of any drinking vessel or open glass bottle, whether empty or containing any beverage.

(This condition shall not apply to patrons who have purchased beverages for consumption off the premises (within the curtilage of the premises licensed area or in the area covered by a Pavement Café Licence) with the express consent of the Licensee, designated premises supervisor or responsible person.)

5.5 There shall be no off sales of alcoholic drinks except for consumption in an area which is covered by a 'Pavement Cafe Licence'.

5.6 No alcoholic drinks shall be sold or supplied for consumption off the premises.

or

Alcoholic drinks will be only be sold or supplied for consumption on the premises (and there shall be no off sales).

5.7 There shall be no sales of alcoholic drinks for consumption off the premises on any day when . . . . is taking place at . . . . (e.g. a 'first class' football match is being played at St. James Park).

5.8 There shall be no sales of alcoholic drinks for consumption off the premises on any day(s) when an event is taking place, subject to notice in writing having been given to the Licensee from the Licensing Authority (in conjunction with . . . Police) at least seven days prior to the respective day(s).

(Note. Examples of when such a notice may be given might be if a major outdoor event (sporting or otherwise) or a parade is scheduled to take place in an area of the local authority, and where it is considered that alcohol off-sales in that area might give rise to or add to potential crime and disorder problems)

6. 6.1 The maximum number of persons permitted on the premises at any one time shall not exceed . . . . persons.

    6.2 The maximum number of persons permitted in each of the following areas at any one time shall not exceed:

    (a)
    (b)
    (c)
    etc,

    but at no time shall the total number of persons on the premises as a whole exceed . . . . persons.

    6.3 The Licensee and designated premises supervisor shall ensure that there are effective management arrangements in place to enable them to know how many persons there are in the premises at all times when the premises are open for a licensable activity.

    6.4 The maximum number of persons permitted on the licensed premises, or relevant part of the licensed premises shall be indicated by a fixed notice bearing the words 'Maximum Occupancy' with letters and number not less than 20mm high, conspicuously sited at each relevant part of the premises and at the reception point.

    6.5 Seating for no less than . . . . persons shall be provided in the premises at all times the premises are open for a licensable activity.

    6.6. Seating must be provided for all customers and alcohol must only be served to those customers who are seated at tables by way of waiter or waitress service only.

    6.7 Except in the area identified and delineated (e.g., hatched, coloured green) on the deposited plan, alcohol drinks shall only be sold or supplied to and consumed by persons seated at a table, by way of waiter or waitress service, save that:

    (a) No more than (number) persons may stand in the area identified and delineated (e.g. coloured blue) at any one time, and
    (b) A person may take a drink from the area marked (e.g. coloured green) and sit in the area marked (e.g. coloured blue).

7. 7.1 All members of staff at the premises including Door Supervisors shall seek 'credible photographic proof of age evidence' from any person who appears to be under the age of 18 years and who is seeking access to the premises or is seeking to purchase or consume alcohol on the premises. Such credible evidence, which shall include a photograph of the customer, will either be a passport, photographic driving licence, or Proof of Age card carrying a 'PASS' logo.

    7.2 A suitably worded sign of sufficient size and clarity must be displayed at the point of entry to the premises and in a suitable location at any points of sale, advising customers that they may be asked to produce evidence of their age.

8. 8.1 The Licensee shall not advertise, promote, sell or supply alcoholic drinks in such a way that is intended or likely to encourage persons to consume alcohol to an excessive extent.

8.2 The Licensee shall not sell or supply alcoholic drinks at a 'reduced price' during any part or limited period of any day.

Reduced price means:

(i) At no cost to the customer, or

(ii) By way of exchange for any ticket or voucher, or

(iii) By inclusion of the price for an alcoholic drink in some other charge or payment for a product, goods or services such as with a 'mixer', food or an entrance/cloakroom charge, or

(iv) At a price less than that being charged either during an earlier or later period of the same day, or

(v) In such a way that types, brands, and mixtures of drinks are sold either singly or in multiples, at a price for greater measures or quantities than those same drinks being sold for the same price but in smaller measures and quantities during an earlier or later period of the same day.

8.3 The Licensee shall not sell or supply alcoholic drinks in such a way which will enable, or which is intended to enable, persons to consume unlimited quantities of alcoholic drinks on payment of a single payment or a payment arrangement which is not related to the quantity or volume of alcoholic drinks supplied.

8.4 The Licensee shall not sell or supply alcoholic drinks at prices less than the 'agreed minimum prices'.

'Agreed minimum prices' are the prices for a variety of specified products or types of drinks, agreed from time to time by all participating members of the 'pubwatch scheme', in conjunction with the Council and . . . . Police,

9. 9.1 A conspicuous notice must be displayed on or immediately outside the premises adjacent to the entrance to the premises which gives details of times when the premises are permitted to be open for any licensable activity.

9.2 A conspicuous notice must be displayed on or immediately outside the premises, or immediately adjacent to the premises, which gives details of any restrictions relating to the admission of children to the premises.

10. 10.1 Suitably phrased, clear and conspicuous notices, shall be displayed near the entrance to the premises and in other appropriate locations such as sanitary conveniences advising patrons;

(i) of any risk of theft or possibility of other criminal activity.
and/or
(ii) to exercise care with their personal possessions to prevent theft.
and/or
(iii) how to report any incidents of theft or other criminal activity.

11. 11.1 All signs required under these conditions shall comply with those conditions, shall be placed in accordance with those conditions and be illuminated or positioned in well-lighted locations.

12. 12.1 A CCTV system shall be designed, installed and maintained in proper working order, to the satisfaction of the Licensing Authority and in consultation with . . . . Police. Such a system shall,

(i)   Be operated by properly trained staff,

(ii) Be in operation at all times that the premises are being used for a licensable activity,

(ii) Ensure coverage of all entrances and exits to the Licensed Premises internally and externally,

(iii) Ensure coverage of such other areas as may be required by the Licensing Authority and . . . . Police,

(iv) Provide continuous recording facilities for each camera to a good standard of clarity. Such recordings shall be retained (on tape or otherwise) for a period of two months, and shall be supplied to the Licensing Authority or a Police Officer on request.

APPENDIX D

Draft pool of model conditions relating to public safety

1. When disabled people are present, adequate arrangements must exist to enable their safe evacuation in the event of an emergency. Staff must be aware of disabilities and react according to a pre-determined plan and disabled people on the premises must be made aware of the arrangements in place to enable their safe evacuation in the event of an emergency.

    All escape routes and exits must be kept unobstructed, in good order with non-slippery and even surfaces, free of trip hazards and clearly identified.

2. All exit doors, whenever the premises are occupied, must be easily openable in the case of an emergency, without the use of a key, card, code or similar means.

3. All exit doors must be regularly checked to ensure that they function satisfactorily and a record of the check kept.

4. Any removable security fastenings must be removed whenever the premises are open to the public or occupied by staff.

5. All fire doors must be maintained effectively self closing and must not be held open other than by approved devices.

6. Fire resisting doors to ducts, service shafts, and cupboards must be kept locked shut to prevent unauthorised access and preserve integrity.

7. The edge of the treads of steps and stairways to be maintained and to be conspicuous.

8. Safety checks must be carried out before the admission of the public. These must correspond with the risk assessment and the conditions of the licence.

9. Details of all safety checks must be kept in a logbook.

10. All licensed premises must have a means of giving warning to persons in the event of an outbreak of fire or other emergency. Where determined by the risk assessment that a mains electrical fire alarm is required, this must be designed to and installed in accordance with British Standard 5838 Current Edition. Activation of the fire alarm must operate an electronically linked automatic cut off switch to silence any amplified music, this device must not infringe compliance of the system with the appropriate British Standard.

11. Fire fighting equipment must be provided in the licensed premises in accordance with the risk assessment with staff suitably trained as necessary.

12. Hangings, curtains and temporary decorations must be maintained in a flame retardant condition.

13. Upholstered seating must meet on a continual basis the pass criteria for smouldering ignition source 0, flaming ignition source 1 and crib ignition source 5 when tested in accordance with section 5 of BS 5852:1990 or equivalent standard.

14. Curtains, hangings and temporary decorations must be arranged so as not to obstruct exits, fire safety signs or fire fighting equipment.

15. Prior advice must be sought from the Licensing Authority before temporary decorations are used, and the risk assessment amended accordingly.

16. Arrangements must be made to ensure that any capacity limit imposed under the premises licence or club premises certificate is not exceeded.

17. The capacity limit imposed under the premises licence or club premises certificate must be displayed conspicuously on the premises.

18. The capacity limit imposed under the premises licence or club premises certificate must be displayed at the entrance to each licensed room/area.

19. The licence holder, a club official, manager or designated premises supervisor must be aware of the number of people on the premises at any time, and must provide this information to any authorised person on request.

20. Notices detailing the actions to be taken in the event of fire or other emergency, including how to summon the fire brigade, must be prominently displayed and protected from damage and deterioration.

21. The responsible person where there is an outbreak of fire, however slight, must raise the alarm, evacuate the building, and call the fire brigade. Following the incident, the responsible person must ensure that the details are recorded in a Fire Log Book. Any remedial work necessary to restore fire precautions to their original standard must be completed with systems fully functional prior to re-admittance of the public.

22. The responsible person must notify the Licensing Authority as soon as possible if the water supply to any hydrant, hose-reel, sprinkler, drencher or other fire extinguishing installation is cut off or restricted.

23. Access to the premises for emergency vehicles must be kept clear and free from obstruction.

24. Adequate and appropriate equipment and materials must be provided for enabling first aid to be rendered to members of the public if they are injured or become ill whilst at the licensed premises.

25. At least one suitably trained first aider per 500 people must be on duty at all times when the public are present up to the first 3,000 and then one per 1,000 for the remainder.

26. If, having regard to the nature of the premises, the number of persons visiting it and the location of the premises, it would be adequate and appropriate to do so, then instead of a person for rendering first aid there must be a person appointed to take charge of the situation relating to an injured or ill member of the public and the first aid equipment and facilities.

27. In the absence of adequate daylight, the lighting in any area accessible to the public, members or guests must be fully in operation when they are present.

28. Fire safety signs must be adequately illuminated.

327

29. Emergency lighting must be provided in accordance with BS 5266 (current edition) or an equivalent standard approved by the Licensing Authority.

30. Emergency lighting must not be altered without prior consent of the Licensing Authority.

31. The emergency lighting system must be checked to ensure it is operating correctly before the admission of the public, members or guests.

32. In the event of the failure of normal lighting, where the emergency lighting battery has a capacity of one hour, arrangements must be in place to ensure that the public, members or guests leave the premises immediately. Where the emergency lighting battery has a capacity greater than one hour the public, members or guests may remain in the premises for the duration of the system less one hour.

    Note **In addition an investigation into any failure of the system must be carried out to ascertain whether it is safe for persons to remain in the premises when only the emergency lighting is operating.**

33. Emergency lighting installations must comply with BS 5266 or equivalent standard.

34. Temporary electrical wiring and distribution systems must not be provided without notification to the licensing authority at least ten days before commencement of the work and prior inspection by a suitable qualified electrician. Premises must not be opened to the public until the work is deemed satisfactory by the above parties.

35. Where it is not possible to give ten days notification to the licensing authority of provision of temporary electrical wiring and distribution systems, the work must be undertaken by competent, qualified persons.

36. Temporary electrical wiring and distribution systems must comply with the recommendations of BS 7671 or where applicable BS 7909.

37. All temporary electrical wiring and distribution systems must be inspected and certified by a competent person before they are put to use.

38. An appropriately qualified medical practitioner must be present throughout a sports entertainment involving boxing, wrestling, judo, karate or similar.

39. Where a ring is involved, it must be constructed by a competent person, supported by any necessary documentation, and inspected by a competent authority. Any material used to form the skirt around the ring must be flame retardant.

40. At any wrestling or other entertainment of a similar nature, members of the public must not occupy any seat within 2.5 metres of the ring.

41. Sporting events involving any public contest, exhibition or display of 'Total Fighting' are NOT permitted under the terms of this licence. The term 'Total Fighting' shall include any 'full contact' martial arts involving the combined codes of judo, karate and ju-jitsu, judo, sombo and Olympic wrestling or any other mixed martial arts.

42. Any Licensee wishing to hold a Total Fighting event on the licensed premises must first apply to the Council for a variation of this licence and, in the event

that such application is granted, must comply with any additional conditions that may be imposed.

43. At water sports entertainments, staff adequately trained in rescue and life safety procedures must be stationed and remain within the vicinity of the water at all material times.

44. No alterations must be made to the premises which make it impossible to comply with an existing licence condition without first seeking a variation of the premises licence proposing the deletion of the condition in question. The applicant will need to propose a new operating schedule reflecting the proposed alteration to the premises and how he or she intends to take alternative steps to promote the public safety objective and amend the risk assessment accordingly.

45. Where special effects are intended for use, including:

   – dry ice machines and cryogenic fog

   – smoke machines and fog generators

   – pyrotechnics, including fireworks

   – real flame

   – firearms

   – motor vehicles

   – strobe lighting

   – lasers

   – explosives and highly flammable substances

   the responsible person must notify the Licensing Authority and submit a relevant risk assessment at least ten days prior to the event.

46. The number of attendants on each floor in a closely seated auditorium must be as set out on the table below:

Number of members of the audience present on a floor	Minimum number of attendants required to be present on that floor
1–100	One
101–250	Two
251–500	Three
501–750	Four
751–1000	Five
And one additional attendant for each additional 250 persons (or part thereof)	

47. Attendants must not be engaged in any duties that would hinder the prompt discharge of their duties in the event of an emergency or entail their absence from that floor or auditorium where they are on duty.

48. All attendants must be readily identifiable to the audience (but this need not entail the wearing of a uniform).

49. The premises must not be used for a closely seated audience except in accordance with seating plan(s), a copy of which is available at the premises and must be shown to any authorised person on request.

50. No article must be attached to the back of any seat which would reduce the clear width of seatways or cause a tripping hazard or obstruction.

51. A copy of any certificate relating to the design, construction and loading of any temporary sealing must be kept available at the premises and must be shown to any authorised person on request.

52. Sitting on floors must not be permitted except where authorised in the premises licence or club premises certificate.

53. Waiting or standing must not be permitted except in areas designated in the premises licence or club premises certificate.

54. In no circumstances must anyone be permitted to –

    (i)   sit in any gangway;
    (ii) stand or sit in front of any exit; or
    (iii) stand or sit on any staircase including any landings.

55. Except as authorised by the premises licence or club premises certificate, no drinks must be sold to or be consumed by a closely seated audience except in plastic and paper containers.

56. Clothing or other objects must not be placed over balcony rails or upon balcony fronts.

57. Any special effects or mechanical installation must be arranged and stored to minimise any risk to the safety of the audience, the performers and staff.

58. All special effects must be tested before the performance in respect of audience safety and to ensure that there is sufficient ventilation and extraction to avoid activation of fire protection equipment.

    Special effects include:

    (a) dry ice machines and cryogenic fog;
    (b) smoke machines and fog generators;
    (c) pyrotechnics, including fireworks;
    (d) real flame;
    (e) firearms;
    (f) motor vehicles;
    (g) strobe lighting;
    (h) lasers (see HSE Guide The Radiation Safety of lasers used for display purposes (HS(G)95) and BS EN 60825: Safety of laser products);
    (i) explosives and highly flammable substances.

    In the case of any other special effects with safety implications prior notification must be given in writing to the responsible licensing authority at least 10 days before the event with details as to their use to enable the Authority to consider if further inspection by the Fire Authority is necessary. It may be required that staff trained in fire prevention and extinction be present during any such performance.

59. Any scenery must be maintained flame-retardant.

60. Where a safety curtain is provided, it must be arranged to protect the audience from the effects of a fire or smoke on stage for sufficient time to enable the safe evacuation of the auditorium.

61. Where a risk assessment requires a sprinkler or drencher all safety curtains incorporating a drencher, all smoke ventilators and sprinklers (where fitted) must be maintained unobstructed and in good working order.

62. Where a stage with a proscenium arch is not equipped with a safety curtain, any curtains provided between the stage and the auditorium must be heavy-weight and be made of non-combustible material or inherently or durably treated flame-retarded fabric.

63. All ceilings in those parts of the premises to which the audience are admitted must be inspected by a suitably qualified person who will decide when a further inspection would be necessary and a certificate concerning the condition of the ceilings forwarded to the licensing authority.

64. Where the potential audience exceeds 250 all seats in the auditorium must, except in boxes accommodating not more than 8 persons, be either securely fixed to the floor or battened together in lengths of not fewer than four or more than twelve.

65. Where premises used for film exhibitions are not equipped with a staff alerting system the number of attendants present must be as set out in the table below:

Number of members of the audience present on the premises	Minimum number of attendants required to be on duly
1–250	2
And one additional attendant for each additional 250 members of the audience present (or part thereof)	
Where there are more than 150 members of an audience in any auditorium or on any floor	At least one attendant must be present in any auditorium or on any floor

66. Where premises used for film exhibitions are equipped with a staff alerting system the number of attendants present must be as set out in the table below:

Number of members of the audience present on the premises	Minimum number of attendants required to be on duty	Minimum number of other staff on the premises who are available to assist in the event of an emergency
1–500	Two	One
501–1000	Three	Two
1001–1500	Four	Four
1501 or more	Five plus one for every 500 (or part thereof) persons over 2000 on the premises	Five plus one for every 500 (or part thereof) persons over 2000 on the premises

67. Staff must not be considered as being available to assist in the event of an emergency if they are:

   (i) the holder of the premises licence or the manager on duty at the premises and therefore responsible for directing operations; or
   (ii) a member of staff whose normal duties or responsibilities are likely to significantly affect or delay his response in an emergency situation; or
   (iii) a member of staff whose usual location when on duty is more than 60 metres from the location to which he is required to go on being alerted to an emergency situation.

68. Attendants must as far as reasonably practicable be evenly distributed throughout all parts of the premises to which the public have access and keep under observation all parts of the premises to which the audience have access.

69. The staff alerting system must be maintained in working order and be in operation at all times the premises are in use.

70. The level of lighting in the auditorium must be as great as possible consistent with the effective presentation of the film; and the level of illumination maintained in the auditorium during the showing of films would normally be regarded as satisfactory if it complies with the standards specified in BS CP 1007 (Maintained Lighting for Cinemas).

71. No flammable films must be allowed on the premises without the prior notification of the licensing authority/fire authority.

72. Drinking water (e.g. tap water) shall be available or served to patrons in sufficient quantities at all times when patrons are present on the premises.

Draft pool of model conditions relating to public nuisance

1. Noise and vibration must not be audible outside the premises.

2. Noise generated by amplified music must be controlled by a noise limiting device set at a level determined by the Local Authority Environmental Health Officer, such level being confirmed in writing to the Licensee.

3. Noise limiting devices, once set, cannot be reset or adjusted without consultation with the Local Authority Environmental Health Officer.

4. The lobby doors at the premises must be kept closed except for access and egress. Door staff must supervise to ensure that the doors are maintained closed as far as possible when public entertainment is taking place.

5. The use of fireworks and pyrotechnics is restricted to the hours of . . . . to . . . .

6. Internal and external lighting provided for the purpose of customer and staff safety and for the security of the premises must be positioned so as not to cause nuisance to neighbouring or adjoining properties.

7. Lighting associated with activities of entertainment must be positioned so as not to cause nuisance to neighbouring or adjoining properties.

8. Lighting provided externally to promote advertising of the premises or activities associated with the premises must be of an intensity such as not to cause nuisance to neighbouring or adjoining properties.

9. Suitable ventilation and extraction systems must be provided to eliminate noxious odours. Such systems must be maintained on a regular basis.

10. The Licensee shall ensure that waste and refuse are removed in a timely manner to a licensed waste disposal facility.

11. [The Licensee of the] premises must enter into a waste removal agreement with a licensed waste disposal contractor and keep documented evidence of the agreement.

12. Empty bottles must be stored in a lidded skip within the curtilage of the premises prior to collection. Operationally bottles must be removed from the public area on a frequent basis and transferred to the skip. It is recommended that transfer to an external skip must not be undertaken after (10.00 pm) to minimise noise disturbance to adjoining properties.

13. No glass or material or bottles shall be deposited in any skip, bin or other container of a like nature, located in the open air outside of the premises,

between the hours of (10.00 pm) and (8.00 am) and any such skip, bin, or container shall not be removed from the premises between those hours.

14. Clear and legible notices must be displayed at exits and other circulatory areas requesting patrons to leave the premises having regard to the needs of local residents, in particular emphasising the need to refrain from shouting and slamming car doors. The sounding of car horns must also be discouraged.

15. The premises licence holder, designated premises supervisor, must ensure that door supervisors and other members of staff monitor the activity of persons leaving the premises and remind them of their public responsibilities where necessary.

Draft pool of model conditions relating to the protection of children from harm

1. Where evidence has been provided that premises are associated with heavy, binge or underage drinking, drugs or gambling, children under 18 years will not be allowed access to those premises.

2. Where the public are admitted to premises not serving alcohol for consumption on the premises, children under 12 unaccompanied by an adult over 18 must not be admitted after 11 pm.

3. Where the Licensing Authority classifies films for the admission of children under 18 years:

   (a) Any film must be submitted to the Licensing Authority at least 28 days before it is shown, for classification.

   (b) The premises licence holder or club premises certificate holder must adhere to the age restriction imposed.

3. Only films that have been classified by the British Board of Film Classification as U, PG, 12A, 15 or 18 or as classified by any other body designated under section 4 of the Video Recordings Act 1984 or as otherwise classified by the licensing authority may be exhibited on the premises. The premises licence holder or club premises certificate holder must adhere to the age restriction in accordance with the following classification:

   - 'U' Universal – means films suitable for audiences aged 4 years and over
   - 'PG' Parental Guidance – means films where some scenes may be unsuitable for young children
   - '12A' – means films passed only for viewing by persons aged 12 years or older or persons under 12 years when accompanied by an adult
   - '15' – means films passed only for viewing by persons aged 15 years and over
   - '18' – means films passed only for viewing by persons aged 18 years and over

4. Immediately before the exhibition of a film there must be exhibited on screen for at least 5 seconds a representation or written statement of the film's classification in such a manner as can be easily read by all persons attending the entertainment and also in the case of a trailer advertising any film.

5. Where a film is to be shown that has been classified as 12A, 15 or 18 the licence holder must cause a notice to be displayed, in a conspicuous position, at the entrance to the premises or room in which the film is to be shown reading:

PERSONS UNDER THE AGE OF [insert as appropriate] CANNOT BE ADMITTED TO ANY PART OF THE PROGRAMME.

This notice must refer to the oldest age restriction where films of different categories are included in one programme.

1. No children under the age of 18 years must be allowed access to premises during any time when an activity or entertainment of a sexual nature is being provided. For the purposes of this condition, entertainment of a sexual nature includes but is not limited to striptease (sometimes referred to as exotic dancing), lap dancing, pole dancing or any other entertainment of a similar nature.

2. No children under 18 must be admitted to any entertainment of an adult nature.

    For the purposes of this condition entertainment is regarded as being adult entertainment if it includes foul or abusive language, nudity or violence or subject matter which is likely to offend against good taste or decency.

3. Where entertainment is provided wholly or mainly for unaccompanied children:

    - There must be at least one attendant per 50 children or part thereof who must be on duty in the area(s) occupied by the children and stationed in the vicinity of each exit and at the head of each stairway
    - attendants must wear distinctive clothing or suitable armbands
    - attendants must be present throughout the entertainment and while the audience is entering and leaving the building

4. The performance of children in shows is regulated by the Children (Performances) Regulations 1968. The show venue must be large enough to safely accommodate the children backstage. All chaperones and production crew must receive the fire instruction procedures applicable to the venue prior to the arrival of the children. You must consider the adverse effects of special effects upon the health and safety of children. Children must be supervised by an adult at all times.

5. Compliance with the Portman Group's Retailer Alert Bulletins is required.

6. Proof of Age evidence must be viewed before admission to the premises and underage persons must not be admitted. The age must be * over 16 years or 18 years (*delete as necessary).

APPENDIX G

Scale of fines

The standard scale of fines for summary offences is:

Level on scale	Amount of fine
1	£200
2	£500
3	£1,000
4	£2,500
5	£5,000

APPENDIX H

Useful websites

Alcohol Education and Research Council	www.aerc.org.uk
Arts Council	www.artscouncil.org
Association of Convenience Stores	www.thelocalshop.com
Association of Licensed Multiple Retailers	www.almr.org.uk
Bar Entertainment and Dance Association	www.beda.org.uk
British Beer and Pub Association	www.beerandpub.com
British Board of Film Classification	www.bbfc.co.uk
British Institute of Innkeeping	www.bii.org
British Retail Consortium	www.brc.org.uk
British Standards Institution	www.bsi-global.com
Chartered Institute of Environmental Health	www.cieh.org
Circus Arts Forum	www.circusartsforum.org
CitizenCard	www.citizencard.net
Department for Culture, Media and Sport	www.culture.gov.uk
Disclosure Scotland	www.disclosurescotland.co.uk
Entertainment Technology Press	www.etnow.com/books
FireNet International	www.fire.org.uk
Health and Safety Executive	www.hse.gov.uk
Home Office	www.homeoffice.gov.uk
Independent Street Arts Network	www.streetartsnetwork.org
Institute of Acoustics	www.ioa.org.uk
Local Authorities Coordinators of Regulatory Services	www.lacors.gov.uk
Local Government Association	www.lga.gov.uk
Magistrates' Association	www.magistrates-association.org.uk
Maritime and Coastguards Agency	www.mcga.gov.uk
Musician's Union	www.musiciansunion.org.uk
National Pubwatch	www.pubwatch.org
ODPM	www.odpm.gov.uk
Portman Group	www.portman-group.org.uk
Stationery Office	www.tso.co.uk
Transport for London	www.tfl.gov.uk
Valuation Office Agency	www.voa.gov.uk
Wine and Spirits Association	www.wsa.org.uk

Index